Doi ng justice Better

Doing Justice Better
The Politics of Restorative Justice

Published by
WATERSIDE PRESS
Sherfield Gables
Sherfield-on-Loddon
Hook
Hampshire RG27 0JG
United Kingdom

Telephone 01256 882250 UK Landline low-cost calls 0845 2300 733
E-mail enquiries@watersidepress.co.uk
Online catalogue and bookstore www.WatersidePress.co.uk

ISBN 978 1904380 34 4

Cataloguing-In-Publication Data A catalogue record for this book can be obtained from the British Library

Cover design © 2007 Waterside Press. Front cover picture depicts a scene from *'n Lam vir die Pase* ('A Lamb for the Passover'), a play written and directed by Nico Luwes and performed by members of the Theatre Arts Department, University of the Free State, Bloemfontein, Republic of South Africa. The scene, entitled: 'An Altercation at the Well', is reproduced by kind permission of Nico Luwes and the members of the cast, to whom the grateful thanks of David Cornwell and Waterside Press are extended.

Printing and binding Biddles Ltd, Kings Lynn, Norfolk, UK.

North American distributor International Specialised Book Services (ISBS), 920 NE 58th Ave, Suite 300, Portland, Oregon, 97213-3786, USA
Telephone 1 800 944 6190 Fax 1 503 280 8832 orders@isbs.com www.isbs.com

Doing Justice Better

THE POLITICS OF RESTORATIVE JUSTICE

David J Cornwell

With a Foreword by

Mark S Umbreit

 **WATERSIDE** PRESS

Acknowledgements

This book has been prompted by discussions with an extensive range of colleagues associated with criminal justice systems across the world. Some of those who contributed to the initial debate are primarily academics, though many more are professional practitioners working within the widely different areas of criminal justice administration in their own countries. The title of this work—*Doing Justice Better: The Politics of Restorative Justice*—was a deliberate choice but one not without its own difficulties. The reasons for this deserve brief explanation.

Experienced criminal justice professionals—whether from a background of law, policing, court services, prison management, probation, social work or many of the well-known voluntary or charitable organizations associated with criminal justice—all have an ethical allegiance to the organizations that they represent and which employ them. These allegiances often make it difficult for them to contribute openly to a debate that is either of a 'political' nature, or which inevitably becomes critical of official policies and practices currently pursued by the national governments of the countries in which they serve. Criminal justice and political expediency have long been incompatible bedfellows, but seldom more so than in the contemporary circumstances of so many nations of the world.

The response from these professional and academic colleagues for assistance in writing this book has been truly overwhelming and I am deeply indebted to them for their support, provision of reference material, comments on draft chapters and suggestions for inclusion and improvement. Without this encouragement, this book simply could not have been completed. Though I cannot acknowledge each of them personally and many of their contributions have been included on an unattributed basis, I trust that they will recognise areas of the text in which their influence has been considerable. Where, however, the published work of these colleagues is a matter of public record, the normal protocols of referencing have been carefully followed.

Two particular texts have proved invaluable in preparing this work: David Garland's *Culture of Control: Crime and Social Order in Contemporary Society* (2002) and Michael Tonry's edited volume *Confronting Crime: Crime Control Policy Under New Labour* (2003). I have quoted widely from both because the accounts offered within each precisely reflect the tenor of the debate within the chapters of this book. I express thanks to both of these authors for the clarity of the arguments and explanations advanced in their writing and trust that I have accurately reflected their intentions.

I am deeply grateful to Mark Umbreit for devoting the time from a very hectic work schedule to providing a foreword for this book. The range and elegance of his own writing within the international promotion of restorative justice is widely known and respected; I am truly delighted that he agreed to set the scene for this work. Sincere thanks are also due to Sir Charles Pollard Q.P.M. and to Nigel Whiskin M.B.E. who have also spared scarce time from busy lives to read and comment on the final manuscript. Their contributions have been extremely valuable and, as ever, totally practical and full of insight.

To Bryan Gibson and the staff of Waterside Press I once again acknowledge a considerable debt of gratitude for their patient handling of the manuscript and for their continued support and encouragement.

Finally, both victims of crime and the offenders who do them harm receive inadequate justice in many contemporary societies. Both groups deserve better outcomes from the criminal justice process and restorative justice seeks to promote these outcomes. This book acknowledges the different needs of victims and offenders and the dedication of those criminal justice professionals everywhere whose lives are devoted to *doing justice better.*

Doing Justice Better:
The Politics of Restorative Justice

CONTENTS

Dedication

For brave Belinda,
with love and admiration.

Also, for criminal justice professionals throughout
the world who constantly strive to do justice better.

Preface

This book represents a deliberate attempt to place the concept of restorative justice within a context that directly challenges, and responds to, the evident inadequacies of contemporary criminal justice practices within Britain and many other 'Western-style' democracies. It is written from a predominantly British perspective that builds upon, and extends, many of the arguments developed within a previous work— *Criminal Punishment and Restorative Justice* (Cornwell, 2006). More to the point, however, it seeks to explain how what I shall describe as the 'politicisation' of crime frustrates the development of more effective and enlightened criminal justice policies and delivery.

Existing criminal justice processes fail almost universally to deliver substantive crime control, lesser use of custodial punishment or a sustained reduction in rates of re-offending. These facts are now accepted as more or less incontrovertibly 'given' as much in North America as in the United Kingdom, and similar situations are also evident in Europe, Southern Africa, Australia, New Zealand and elsewhere. While explanations of these situations differ to some extent according to the national contexts within which they occur, there seems to have emerged a discernible common thread: this is that governments, increasingly frustrated by an inability to control crime, have turned to strategies of risk management and incarceration, rather than of crime reduction, in order to retain some measure of electoral credibility.

Within the so-called 'liberal' democracies, it has become the case that crime control, more than any other contemporary social issue, has risen rapidly in recent years to become one of the central, and probably the most controversial, political agendas of governments. In addition, it is scarcely surprising that as social inequalities within these democracies have increased, so too have the perceived risks of crime within all sectors of their societies. As a result, increases in, or the prevalence of crime have come to be widely attributed predominantly to the criminal behaviour of those consigned to the socio-economic margins. These are the apparently inevitable outcomes of criminal justice policies demonstrably promoted to be 'tough on crime', without being similarly 'tough on the causes of crime'.

Preoccupation with crime control rather than with crime reduction leads inevitably towards policies of incapacitation and exclusion, rather than towards those of restoration and inclusion. Incapacitation may achieve the short-term objectives of social risk management, but, ultimately, it further exacerbates the dysfunctional circumstances of those already marginalised. Small wonder, then, that so many of those released from prisons re-offend within short periods following upon release. Worse still, when prisons are routinely constrained to operate above operational capacity, little can be done to encourage attitudinal change or law-abiding behaviour on release. It is precisely this cycle of despair that forms the focus for this book.

Within normally developed societies, community corrections should surely provide the dominant punitive strategy for dealing with all offenders unless, or until, it becomes evident that their removal from society is strictly unavoidable due to the heinous nature of their offences or the quantifiable risk through offending that they pose to the general public. Only in such circumstances should the use of custody become the strategy of first resort. Sadly, our contemporary infatuation with, and reliance upon custodial punishment for the primary purposes of incapacitation serves only to mask the problems of criminality rather than resolve them.

Restorative justice has, over recent years, emerged as an increasingly reasoned response to criminal offending, simply because it asks more pertinent questions of criminal justice and seeks to promote more positive outcomes of the processes of justice than those that the existing framework can provide. Its potential for the future lies in its evidently inclusive prescription for *better justice* that embraces offenders, victims of crime and communities as essential stakeholders within criminal justice. In so doing it seeks a wider distribution of justice, a more compassionate approach towards victims of crime and an infinitely more considered and constructive approach towards the punishment of offenders.

There is no doubt, however, that the questions restorative justice asks of present day penology are searching to the point of being directly challenging. Its entirely justifiable claim that 'crime violates people and relationships to a greater extent than it violates the state and its laws', is just the starting point for what, inevitably, becomes an 'uncomfortable' discussion within contemporary penal politics and jurisprudence. The subsequent question of: 'Who has been harmed and whose responsibility is it to put this right?' rather than: 'What law has been broken and how much punishment is deserved?' becomes equally pertinent and demanding of satisfactory explanation. These two questions alone speak volumes in terms of the agenda that restorative justice sets for a fairer and more humane administration of justice in modern societies.

This book unashamedly promotes the cause of restorative justice, but it does so from a basis of pragmatism and in the genuine belief that significant change within criminal justice is not only long overdue but also inevitable. It is morally and socially irresponsible and unreasonable to continue to exclude victims of crime from due consideration; it is pointless to incarcerate offenders without addressing their social deficits or enabling them to make reparation; and it is mindless to be 'tough on crime' without being equally energetic about redressing the causes of crime. These are simple messages with massive implications that politicians and penal policy-makers presently prefer to ignore as far as possible, but which, due to the worldwide movement towards restorative justice, will not now remain in the shallow margins of criminal justice.

Policy-makers and political advisers within criminal justice are increasingly noted for expressing a preference for initiatives that are 'evidence-led', measurable in terms of performance criteria and which have the potential for cost reduction.

There is an ever-growing body of sufficiently rigorous research material worldwide that indicates a strong correlation between the implementation of restorative justice programmes and reduced levels of recidivism within the non-custodial sector of corrections. Within custodial corrections, however, the situation is much more open to speculation as we shall see in later chapters. This is because, as yet, few if any prisons are operated on truly restorative justice models involving reparative and restorative regimes. What is demonstrably certain is that the currently prevailing mode of penal incapacitation (at least in the United Kingdom) is in the order of 60 per cent *ineffective* in reducing recidivism and that this comes at a cost per inmate place far in excess of the total net operating cost of prisons specifically designed to deliver restorative outcomes.

Finally, politicians and policy-makers are notoriously eclectic in their selection of penal policies, being ultimately far more influenced by media reaction and considerations of electoral credibility, than by either research evidence or the advice of criminologists or of experienced criminal justice practitioners. This situation is exacerbated by the presence in many countries of influential and change-aversive 'interest' groups whose commitment to the *status quo* favours increasingly punitive measures as the only means of dealing with criminal offenders. Against such a backdrop, any initiative for radical change within criminal justice systems is bound to face an uphill struggle, at least until the necessity for change is recognised and acknowledged. This book proposes a more reasoned and persuasive argument for '*doing justice better*'.

David J. Cornwell
Kersoe, Worcestershire, United Kingdom
May 2007

Foreword

Mark S. Umbreit, PhD
Centre for Restorative Justice and Peacemaking
University of Minnesota, School of Social Work

Restorative justice in the twenty-first century is a social movement that has moved far beyond its humble and rather marginal, beginnings in North America and England more than a quarter of a century ago. Today restorative justice policies and practices are developing throughout the world in diverse cultural and national settings, with recent endorsements by the European Union and the United Nations. While still not the mainstream in any nation, restorative justice has clearly moved beyond the margins of social change in many locations and is entering the mainstream of criminal justice policy.

Restorative justice emphasises positive human development, accountability, mutuality, empathy, responsibility, respect and fairness. There is growing empirical evidence from different parts of the world community that restorative justice interventions (particularly those involving some form of dialogue with offenders, victims and other support people) yield positive outcomes on victim satisfaction and reparation, perceptions of fairness by both victim and offender and reduced recidivism. Increasingly rigorous research is being conducted in numerous settings, including a series of meta-analyses initiated by the Canadian Department of Justice and several universities in the United States. Yet the principles and practices of the restorative justice movement are not inherently benign, incapable of doing harm or resulting in bad public policy. In fact, as in so many other movements and interventions grounded in lofty values and good intentions, reports of unintentionally harmful consequences or outcomes are inevitable.

In large part, these unintended consequences derive from the inherent difficulty of attempting to balance so many valid needs: needs of victims, needs of offenders, needs of their community and ultimately the needs of the state that has come to represent them. Small programmes that are accountable to a finite and immediate constituency may be less prone to such errors than large institutions and governments, but even so, examples of unintended harm and policy abound.

Sometimes the problem arises from inattention to some of the basic principles and guidelines that have by now become well established and widely known. Examples include: lack of crime victim involvement and preparation for specific interventions; inappropriate referrals; inadequate training of staff and volunteers; policies and practices that fail to address the reality of the disproportionate number of people of colour who are in the justice system; continued over-reliance on costly incarceration and other offender driven policies of retribution.

Other examples derive from attempts by the formal criminal justice system to take over the movement and fashion it to meet the traditional needs of the system and its bureaucracy. Such actions can threaten the soul of the restorative justice movement and even neutralise its impact. A frequent example of this type is excessive focus on offender rehabilitation, to the exclusion of the needs of the victims and the community. Within North America and Europe there are several examples of nations or states that have adopted legislation to support restorative justice principles and practices yet focus entirely on offender orientated treatment and rehabilitation.

For all of these reasons, *Doing Justice Better: The Politics of Restorative Justice* is an important and timely contribution to the literature, for policymakers, practitioners and researchers. David Cornwell addresses many critical and difficult issues related to the practical reality of effectively implementing restorative justice policies and practices on a large scale. Most importantly, he anchors his analysis in the greatest core principle and distinguishing characteristic of restorative justice: the victim. Cornwell makes it clear that it is morally and socially irresponsible to continue to exclude people who have been victimised by crime from involvement in the process of holding offenders accountable and repairing the harm caused by their actions. Similarly, he argues that it makes little sense simply to incarcerate offenders without addressing their social deficits and enabling them to make reparation to their victims. Cornwell's emphasis on the politics of restorative justice and his insightful analysis is a much needed voice addressing what he calls the mindlessness of common political rhetoric that continually speaks to being tough on crime without ever being equally passionate about addressing the causes of crime.

More literature addressing the messy and complex issues related to the politics of restorative justice and effective policy implementation is desperately needed in the world community. David Cornwell offers a valuable text to stimulate this dialogue.

Introduction

In the closing chapter of a recent work, *Criminal Punishment and Restorative Justice*,[1] I advanced the view that criminal justice within Britain and a number of other developed democracies worldwide, presently stood at a crossroads. This crossroads was formed by the intersection of two highways: the one carrying the traffic of 'traditional' justice; and the other, the lesser but increasing volume of restorative justice traffic. It was further suggested that eventually and inevitably, choices would have to be made about which of these highways offered the preferable route for the delivery of 'better justice' to all the stakeholders involved in the processes of contemporary criminal justice administration.

THE NEED FOR THIS BOOK

Completion of the book mentioned above had resulted in widespread discussions with colleagues drawn from the very different backgrounds of academic research, penal policy development, criminal law and day-to-day employment within criminal justice systems across the world. In these days of electronic communication, exchanges of views and research material quickly result in the accumulation of papers, articles and correspondence that can become quite overwhelming in its diversity and points of origin—some of it emerging from sources both unexpected and infinitely informative.

These exchanges indicated one pervading thread that effectively made the present crises of policy stagnation experienced within so many jurisdictions assume a common and discernible form: this lies in the evident fact that criminal justice policy, presently and almost everywhere, is influenced and informed much more by prevailing political ideologies and electoral considerations than by criminological principle and rigorous research. The more cynically disposed person would maintain that there is nothing particularly new about this situation, that criminal justice is part of the spectrum of activities that routinely attract political attention within every democracy and that there is a certain inevitability about the reality of this state of affairs. Indeed, enlightened pragmatism would insist that it is naïve to believe otherwise.

Another and perhaps more disturbing strand accompanied the one previously described. It revealed the extent to which a number of criminal justice practitioners found themselves unable, for entirely professional reasons, to express openly views that might be considered critical of the organizations that employed them, because to do so would be considered unacceptably disloyal or disingenuous. Put together, these two situations might, when combined with others relating to a perceived requirement for 'apolitical neutrality', go a long

---

[1] DJ Cornwell (2006), *Criminal Punishment and Restorative Justice: Past, Present and Future Perspectives*, Winchester, UK: Waterside Press, p.176.

way towards explaining why a preference for the *status quo* rather than for progressive reform is so deeply embedded in so many criminal justice systems today.

In his own account of this situation, David Garland ascribes it to a significant shifting effect within criminal justice that has taken place over the past four decades almost universally. The demise of rehabilitation, the rise of and subsequent retreat from the 'justice model' and the move towards 'populist punitivism' have all led more to confusion than to clarification of the role of criminal justice within many societies. This has left the landscape featureless, devoid of the former reference points that guided the processes of justice and, in Garland's own words:

> No one is quite sure what is radical and what is reactionary. Private prisons, victim impact statements, electronic monitoring, punishment in the community, 'quality of life' policing, restorative justice—these and dozens of other developments lead us into unfamiliar territory where the ideological lines are far from clear and where the old assumptions are an unreliable guide …
>
> For at least two decades now, criminal law and penal policy have been working without clear route maps on a terrain that is largely unknown. If this field is to have any self-consciousness and any possibility of self-criticism and self-correction, then our textbooks have to be rewritten and our sense of how things work needs to be thoroughly revised. (Garland, 2002: 4-5)

There is truth in all of this, much of which emerges in the chapters of this book, but that, to some extent, is history that cannot be rewritten. It may be the legacy of the past, but it is not the foundation for the future.

Restorative justice certainly leads us into waters that, though not entirely uncharted, are at the least tidally uncertain. Its politics and principles are those of inclusiveness, responsibility, reparation and restoration in relation to criminal offending, the administration of justice and penology.[2] The difficulty with promotion of restorative justice is that it sits uncomfortably alongside the prevailing images of 'contemporary' justice that are predicated on retribution, deterrence, incapacitation, exemplary punishment, social exclusion and social control. In an era in which every social risk has to be 'managed' and if possible reduced or neutralised, restorative justice conveys the message that many of today's politicians and policy-makers least want to hear. That is what the title of this book, *Doing Justice Better*, is all about.

---

[2] Here it is important to define the nature of the approach adopted towards the term 'politics' in this work. The sense implied is that which deals with what dictionaries define as 'the complex or aggregate of relationships of men in society, especially those relationships involving authority or power'. This includes the policy-formulating aspects of government, as distinguished from the making of laws in a particular sense.

'RESTORATIVE JUSTICE' AND 'COMMUNITY JUSTICE': A RECIPE FOR CONFUSION?

This book is essentially concerned with the implementation of restorative justice principles within the processes of criminal justice and the implications of such a development for the delivery of 'better justice'. It is not specifically about the endorsement of what has, since the early years of this decade, emerged as the concept of 'community justice', however desirable that initiative may appear to be, or whatever the political motivations for its promotion on an increasingly worldwide basis.[3] The reasons for this distinction are important and require clarification at the outset of this entire discussion.

Adoption of restorative justice principles within criminal justice processes requires that structural change be made throughout the spectrum of policies and practices that include punishment philosophy, court procedures, sentencing practices, the use of imprisonment, non-custodial corrections, the status of victims of crime and the involvement of communities in the delivery of justice. As will become evident in later chapters, restorative justice asks different questions of and proposes alternative answers to the way in which contemporary justice systems are administered on behalf of societies. It seeks to liberate justice from what McElrea (2002a and b) has so aptly described as the 'shackles of the past', by making it more humane, appropriate and considerably more likely to reduce re-offending.

'Community justice' has an altogether different agenda. For while, as McCold (2004) points out, it has superficial similarities with restorative justice, it seeks to work within the structures and assumptions that underpin existing criminal justice systems and which protect these processes from precisely those forms of change that restorative justice proposes. At the same time, 'community justice' implies a proliferation in the spectrum of justice-related agencies within modern democracies through its apparently widely 'inclusive' involvement of politicians, legal professionals, criminal justice policy formulators, police and local government authorities, courts, and charitable and voluntary bodies associated with crime and community protection.[4]

These diverse 'community justice' programmes have adopted a linguistic and practical formula within their broadly stated remits that refers variously to restorative justice, reparative justice, restitutive justice, mediation projects, victim–offender mediation, conferencing, community protection, and services for

---

[3] Community justice initiatives have already been developed in the USA, Canada, Australia, South Africa and, latterly, the UK, albeit on different models and with variations in the public and private sector agencies involved (See, for example, Karp and Todd, 2002; Schärf, 2000; Rodgers, 2005; Scottish Parliament, 2006.)

[4] In England and Wales, the latter include notably the National Association for the Care and Resettlement of Offenders (NACRO), the Prison Reform Trust, the Howard League and Crime Concern, amongst others.

victims, survivors and witnesses, in almost equal measure (*New Statesman,* December 2003). Here, it is of interest to note that at an early British conference held in London in November 2003, the (then) UK Minister for Crime Reduction, Policing and Community Safety (Hazel Blears) advanced the view that 'the future of justice does not exist in isolation, but as part of a wider push to transform public services' (*New Statesman,* December 2003: 2). Such a portmanteau approach is far removed from the prescriptions for restorative justice that lie at the core of this work.

Paul McCold is, I believe, entirely right in suggesting that the greatest threat to adoption of restorative justice principles lies in its becoming submerged in the 'community justice' initiative. This agenda places a focus on the restorative ethos without any essential commitment to the reforms within criminal justice that would be necessary to make reparative and restorative justice operational. 'Community justice' is not specifically about changing court practices to empower victims of crime, not primarily about sentencing reform or making lesser use of custody, not particularly about expanding community corrections and, in fact, not fundamentally about any of the central issues that will concern us in subsequent chapters of this book. However, by apparently adopting some of the language of restorative justice, it may be the case that support for, or endorsement of 'community justice' becomes a preferable political tactic, deliberately designed to confine truly restorative justice to the margins of criminal justice, rather than to confront its central prescriptions.

The explanation offered by McCold has, however, generated its own debate[5] and while broadly supported by Strang (2004), it has been criticised by Karp (2004), Umbreit *et al.* (2004) and by Mara and Bazemore (2004), though for somewhat different underlying reasons. The latter authors, in particular, regard McCold's explanation as being to an extent incomplete and, in some respects also, of itself confusing. Karp, in particular, views restorative and community justice as being to an extent complementary, with more similarities than essential differences. The central issue for Karp is, importantly, the significant divide between either model and the traditional retributive court and its practices. The same view has been endorsed by Blad (2006a and b) and we return to its implications on a number of occasions within the course of this debate.

These differences in approach notwithstanding, the central issue for restorative justice is that it robustly challenges the *status quo* within contemporary criminal justice in a way that 'community justice' does not, being as the latter evidently is, accommodating of the present situation, though perhaps seeking a wider context for crime control and reduction. As Strang points out, it would be unfortunate if the development of restorative justice were to be circumscribed by the limits of 'community justice' and for this reason alone it seems desirable to maintain a clear distinction between the two prescriptions

---

[5] See *Contemporary Justice Review*, Vol.7, No.1 (March 2004) in which responses to McCold were submitted by Strang, Umbreit, Coates and Vos, by Mara and Bazemore and by Karp.

within this work. There are, however, some disturbing signs that within recent approaches to changed practices within the custodial sector of corrections, the emphasis more closely resembles that of a 'community' rather than a restorative justice model. It is largely for this reason that the discussion in later chapters focuses on making prisons reparative and restorative, and on designing for these particular outcomes rather than adopting a wider 'rehabilitative' approach.

THE NECESSITY FOR CHANGE

This book would be unnecessary were it not for the recurring and, in some instances, deepening penal crises that have afflicted so many of the developed democracies over the course of the past two decades. The reasons for these crises are complex, deep-seated and in many respects historical in origin, but it may be contended that they display common features even though they have arisen at different times and in different places. The first of these features is the widespread growth in serious crime; the second is increased severity in sentencing; and the third is the over-use of custodial punishment. Some observers would insist that these features are logically consequent one upon another, though such a contention is not supported in this analysis. If it were demonstrably true that increased use or duration of custodial sentences led to a reduction in serious crime, then the argument would have some force. Since, however, recidivism statistics and evidence-based research provide indications to the contrary, the conclusion is, at the least, equivocal.

Crime apparently reduces for a variety of reasons. One is that it becomes more risk-laden to would-be offenders because the likelihood of detection becomes unacceptable.[6] Another is that offences become re-specified, downgraded or made non-criminal.[7] A third is that detection and prosecution rates decrease because police effort is diverted towards other more prevalent or serious crime, or rates of reporting of certain offences by the public decrease because no substantive outcome is likely. Whatever the reasons, however, comparative crime surveys covering the continent of Europe and North America reveal fluctuating patterns of activity that defy generalised analysis and data definitions that are not strictly comparable. Tonry (2003: 3) indicates that crime rates across Europe have fallen since the mid-1990s, though there is some evidence to show that this amounts to a broad generalisation and that in fact the

---

[6] There is some evidence to show that in Europe and North America the rate of domestic burglary has reduced significantly as a result of the development and widespread installation of domestic surveillance and alarm systems linked to response organizations.

[7] As in the UK where cannabis has been downgraded from a Class B to a Class C drug, the possession of which, although still illegal, is now widely considered by police not to warrant prosecution where individuals are found in possession of small amounts for personal use. See: A. Woodcock (2006), 'Cannabis Law Back in the Spotlight', *Independent*, January 5. The Netherlands decriminalised possession of cannabis in 1975, Germany in 1994 and Belgium in 2003 for those aged 18 or over.

more detailed picture is a variable one, with increases in some areas and decreases in others.[8]

Within England and Wales it is certainly the case that overall crime rates have been falling over recent years, though since 2003 rates of non-injurious violence and robbery have shown significant increases.[9] The *British Crime Survey 2006* indicates a 42 per cent decrease in all offences since 1995, with steadily decreasing trends for crimes of violence, domestic burglary and the volume of overall offences recorded by the police.[10] It therefore seems surprising that over much the same period, the prison population has risen dramatically by a factor of over 50 per cent.[11] In 2004-5, the last full year for which statistics are currently available, of an average daily prison population of more than 75,000, 58 per cent were serving sentences of six months or less. As we shall see later, such sentences are altogether unlikely to reduce the high incidence of re-offending and reconviction.[12]

Correctional services in England and Wales[13] consumed a total resource budget of £3.5 billion in 2003-4, an increase of more than 50 per cent since 1998-9. Home Office estimates indicate that this figure will rise by a further 15 per cent in the financial year 2005-6. Of the increase since 1998-9, £340 million has been invested in prisons and £488 million in additional funding has been absorbed by the (now) National Probation Service. Moreover, capital investment in prisons has risen by only £6 million over the same period, despite the rapid growth in the prison population. In October 2006, 88 of the 142 prisons were overcrowded

---

[8] These comments refer to offences recorded by the police. The *International Comparison of Criminal Justice Statistics* (Barclay and Tavares *et al.*, 2003), indicates rising rates in France, Greece and Portugal (all 11 per cent), Holland and Spain (both 10 per cent) and the entire European Union (4 per cent) and falling rates in Italy and Denmark (both 11 per cent), Finland (3 per cent), England and Wales (2 per cent) and Sweden (1 per cent). Source: www.homeoffice.gov.uk/rds/pdfs2/hosb

[9] Home Office (2005a), *Crime Statistics – England and Wales*, www.crimestatistics.org.uk/output/page 63.asp

[10] The same trends are indicated in the British government's own most recent analysis: *Crime in England and Wales 2005/6* (A. Walker, C. Kershaw and S. Nicholas (eds)), London: Home Office Research, Development and Statistics Directorate (Home Office, 2006a) .

[11] In fact, since 1993 in England and Wales, the average daily prison population has risen by 70 per cent from 44,500 to 79,500 in October 2006. Home Office median level projections indicate a further rise to some 98,190 by 2010. The average daily prison population in 1997 was 60,000 — 19,640 fewer than the present level of occupancy. Sources: Reform International — www.reform.co.uk/website/crime/factfile.aspx. and Home Office (2006b), *Prison Population Projections 2006-2013, England and Wales* (Statistical Bulletin 11/06), London: Home Office Research, Development and Statistics Directorate (N. deSilva, P. Cowell, T. Chow and P. Worthington (eds)), (July).

[12] In 2003-4, the latest year for which recidivism statistics are available, 61 per cent of all offenders were reconvicted within two years. For the 18-21 year age group the rate was 73 per cent and for male adolescents (aged 15-18) the rate was 82 per cent (Home Office) (2005a *supra*, p.2).

[13] These include the Prison and Probation Services and the Youth Justice Board (YJB). The former two organizations form the National Offender Management Service (NOMS).

and overall occupancy levels were six per cent in excess of the authorised operational capacity of the total prison estate.[14]

These broadly stated statistics give rise to a number of serious questions. Why, when crime recorded by the police has shown a consistent trend of decreasing, have increasing numbers of offenders been sentenced to custody? Why are reconviction rates so high within two years of a sanction having been imposed? Can it be claimed that short custodial sentences are effective and if not, why are so many offenders thus sentenced? What does this all cost the government and the tax-paying public? Is a 60 per cent failure rate in any sense 'value for money'? Are there ways of 'doing justice better'? The even larger question that over-arches all these considerations is that of what ideological imperatives drive the penal policies that produce these results. In short, what are the politics of this penology? These questions and a number of others that derive from them will all be addressed in the chapters that follow.

The statistics do certainly indicate that there is a considerable discrepancy between aspirations and outcomes within the British penal system at the present time. Moreover, the British situation is mirrored in a number of other Western-style democracies throughout the world today. High rates of incarceration and of recidivism together suggest strongly that there is something fundamentally wrong with existing penal policies and practices. Penal policies do not, however, function in a vacuum, or at the very least should not do so. These are a part, albeit a significant part, of the broader spectrum of national social policy that encompasses the welfare and quality of life of all citizens within a state. Prisons are, or should be, part of the communities within which they operate, not fortresses remote from the social environment that surrounds them.

Community corrections should also form part of the social fabric that binds the day-to-day functioning of living communities together, rather than being seen as something that is carried on in an isolated manner that enables offenders to be ostracised and stigmatised. In ideal circumstances, community-based sanctions can provide added value to the amenity of community life by undertaking purposeful work and activities that would, otherwise, remain undone or neglected. Within most countries there is a vast scope for such undertakings that can serve to enhance the quality of life of citizens, providing that the projects selected are properly planned, resourced and supervised.

'Doing justice better' means changing attitudes towards offending and offenders, perceiving offending differently, and attempting to understand its causes and effects within the *total* social structure rather than in a narrower legalistic frame of reference. It also means changing political attitudes and the extent to which these are shaped by short-term electoral ambitions driven significantly by pressures exerted by the mass media. In countries like Britain,

---

14 The latter statistics were compiled by the Prison Reform Trust on 23 September 2006 and quoted in *The Observer* newspaper in an article by Jamie Doward (Home Affairs Editor) entitled 'Police Cells Ready as Prison Population Hits Limit of 80,000', London: *The Observer* (2006a), 24 September p. 9.

the need for penological change has become one of the most urgent social priorities that confront governments—regardless of their political preferences and persuasions.

THE POLITICS OF JUSTICE: A BRITISH PERSPECTIVE

Recent experience, particularly in Britain, has confirmed that ideological differences between political parties narrow considerably in relation to crime control and reduction[15] (Garland, 2002: 131-6; Tonry, 2003: 16). Perhaps, stated somewhat differently, the same besetting problems caused by crime and offenders have to be faced by whichever government holds power and the means at their disposal to attempt this (the police, courts and correctional services) tend, ostensibly, to be 'given' factors—at least initially. Thus, within this work, we are concerned with a form of politics that operates less from a distinctive ideological base and rather more from reactive strategies eclectically selected to address presenting situations.

During the mid-1990s there occurred a transition within British penal politics that was to have a profound effect in shaping the nature and extent of the contemporary penal crisis. The sudden switch of emphasis in 1993 from what might be described as 'Nothing Works'[16] to 'Prison Works',[17] and the proposal of mandatory minimum sentences for specific forms of offending by Michael Howard (then Home Secretary) were as perplexing as they were dramatic in their effects upon the custodial penal system. Almost immediately, the prison population began its inexorable rise from an average daily level of 44,500 to the present figure of over 79,500. It was perplexing because only a short time earlier, the same government, in its White Paper *Crime, Justice and Protecting the Public* (Home Office, 1990), had declared that 'prison is an expensive way of making bad people worse'. Garland describes this type of political behaviour as 'acting out', or 'engaging in a form of impulsive and unreflective action, avoiding

---

[15] This situation has been particularly noticeable in the 1997 transition from a Conservative government to a New Labour one and the striking continuity of policy determination between the respective Home Secretaries Michael Howard and Jack Straw. It is particularly notable insofar as Michael Howard had, shortly before the general election, brought forward extensively punitive proposals for Mandatory Minimum Sentences for the crimes of violence, drug-trafficking and burglary. Though it was widely considered that a traditionally less punitive Labour government would not bring these measures into legislation, the new Home Secretary Jack Straw did so within The Crime (Sentences) Act 1997.

[16] The term somewhat inaccurately attributed to Robert Martinson in his (1974) assessment of programmes for the treatment of offenders within a research study conducted in collaboration with Lipton and Wilks, published in Lipton *et al.* (1975).

[17] The now (in)famous declaration by Home Secretary Michael Howard to the Conservative Party Congress in October 1993: "Let us be clear. Prison works. It ensures that we are protected from muggers and rapists—and it makes many who are tempted to commit crime think twice." See here, for example, the commentary of Cavadino and Dignan (1997a: 38).

realistic recognition of underlying problems, the very fact of acting providing its own form of relief and gratification' (Garland, 2002: 132-3).

Cathartic though such 'acting out' episodes may be for politicians, and there are plenty of other examples of similar behaviour in the past and since,[18] the effects that they have within the penal system are considerable. Worse, the messages that they convey are ones of confusion, lack of wide consultation and precipitance. Neither are such situations greatly helped by the increasing tendency of governments and their policy-drafting civil servants to disregard the expertise of correctional professionals and research-based academic evidence in favour of internally generated prescriptions consistent with prevailing political ideologies. As Garland suggests:

> The standing of social professionals within the criminal justice system has been challenged from the late 1970s onwards and this was exacerbated in the 1980s by organizational reforms that shifted decision-making power away from clinicians and practitioners towards accountants and managers. This reduction in the credibility and political influence of criminal justice experts and social professionals has had major consequences for criminal justice policy. Up until recently, these professionals functioned as a kind of buffer, shielding the processes of policy-making and day-to-day administration from the full impact of public opinion. The declining influence of these groups, together with the politicisation of crime policy, has altered the dynamics of policymaking in this area, making it much more open to populist pressure from the outside. (Garland, 2002: 151)

The development described here has also removed from the formulation of penal policies a moderating influence that was capable of offering wisdom and practical experience of 'what works' and what does not. Not all reliable evidence derives from research alone: the observations and experience of professionals working within criminal justice systems are often of equal validity and are frequently more pragmatic.

The emergence of restorative justice during the 1990s and into this present decade on an increasingly worldwide basis has added a new dimension to the debate concerning crime and punishment. It has done so because it vigorously challenges some of the hitherto relatively unchallenged assumptions that underpin contemporary justice administration, definitions of crime, court processes, the use of sanctions, the virtual exclusion of victims and the relationship between offenders, victims, communities and society as a whole.

The title of this book was deliberately selected to indicate that the agenda advanced by restorative justice conveys a wider meaning to the term 'politics'. In the brief overview provided up to this point, we have been confronted with a

---

[18] Most notably, perhaps, William Whitelaw in relation to detention centres in the early 1980s, Leon Brittan in suddenly changing parole criteria in November 1983 and more recently by David Blunkett in apparently supporting measures to reduce the prison population in a speech to the Prison Service Conference in 2002 and subsequently calling for longer sentences for violent and sexual offenders in the Criminal Justice Bill published in the same year.

narrow and somewhat dogmatic concept of doing justice, much of which has been more responsive to pressures external to penal systems themselves. Crime does not only violate state laws, and to perpetuate such a constricted definition of crime enhances the likelihood of unreasoned responses towards those who commit offences. Crime violates *people* whom we commonly describe as victims. It also violates families and the communities within which victims live and to which, in the main, offenders have to return having been sanctioned. Crime also creates obligations, particularly on offenders, but these obligations extend much wider than might, at first sight, be supposed.

It was mentioned earlier (at *fn. 2 supra*) that the definition of 'politics' advanced here is one that embraces 'the complex or aggregate of relationships of men in society, especially those relationships involving authority or power.' Commission of crime challenges the authority of the state and places the offender in the power of the state to a considerable extent. The state has a reciprocal responsibility to ensure that offenders are dealt with responsibly, temperately, impartially and without resort to vindictiveness. But the complex or aggregate of relationships necessarily includes victims, communities and the wider society in which reciprocal responsibilities also exist in relation to offenders. This theme is developed further in the chapters that follow and represents the central theme of this work.

'INSTRUMENTALISM' IN CRIMINAL JUSTICE

One of the main difficulties that has arisen within criminal justice during the past decade is that in the wake of the vacuum left by the demise of the 'justice model', the purposes of criminal punishment have become heavily invested with a political rhetoric that has deliberately set out to 'emotionalise' its crusading 'war on crime'. The linguistics of punishment are replete with slogans intended to idealise the way in which this 'war' is being waged in a pro-active manner in many democracies—not least in Britain and America. 'Tough on crime and the causes of crime'; 'Three strikes and you're out'; 'Prison works'; 'Truth in sentencing'; 'If you don't want the time, don't do the crime'; 'No frills prisons'; 'Decent but austere prison conditions': all represent what Garland has described as the 'sound-bite' nature of penal politics designed to convey a punitive message to both offenders and the public (Garland, 2002: 143).

I agree strongly with Blad's assertion that we now live in an era in which 'penal instrumentalism' reigns (Blad, 2003 and 2006a: 137).[19] This strongly implies that criminal punishment becomes used deliberately as an instrument of social policy and that proper limitations on its use are of secondary importance

---

[19] Penal instrumentalism , viewed strictly, means the use of criminal punishment for the pursuit of objectives within social policy other than the punishment of offenders. It has, as will be seen later, significant implications for sentencing practice and, in particular, the justification of specific measures for those considered to be criminally dangerous.

to the necessity to be perceived to be 'winning the war' on crime. As we shall see later (*Chapter 6*), this has significant implications for the necessary linkage between community-based corrections and the custodial sector. Hutton (2003: 118) suggests that this trend has much to do with a political consciousness heavily influenced by perceptions of a 'populist punitiveness'[20] that may be more imagined than real. We shall return to this discussion in *Chapter 3*.

The importance of 'instrumentalism' for this analysis lies in the difficulties it presents for the development of restorative justice practices that seek a strict limitation on the use of custodial penalties where these can reasonably be avoided. The 'tough on crime' rhetoric enables those antipathetic towards restorative justice to label it as a 'soft on crime' option, as we shall subsequently see in *Chapters 5* and *6*. A further and important consideration that arises from Blad's analysis is the inevitability of punishment that flows from penal policies based predominantly on retribution and deterrence. 'Tough on crime' policies, framed in response to mass media pressures for selective punitive responses to certain forms of crime,[21] can be pursued for the purposes of short-term electoral advantage. The outcome of adopting measures such as mandatory minimum and extended sentences is that excessive use of imprisonment becomes an almost inevitable outcome. Moreover, punishment for its own sake becomes unavoidable, since to refrain from imposing such penalties undermines the credibility of the penal policies upon which these are predicated.

However it is viewed, penal instrumentalism has serious implications for restorative justice and *vice versa*. Parsimony in sentencing has long been held to be a virtue, but its insistence upon punishing to the least extent consistent with justice has been widely overlooked in the contemporary 'war on crime'. Indeed, as matters stand, there is a voluble faction within every national population that believes that sentences and judges are altogether too lenient (Tonry, 2003: 5). It is within this particular area of discussions about what is assumed to be 'the essential rightness' of criminal punishment that we run into the difficulties associated with the notion of desert.

Desert, of course, means different things to different people. The 'justice model' was predicated on the principle of 'commensurate desert' (von Hirsch, 1976: 66; Hudson, 1987: 37-40), widely interpreted as the proportionality of punishment to the harm caused by crime. This concept acknowledged that

---

[20] A term first used by Sir Anthony Bottoms in 1993, but which has since been taken up by a number of influential criminologists such as Tonry (2003) and Garland (2002). See Sir A. E. Bottoms (1995), 'The Philosophy and Politics of Punishment and Sentencing', in C. Clarkson and R. Morgan (eds), *The Politics of Sentencing Reform*, Oxford: Oxford University Press. As Tonry (2003: 4-5) points out, explanations of the supposed phenomenon of 'populist punitiveness' vary in approach. Most, however, suggest that media sensationalism of serious crime inflates the public perception of the prevalence of such offences and politicians are generally reluctant to correct these misconceptions since it suits their electoral ambitions to allow them to persist in order to justify 'tough on crime' policies.

[21] Particularly against sexual and violent offenders, as will become evident in *Chapters 6* and *7*.

punishment should not be excessive, but also insisted that it should not be too lenient either. The difficulty caused by the legacy of the model is that it meant all things to all people and interpretations of desert can become value-laden in relation to the seriousness of offences (harm) and the culpability of offenders (blame). For those anxious to pursue increasingly punitive agendas, the justice model presented a perfect justification: ratchet up both the harm and the blame and the extent of punishment must increase accordingly.

Advocates of restorative justice argue the case altogether differently. Acceptance that punishment should be imposed because it is *deserved* does not allow of penalties that are in any way excessive, arbitrary, or imposed for reasons other than to mark the extent of the harm occasioned to victims of crime. Thus, where offenders accept responsibility for the harm done and are prepared to make reparation to victims, a strong case emerges for parsimony—or the infliction of the minimum (or lesser) amount of punishment consistent with achieving a just outcome. It will be evident here that instrumentalism is significantly at odds both with securing just outcomes and limiting punishment when it becomes appropriate to do so.

THE STRUCTURE OF THIS BOOK

The main chapters of this book are each devoted to particular issues that arise directly from the foregoing discussion. The central thesis pursued within each successive chapter is that restorative justice provides a long overdue means of 'doing justice better' than is possible in existing circumstances. The reasons why significant change has become so urgently necessary have been outlined earlier, but change will not occur until those responsible for penal policy development can be persuaded that there are preferable, fairer, more humane and less expensive ways of doing justice than are used at present. That these ways may also ultimately lead to crime reduction and lesser use of custodial corrections becomes a major incentive towards change.

In *Chapter 1, The Politics of Restorative Justice*, an assessment is made of the extent to which restorative justice challenges what might be regarded as traditionally accepted approaches to the administration of criminal justice. Implicit within this assessment is the assumption that matters presently stand as they do because national populations and politicians wish it to be so and that the apparatus of criminal justice in most democracies represents policies of deliberate choice.[22] If this is the case, then it is necessary to question why, when these policies are defined and put into effect, the outcomes are so consistently

---

[22] This conclusion is advanced by both Tonry (2003: 6) and, somewhat differently by Garland (2002: 142-3). The important issue that this raises is why such political choices are made when evidence is available to show that pursuit of such policies neither significantly reduces recidivism nor changes the behaviour of offenders. The inevitable result is seen in increasing use of custody and an escalation in prison populations.

unsatisfactory and ineffective in terms of reducing recidivism and curbing the social and fiscal costs of criminal justice.

Within the same chapter the motivating factors apparently responsible for the maintenance of the *status quo* are examined in the context of their effects upon the broader spectrum of social policy within modern democracies. Drawing primarily on developments within criminal justice in Britain[23] over the past decade-and-a-half, an analysis is made of the main trends in criminal justice legislation and their potential effects upon the promotion of restorative justice principles and practice.

The inevitable conclusion that emerges from the analysis within this chapter is that implementation of restorative justice principles within existing criminal justice systems would require a new penology of corrections. This becomes necessary because restorative justice seeks altogether different outcomes from the processes of criminal justice and is not tolerant of approaches to justice that imply or promote the inevitability of punishment based primarily upon retribution and deterrence.

In *Chapter 2, Making Justice Restorative*, the need for a new restorative penology is discussed in some detail and the differences of approach between restorative and 'traditional' justice are explored with a view to defining the implications of these differences for delivery of 'better justice'. The difficulties associated with the legacy of the rehabilitative ethic are analysed, particularly in relation to the effect that these have upon sentencing patterns and custodial regimes. The outcome of this discussion suggests the need for a new and significantly different concept of what has previously been described as 'rehabilitation' and the potential implications that this has for operational penology.

One of the problems that assume a measure of inevitability is that of dealing differently with offenders who wish to engage with restorative practices and those who decline, for whatever reasons, to do so. This suggests the necessity for an extent of 'bifurcation' in penal practice that has, hitherto, been regarded as largely undesirable. Though this differential approach is discussed in more detail in later chapters, the issue is raised at this stage because it critically affects the potential effectiveness of sanctions designed to secure restorative outcomes.

Within this chapter also, the different demands of restorative justice on offenders, victims of crime, communities and the legal system are identified, particularly in relation to the more obvious counter-arguments that might be deployed against acceptance of the implications of the need for a new penology. In the final section of *Chapter 2*, an attempt is made to draw together the diverse strands of this discussion and assess the extent to which a new penology is an

---

[23] The term Britain used here relates primarily to England and Wales, since Scotland and Northern Ireland have separate penal systems and criminal justice legislation specific to their particular geographical situations and devolved administrations.

essential starting point if restorative justice is to enter successfully the mainstream of correctional theory and practice.

In *Chapter 3, Victims' Voices,* the focus of attention is turned towards victims of crime and the extent to which they can or should be regarded as 'key' stakeholders within the concept of restorative justice (Zehr, 2002a: 14; Zehr and Mika, 1998: 47-55). This is a contentious issue raised by advocacy of restorative justice practices and the debate that it gives rise to merits careful consideration. Within the 'traditional' model of criminal justice it is clear that victims, particularly the needs of victims, have not received adequate consideration and, as a matter of essential fairness, a significant change to this situation is long overdue. The debate concerning how far and in what particular respects this change is necessary is bound to have a major impact upon future court practices, custodial correctional regimes and community justice. For all these reasons, the situation of victims becomes an appropriate matter for attention, since it derives from the requirement for a new penology discussed previously and significantly affects the discussion within following chapters.

That chapter, *Chapter 3,* highlights the implications of viewing crime as imposing obligations, violating both victims and communities, and also of creating opportunities for reparative action by offenders. Discussion of these issues leads logically to an analysis of existing provisions for victim support and the question of the extent to which victims enjoy statutory 'rights' in any significant manner at the present time. Though this discussion is based primarily upon the British criminal justice system as it presently operates, there is considerable evidence to suggest that parallel situations exist in many of the world's developed democracies also.

Obligations involve the practical necessity of 'putting things right', but the extent to which this moral imperative is interpreted in contemporary penal practices becomes a matter of considerable conjecture. So also, is the extent to which victims of crime should be permitted to participate within the processes of criminal justice and the implications of this participation for courts, offenders and victims themselves. *Chapter 3* concludes with a brief overview of the reasons why victims occupy such a central place within restorative justice prescriptions and of the desirable, though perhaps contentious, outcomes that might flow from affording victims greater consideration.

Chapter 4, Penal Politics, Reparation and Restoration, is, in many respects, the pivotal one within *Doing Justice Better*. It brings together the currently problematic political aspects of justice and criminal punishment alongside the prospective concepts of reparation and restoration that are central to the operation of restorative justice. The difficulty that this presents is one of reconciling two systems: the one predominantly retrospective, retributive and inevitably punitive; the other prospective, reparative, restorative and impatient of excessive punishment. The suggestion that in present circumstances criminal punishment is used in an 'instrumental' manner becomes a key issue within this debate,[24] since it can be said to be used as much for political ends as for the administration of justice.

Another problem that has to be faced squarely is that of reducing reliance on punishment for the purposes of general deterrence. I have addressed this issue in some detail in earlier work (Cornwell, 1985 and 2006: 53-65), but find the general objection admirably summarised by Beyleveld in the following words:

> Deterrence has for too long been associated with the sorts of policies which I regard as extreme. This has made the notion [of deterrence] a politically loaded one. This is unfortunate, for deterrence is, in fact, a pervasive fact of human existence ... It is important to understand its limits and operation, not only for purposes of control, but also for purposes of understanding human behaviour generally. If deterrence is not studied seriously or if deterrence policies are suggested and implemented without adequate grounding, we will achieve neither of these purposes, but merely add fuel to the flames of political passion. (Beyleveld, 1973: 148)

There is no doubt that sentencing offenders for the supposed beneficial effects of general deterrence—whether or not in conjunction with retribution—effectively increases the severity of sanctions and also results in the escalation of prison populations. That its effects in practice are largely unknown and unknowable makes the practice the more arbitrary and cynical, however much it may have attractiveness in a political sense.

Within the same chapter it has also been necessary to clarify the fact that restorative justice is not primarily anti-retributive, neither does it propose itself as a substitute for retribution (Brunk, 2001: 31-56; Zehr, 2002a: 58-9).[25] What restorative justice does propose is the general principle of punishing *less*, particularly in instances in which there is no utility in extending punishment and its unpleasant consequences. In other words, we need to move away from the 'inevitability' of punishment chiefly to maintain its own credibility and move more towards limiting its use where mitigating factors (such as an offender's willingness to accept blame and make reparation) indicate more favourable outcomes.

This particular discussion leads logically to the further analysis of the role of reparation within criminal justice and the suggestion that it may be helpful to view reparation, restoration and social reintegration as a sequential process.[26] As

---

[24] (See also fn.19 *supra*). Penal instrumentalism refers primarily to the use of punishment for purposes other than those normally expected to flow from it. Here see, for further clarification, the explanation of 'instrumentalism' provided by Dworkin (1986: 249-52).

[25] As Howard Zehr points out, Conrad Brunk (2001) has argued that at the theoretical or philosophical level, retribution and restoration are not the polar opposites that we frequently assume them to be. In fact, they have much in common. A primary goal of both retributive theory and restorative theory is to vindicate through reciprocity, by evening the score. Where they differ is in what each suggests will effectively right the balance (Zehr, 2002a: 58).

[26] Helpful to the extent of assisting us to revise the former concept of rehabilitation in a more practical manner that does not allow the possibility of extended punishment (or indeterminacy) for

will become evident in *Chapters 5* and *6*, the concept of reparative justice may have more immediate appeal to politicians and policy-makers than that of restorative justice with all its challenges to the *status quo*. This does not, in any sense, negate the principles of restorative justice as it is proposed here: rather it represents a pragmatic attempt to cross one bridge at a time, rather than a bridge too far.

In the concluding section of *Chapter 4* the difficult issue of the social reintegration of ex-offenders is considered in relation to prevailing social attitudes and contemporary penal policies. As will be seen in the chapters that follow and in particular in *Chapter 7*, only a new image of corrections will enable public attitudes, shaped and hardened by media sensationalism of crime, to be changed. It will also become clear that—at least in Britain and also in a number of other countries in Europe and elsewhere—politicians anxious to be seen to be 'tough on crime' have cynically exploited the 'fear of crime' scenario presented by the media both for short-term electoral advantage and to promote increased severity in sentencing and use of custody. This is a principal reason why there is a widespread reluctance to examine the true credentials of restorative justice and a consequent agenda to consign it to the shallows rather than allow it to move into the mainstream of criminal justice policies.

The discussion in *Chapter 5, Making Prisons Reparative and Restorative*, is devoted entirely to the issues involved in transforming prisons to deliver reparative and, ultimately, restorative regimes. From the rather unpromising starting point of the present situation that exists in many countries, it becomes clear that if any progress is to be made, either considerably less use has to be made of imprisonment or many more prisons have to be provided. Prisons filled to, or above capacity simply cannot deliver the quality of regime that allows even the most unrefined of reparative programmes to be made available to all inmates on a consistent basis. These programmes, at the least, require the capacity to address offending behaviour, the facilities to provide reparative work on a daily basis and a staged custodial process that tests the reliability of inmates with external employment within local communities as they approach the time for release.

Changing the ethos of prisons involves abandonment of the present concept of 'negative' sanctions.[27] Prisons that merely 'warehouse' inmates for specified periods of time are unlikely to promote changed behaviour or attitudes to offending and may well release back into communities ex-offenders prone to

---

the purposes of 'treatment', therapeutic intervention, or the exemplary sentencing of certain types of offenders for public protection. This practice is discussed further in *Chapters 6* and *7*.

[27] 'Negative sanctions' is a term used to describe prison regimes that demand no necessary constructive responses from inmates other than the passing of time in custody until the date of their scheduled release arrives. Overcrowded prisons cannot provide for all inmates regular daily employment that enables wages to be earned, a proportion of which is allocated to victims of crime. In addition, every sentence should commence with a period of induction within which individual offending behaviour is analysed and victim-awareness is promoted.

recidivism. If, however, the perceived purpose of imprisonment is predominantly that of social incapacitation, then existing conditions may be said to meet this aim. In such circumstances it should not be a matter of particular surprise that more, rather than fewer offenders appear before the courts charged with new offences within short periods of time from release. The most recent statistics in Britain indicate rates of reconviction within two years of discharge from custody of 60 per cent for certain forms of offending (Home Office 2001a; Office for National Statistics, 2006: 137-8).[28] This is widely believed to be a conservative estimate, but it indicates strongly that under existing circumstances the deterrent effect of imprisonment is low (Home Office, 2002a and b; Roberts and Smith, 2003).

Within many contemporary democracies the purpose of prisons, as expressed in the ideological rhetoric of ruling political parties, is manifestly that of incapacitation justified on the grounds of retribution and deterrence. Imprisonment represents a very high-cost option for delivering retribution where the deterrent effect is so evidently meagre and large numbers of offenders quickly return to prison for 'more of the same'. In *Chapter 5* the logic of this situation is robustly challenged and an altogether more constructive concept of reparative custody is proposed. The regime design and operational ethos of reparative prisons is not difficult to conceive, the under-pinning rationale being provided by clearly specified rules of behaviour, the necessity for addressing offending behaviour and a work-based regime of productive employment that generates revenue for victims of crime and, at the same time, inculcates a regular work pattern in offenders.

The difficulty has to be faced of dealing differently with those offenders willing to engage with reparative regimes, take responsibility for their offences and make reparation to victims and those who refuse to do so. This situation envisages a measure of inevitable 'bifurcation', the implications of which are discussed in *Chapter 5*. In ideal circumstances it would be preferable for entire prison establishments to be given over to reparative regimes and others used to accommodate those who decline to participate in reparative custody. It is not, however, inconceivable that dual regimes might be operated within single prisons, though in such instances, a measure of physical separation would clearly be necessary.

The recommendation is made that reparative regimes should operate the 'direct supervision' model of discipline and control, since this places a clear responsibility on each individual inmate to comply with 'house rules' and

---

[28] The 2006 Edition of *Social Trends*, published by the Office for National Statistics, provides a detailed analysis of reconviction rates for Standard List offences for prisoners in England and Wales discharged in 2001. The rates of reconviction for re-offending within two years are variable as between males and females and reflect particularly high rates for theft (80 per cent and 76 per cent), burglary (76 per cent and 72 per cent) and robbery (56 per cent and 30 per cent), but lower rates (less than 50 per cent) for all other offences. Source: Office for National Statistics (2006), *Social Trends* (No.36), *Chapter 9*, pp. 137-8.

significantly reduces the number of staff members routinely employed on general duties within living units.[29] Use of direct supervision methods also enables a greater proportion of staff to be deployed to productive aspects of the regime, delivery of offending behaviour counselling and analysis, recreational activities and similar duties.

Within the same chapter it is also proposed that for a number of reasons, closer links should be established between prisons and the local communities within which they are situated. There is an evident need to reduce what might be termed the 'fortress effect' of prisons, to make these facilities more 'community friendly' and to involve communities to a greater extent in prison regimes. Ultimately, the reparative regimes suggested here would incorporate a logical progression from custody to community-based work for inmates approaching the end of their sentences. It is acknowledged that this carries an inevitable element of risk, but this risk, it is suggested, is far outweighed by the benefits that flow from accepting it. The potential risks and benefits for communities, offenders and criminal justice systems are discussed in some detail toward the end of *Chapter 5*.

Perhaps the most important aspect of reparative regimes lies in their potential to make prisons more humane and purposeful, while at the same time making them a more integral part of the communities in which they are located. The 'community: custody gap' has traditionally been preserved to emphasise the socially exclusive role of prisons, the isolated nature of the custodial process and perceived merit of 'banishing' criminal offenders from contact with wider society. Understandable though such motivations may be in pursuit or reinforcement of a collective morality, the dysfunctional outcomes also have to be weighed and acknowledged. At the least, reparative prisons and their regimes might restore some measure of public confidence in the effectiveness of custodial corrections and the need for victims of crime to become at least a considered part of the penal process.

Chapter 6, Community Justice, forms a natural extension of *Chapter 5*, with its analysis of the non-custodial sector of corrections and of the potential for its expansion. Indeed, it is important that these two chapters are viewed as complementary in nature, since it was suggested in *Chapter 5* that every reparative custodial sentence should include a final period of time spent working within the community from prison. There is, undeniably, an element of public risk inherent in 'work-out' or 'working-out' schemes, but this is probably no

---

[29] Direct supervision regimes have been introduced with considerable success in some prisons within the USA and recently also in South Africa. The Mangaung Correctional Centre in Bloemfontein, Free State Province, is a 3000-bed maximum security facility operated by the private correctional company Global Solutions Limited (GSL) (SA) Pty. Ltd. Since the facility was opened in July 2001, it has operated on a direct supervision basis with a significant reduction in rule-infracting behaviour, inter-personal violence and non-compliant behaviour compared with other penal institutions of a similar nature.

greater than the risk of releasing prisoners from custody into the community on the expiry of sentences without any period of probationary external activity.

The major problems associated with the expansion of non-custodial corrections are two-fold: the allegedly widespread public fear of crime and the 'tough on crime' political ideology that has pervaded penal policies over the past decade, particularly in Britain. Both are discussed in some detail in the opening section of this chapter. There is much evidence that the former is driven by the sensational treatment of serious violent and sexual crime within the mass media which has, to some extent, provided an apparent justification for the development of 'tough on crime' policies by politicians. Some commentators on this situation have strongly expressed the view that it has been cynically and quite deliberately manipulated by politicians anxious to be perceived as 'waging the war on crime' for electoral advantage (Garland, 2002; Tonry, 2003). Moreover, if the truth about crime rates were to be made more widely known, 'tough on crime' policies would lose some of their public appeal and impetus.[30] It is of interest that a general downward trend in Europe over the past decade in offences against property and the person should have been accompanied by a widespread increase in the use of custodial sentences. This situation forms the backdrop against which an expansion in the use of non-custodial sanctions has to be viewed.

The confused nature of recent criminal justice policy development and legislation in England and Wales relating to community sanctions is discussed at some length in the second part of this chapter. This discussion is particularly relevant in the light of two separate and influential reports compiled during the early years of the present decade. The first of these reports became known as the Halliday Report[31] and the second was the independent report commissioned by the Esmeé Fairbairn Foundation (EFF) under the chairmanship of Lord Coulsfield.[32] As will be seen in *Chapter 6*, both of these reports were to present some significant difficulties for a government pledged to pursuit of 'tough on crime' policies, and the Halliday Report, in particular, revealed some strange inconsistencies with evidence-based research. The subsequent legislation which was broadly based on it (the Criminal Justice Act 2003) will be seen to have added more confusion than clarity to the entire sector of non-custodial corrections in England and Wales and also to have promoted a further measure

---

[30] The available evidence points strongly to the fact that over the past decade in Europe in particular, rates of domestic burglary and violent crime have fallen significantly, though not uniformly (Home Office, 2001a and 2004). These offences, it is widely claimed by the media, are the two main components of public fear of crime.

[31] Home Office (2001b), *Making Punishments Work: Report of a Review of the Sentencing Framework for England and Wales*, London: Home Office Communications Directorate. The report was named after its director John Halliday and included, significantly, the proposals for 'custody plus', 'custody minus' and 'intermittent custody' that subsequently became part of the White Paper *Justice for All* (Home Office, 2002a) and the Criminal Justice Act 2003.

[32] EFF (2004a), *Crime, Courts and Confidence: Report of an Independent Inquiry into Alternatives to Prison*, London: The Stationery Office (TSO).

of crisis within a custodial penal system already operating at all-time record levels of occupancy.

In the third part of *Chapter 6,* the focus of attention is turned to an altogether different and more encouraging situation in Finland and to a brief analysis of how that country deliberately set about reducing its overburdened prison system and simplifying, rather than complicating, its non-custodial sector of corrections over recent decades. The Finnish experience clearly demonstrates that massive prison populations are both undesirable and completely avoidable and, moreover, that crime rates need not increase if greater dependence is placed on community-based sanctions. It is an object lesson in criminological pragmatism that serves to demonstrate, in the starkest terms, the extent to which ideological dogmatism lies at the heart of the crises that afflict so many of our contemporary penal systems.

In the light of the discussion within *Chapter 6* it is difficult to be other than pessimistic about the potential in Britain and many other democracies for an expansion in community-based corrections and lesser use of custody: that is, unless there is a sea-change both in attitudes towards offenders and in the intransigent ideological approaches to penal politics. Restorative justice offers a means of facilitating this change and the Finnish model of justice provides evidence that it is not impossible of achievement. As the old proverb has it: one can take a horse to the water, but one cannot make it drink. Community sanctions are thus likely to remain confined in the present *cul-de-sac* until a serious re-assessment of social priorities allows a more enlightened approach to be adopted.

Perhaps the most distressing aspect of this situation is that it is caused to a considerable extent by a form of intellectual dishonesty. The first strand of this dishonesty is the failure of those making penal policies to acknowledge that to a notable extent recorded crime has diminished, not just in Britain but widely also elsewhere across Europe and North America (Tonry, 2003: 3; Garland, 2002: 106). The most notable decreases have occurred within the offences of domestic burglary and violence against the person—both offences for which conviction normally carries a custodial sentence. Thus to make increased use of imprisonment in such circumstances seems, on the face of matters, particularly perverse.

The second strand of this dishonesty lies in the much-advertised predisposition of some governments—particularly the British government—to rely on evidence-based research in policy determination and then, when this is made available, ignore it to a very significant extent and for entirely ideological reasons. We return to this particular issue in *Chapter 7, Doing Justice Better,* that forms the final part of this work.

DOING JUSTICE BETTER—WHAT RESTORATIVE JUSTICE PROPOSES

The final chapter of this book, *Chapter 7*, is devoted to an appraisal of the ways in which approaches to criminal justice administration would have to change in a restorative justice era. In many respects this chapter draws together the main areas of discussion within the preceding chapters and locates these within a restorative justice framework designed to 'do justice better' in the future.

The first part of the chapter deals with the need to change the way in which criminal justice policies are conceived and to move away from the self-consciousness of an era dominated by media sensationalism of crime and reactive policy-making designed, primarily, to secure short-term electoral support for being seen to be 'tough on crime'. This means, essentially, telling the truth about crime, resolving to use expensive custodial punishment only when it is strictly unavoidable and, when it is used, making it purposeful for offenders, victims and the wider society.

Strategies to *reduce* crime may be altogether different from those designed to *control* crime and this prompts the need to think within a changed conceptual framework that recognises this possibility. This may require the formulation of a new penology as suggested in *Chapter 2*, acceptance of a measure of 'bifurcation' within operational penal practice and reconsideration of the use of prisons. Restorative justice may assist us in doing this simply because it proposes a different set of definitions of criminal justice and asks different questions about the preferable outcomes of the justice process.

Giving victims of crime greater consideration within the processes of justice requires that courts operate differently and suggests a measure of pre-trial conferencing and diversion where this is possible and appropriate. Statements made by victims (other than as witnesses)[33] become a sensitive issue both for offenders and for those involved in sentencing. The discussion within *Chapter 7* addresses these issues and their implications for courts, offenders and victims of crime.

The desirability of offenders making reparation to victims of crime is a central feature of restorative justice practice and recurs in the discussion within every chapter of this book. It is, however, only a part of the envisaged process through which restorative justice seeks to vindicate victims and reintegrate offenders within communities. In *Chapter 7* the case is made for reparation, restoration and reintegration to be perceived as a sequential process by which offenders become reconciled with all the stakeholders within the criminal justice process.

---

[33] Whether in the form of Victim Impact Statements (VISs) that are permitted in the USA or of Victim Personal Statements (VPSs) that have become the pattern in the UK.

The chapter concludes with a number of practical recommendations for making custodial corrections reparative in nature, bridging the conceptual and operational divide between prisons and communities and making more purposeful use of community-based sanctions. The discussion acknowledges the difficulties that have to be surmounted in each of these sensitive areas if restorative justice is to become a reality. It also indicates the many advantages that would flow from such an initiative, not the least of which is to punish less and punish differently. This is, in essence, the motivating rationale for 'doing justice better'.

The Politics of Restorative Justice, Critique, Analysis and the Basis of the Discussion

The increasing interest in restorative justice over the past decade or so has been accompanied by a burgeoning literature worldwide, and has attracted the support of many academics, criminal justice practitioners and a number of far-sighted members of the legal and other professions. Restorative practice has a wide range of actual and potential applications beyond the more obvious field of criminal justice, ranging from civil dispute mediation, family breakdown and communal conflict resolution, to work-place relations, schools administration and the like. Though this particular work focuses directly (and solely) on the application of restorative justice principles within the criminal justice systems of developed and developing nations, it should be recognised that many of these same principles guide its wider operation in a remarkably similar manner.

The title of this book reflects the extent to which implementation of restorative principles within many areas of public life, and within criminal justice specifically, becomes a profoundly political issue.[1] A restorative penology challenges politicians and governments, as well as their advisers and state servants, to review and possibly abandon outmoded or failing policies and/or practices in favour of an altogether more socially cohesive and less precedent-driven agenda for resolving dysfunctional aspects of community existence. This work expresses no preference for any particular political persuasion or orientation, since to do so would be invidious and altogether counter-productive. It does, however, identify the widely evident contemporary *malaise* within the criminal justice systems of many 'Western-style' democracies: a phenomenon that has led to recurring penal crises of one form or another (Evans, 1980; Cavadino and Dignan, 1997a: 8-31; Morris, 1989: 125; Prison Reform Trust, 1995).

Crime control and, ideally, crime reduction are the 'grails' of criminal justice policies almost universally. The behaviour of criminal elements within many modern societies obstinately defies achievement of these ideals, in spite of escalating use of custodial punishment almost everywhere and the incarceration of serious offenders for increasing periods of time. These facts call into question the effectiveness of contemporary criminal justice policies, the appropriateness of existing sanctions and, in short, the entire basis upon which criminal punishment

---

[1] Political in the sense that it affects what dictionaries describe as 'the complex or aggregate of relationships of men in society, and especially those relationships involving authority and power'. See, for instance, P. Hanks (ed.) (1979), *Collins Dictionary of the English Language*, London and Glasgow: Collins, p. 1134.

is justified and implemented. Restorative justice, both in theory and practice, challenges the implicit assumption that there are no alternatives to the *status quo* in a very clear and direct manner. Its logic is, at the core, both simple and persuasive, but as we shall see in the following chapters, it implies a fundamentally different rationale for the administration of justice in the circumstances of many modern societies.

At the outset of any discussion concerning the implementation of restorative justice principles within contemporary (or even prospective) criminal justice administration, it is difficult not to adopt an approach that focuses predominantly on its humanistic rather than its moralistic potential.[2] Here it should be explained that a subtle, though important, difference is perceived between a concept of humanism that seeks to promote a general welfare model of justice and a moral legalistic one that insists primarily that the law be upheld as a matter of essential principle.[3]

Over a century ago now, Henry Sidgwick, a renowned ethical scholar of the late Victorian era in England, proposed a distinction between what he termed 'conservative' and 'ideal' justice respectively. The former, he suggested, subsumed general observance of the law, of contracts and of definite understandings, based on the fulfilment of natural and normative expectations. In breach of such conditions, fixed and appropriate penalties might be imposed for non-compliance. In the latter instance relating to 'ideal' justice, Sidgwick argued a utilitarian case for individual freedom from legal intervention providing that no harm or injury be caused to others. Moreover, he also advanced a socialistic case for penalties requiting desert in the event that harmful or injurious offences were committed. In both instances, the distributive principle implied, in Sidgwick's view, the need for adequate reparation of those offended against as a necessary and indispensable aspect of true justice.[4]

Thus, within the concept of 'justice as fairness' outlined above, there is no essential antithesis between justice and retribution in relation to offences committed, neither is the notion of desert absent from considerations relating to the extent of punishment which might be appropriate in individual cases. In many

---

2   The distinction is, for the purposes of the discussion hereafter, an important one. The humanist would insist that the primary justification of legal processes ultimately resides in the promotion of the general welfare of societies, whereas the moralist would propose that these are necessary to regulate the behaviour of citizens in compliance with legal prescriptions. Though the two concepts are not mutually exclusive, it will be argued that from a political viewpoint they contain significant elements of incompatibility.

3   At this stage it will be noted that the notion of ethical principle may be said to confuse rather than clarify the issues discussed here. For while it may be conceded that the study of ethics embraces the concept of identifying and promoting codes of moral principle, these, in turn, most often reflect the value systems of groups holding positions of power within societies. Politics is ultimately concerned with the distribution and use of power and authority within social structures, and within democracies, in particular, by those freely elected to do so on behalf of the general population.

4   See Henry Sidgwick (1893), *The Methods of Ethics*, Book III, Chapter 5 (5th Edition), re-printed in F.A. Olafson (ed.) (1961), *Justice and Social Policy*, Englewood Cliffs NJ: Prentice Hall, pp. 3-28.

respects, Sidgwick's prescription has been echoed in the subsequent analyses of a number of penal philosophers and most particularly those within the utilitarian tradition.[5] The growth of interest in restorative justice over the past decade or so reflects not only a welcome and long-overdue attempt to make the administration of criminal justice fairer, but an equally important initiative to give the victims of criminal acts adequate consideration.

To many observers of contemporary criminal justice systems throughout the world, such a development seems both logical and entirely reasonable. It is logical because it seeks to identify the nature and extent of the harm occasioned by criminal acts in terms of the impact these have on victims who are directly affected by the commission of them and on the communities within which they are committed. It is also reasonable insofar as it seeks to allow for some measure of reparation to be made to victims by those convicted of criminal wrongdoing as the central purpose of any retributive process (Walgrave, 2003; Strang, 2004; Kaptein, 2004). In some respects also, it goes part of the way towards resolving the objections of writers such as Blad (2006a) in relation to the 'instrumentalism' of retributive punishment.

There is nothing new about the concept of harm involved in the commission of crime, the gravity of offences having traditionally been measured by the extent to which laws are broken and offenders are culpable. What is new is the relationship that restorative justice seeks to establish between offenders, offences, victims and communities, rather than offenders, offences and the law.[6] It is this important change of emphasis that provides both the motive energy of the restorative justice agenda and, at the same time, the principal area of objection to it among its detractors (Cavadino and Dignan, 1997b; Zedner, 1994).

SKETCHING THE CONTEMPORARY BACKGROUND

To a significant extent, the traditionally held concept of criminal offending within the world dominated by Western ideologies has been that the primary harm caused by crime lies in the breach of the law rather than in the violation of social relationships and victims. Within such a concept of harm, the collateral damage to those harmed is of secondary importance to the need for the law to be upheld and offenders punished. It may be suggested that this single notion is, more than any other, responsible for the prevailing culture of retributive 'punitivism' that pervades the penal policies of many developed nations throughout the world. Within such a view of criminal offending, punishment becomes an inevitable consequence of the law being broken, rather than as a means of restoring the social equilibrium that crime disturbs.

---

[5] Notably by John Rawls (1958), 'Justice as Fairness', *The Philosophical Review*, vol. LXVII, pp. 164-94, and to some extent by H.L.A. Hart (1968) in *Punishment and Responsibility*, Oxford: Oxford University Press.

[6] This situation is admirably summarised by Howard Zehr (2002) in *The Little Book of Restorative Justice*, Intercourse, PA: Good Books, p. 21.

It will become clear, as the chapters of this book unfold, that much of the present predicament within the British penal system flows directly from the emergence of the 'law and order' ideology of the mid-1990s. Though this occurred during the tenure of a Conservative government[7] that deliberately adopted penal policies that encouraged increasing use of imprisonment and longer custodial sentences, such is only a datum point within this analysis. In fact, the New Labour government that assumed power in 1997[8] not only implemented a number of the draconian sentencing measures drafted by its Conservative predecessors, but also added its own brand of punitive sanctions as the early years of the present decade elapsed.[9]

This 'law and order' ideology became grounded in the belief that with sufficient persistence, severity of sentencing and 'decent but austere' prison conditions, crime could be controlled. Strict retrenchment in the use of parole, accompanied by expansion of the penal estate would house more criminals in custody and for longer periods of time. Such, it was proposed by Home Secretary Michael Howard, would justify his assertion that 'prison works', that society would feel more secure in its protection from 'muggers and rapists' and that the new severity would 'make many who are tempted to commit crime think twice.'[10] Moreover, provision for mandatory minimum sentences for drug trafficking, violence and burglary (and later for serious sexual offences) would ensure that the judiciary complied with these general intentions and that the law and order symbolism would be perpetuated (Tonry, 2003: 16).

Though such ideological posturing is evidently closely allied to political motivations and electoral 'survivability', this is neither unusual nor the central issue for this analysis. The fact that it has been perpetuated by successive governments with traditionally divergent approaches to criminal justice legislation makes it represent an institutionalised and largely unquestioned pattern of behaviour and one from which it is difficult to envisage an early retreat. This has significant implications for the promotion of restorative justice and accounts, in some part, for its deflection to the margins of criminal justice practice at the present time.

Garland (2002) charts a broadly similar pattern of events in the USA over much the same period of time and, in particular, the marked increase in the use of custodial sentences and escalation of the prison population. The pattern is reflected in Europe also, though by no means universally. The prison population of The Netherlands has increased markedly since 1985 (Blad 2006a), but it has remained more or less constant in Sweden, Germany and Scotland. Significantly, however, it

---

[7] The government in which John Major replaced Margaret Thatcher as Prime Minister, and Michael Howard was appointed Home Secretary.

[8] New Labour under Prime Minister Tony Blair took office in 1997, with Jack Straw as Home Secretary. Straw has since been succeeded by David Blunkett, Charles Clarke, and, latterly, John Reid in this post.

[9] These measures are described in some detail in *Chapter 6*.

[10] The words in quotation marks are taken from Michael Howard's address to the Conservative Party Conference in October 1973.

has fallen in Finland, Canada and Denmark and this, at least is encouraging (Tonry, 2003: 3). The Finnish situation is the most remarkable, as will become evident in *Chapter 6*.

How has this reliance upon the use of imprisonment become so much a feature of the criminal justice landscape in so many of the developed democracies worldwide? The use of custody is a high cost option by any standard of assessment and there is considerable evidence to suggest that short prison sentences, in particular, achieve little in terms of reducing recidivism and may, in fact, make it more likely to occur (EFF, 2004a: 5; Home Office, 2002a: 102; Roberts and Smith, 2003: 182). The answer would seem to reside in a widespread, though somewhat uncritical belief in 'Howard's *dictum*' that was cited previously: if 'prison works', then it is worth having, regardless of the cost.

The cost is not confined to fiscal considerations alone. More to the point, there are what might be termed 'collateral costs' of using imprisonment indiscriminately, and these are borne, in the main, by the victims of crime and the immediate family groups of those sentenced to custody. Many victims of crime remain unsatisfied by the criminal justice process even though it may punish those who offend against them directly. Many also would not wish punishment to extend to the families of offenders if this could be avoided through some process of mediation and reconciliation, and providing that the offender made reparation. The social effects of imprisonment frequently destroy family relationships, most particularly when they result in financial hardship, debt and the subsequent reduced employability of the main bread-winner. This means that released offenders often find themselves homeless, unemployed and unsupported and at increased risk of further criminal offending (Lewis, 1997: 54; Box, 1987: 47-8; Thornberry and Christenson, 1984).

There are, however, belief systems abundant in more ancient cultures that view matters entirely differently.[11] Such peoples perceive the need for a mediated resolution of wrongful acts and the reparation of victims as categorical imperatives within the overall purpose of maintaining social stability and structural cohesiveness (Green, 1998; Ross, 1996; Yazzie, 1998; Zion, 1985 and 1998). Though such cultures in no sense deny the necessity for punishment of criminal acts, the principle of parsimony is expressed much more vividly within deliberations concerning the extent and nature of its imposition. In such a view of justice, punishment (for its own sake) becomes a strategy of last, rather than of primary resort, and the social consensus demands that it be strictly limited and constructive rather than destructive towards both victims and offenders (La Prairie, 1992; Blad, 2006a).

Why, then, has it become the case that the concept of restorative justice—with all its evident potential to promote fairer justice—has encountered such apparent difficulty in establishing its rightful place within the mainstream of criminal justice

---

[11] These are to be found within the cultures of Aboriginal peoples in Australia, New Zealand, the Pacific islands, Africa and the First Nations settlements of the North American continent in particular.

practice? Far from being of a rhetorical nature, such a question suggests that there are aspects of restorative justice that are essentially problematic in a structural, rather than a moral or ethical dimension.[12] For even if implementation of restorative justice principles is beset with difficulties of an operational or logistical nature, such do not negate either its 'rightness' or its claims to provide better justice. This is not to suggest that there has developed some sort of world-wide conspiracy to obstruct the development of restorative justice, but rather that the challenges it poses to established justice systems are such as to make it, at the least, a questionably welcome bed-fellow.

It is the central contention within this work that the situation in which restorative justice finds itself at the present time is very much of the nature described above. It becomes important, therefore, to discern why this should be so and seek ways of making it less threatening and ultimately more welcome. Here it will be noted that reluctance to embrace restorative justice whole-heartedly both in principle and in practice is far from a British or Northern European phenomenon: it is evident also in the North American, African and Pacific continents in broadly equal measure. More important still, perhaps, the reasons that underlie the reluctance are remarkably similar within each of these widely dispersed areas.

It would be tempting to suggest that these reasons reside principally within the confines of criminal justice policy determination, but to do so would represent a gross over-simplification of the situation, and ignore the much wider social policy implications involved in the restorative justice arena. Certainly there are issues of criminal justice policy that become to an extent pivotal, but these are in many respects less significant than might, at first sight, be imagined. Much more central to the debate lie a range of socio-political factors that play a considerable part in fashioning responses to the challenges implicit in adopting restorative justice principles. Foremost among these is the nature of public attitudes towards crime and criminals and thus the extent to which there exists a measure of tolerance or intolerance in relation to overall levels of offending within each society.

Within societies that have a relatively low threshold of tolerance towards crime, it becomes altogether likely that politicians will feel confident in adopting 'hawkish' approaches to crime control and the measures selected to maintain law and public order. Such societies are typified by the existence of an extensive and relatively affluent, educated, property-owning middle-class and a much less well-off and more socially deprived 'underclass' with lower levels of physical and environmental health, education, housing, employment and access to social amenities. This latter social grouping, it will be noted, frequently displays a significantly more extensive tolerance of 'crime' than the former, perceiving criminal and anti-social behaviour as a 'rational' response to the disparities of opportunity and the impact of lesser eligibility.

---

[12] Here see, for instance, the analysis offered by James Dignan in L. Walgrave (ed) (2002), *Restorative Justice and the Law*, Devon: Willan Publishing, pp. 168-90.

Many of the so-called 'Western-style' democracies exhibit a number of the characteristics described briefly here, and definitions of 'prevalent crime' tend to become those of the relatively affluent 'middle-class' that forms the majority of the voting population. It is no accident either that this affluent middle-class displays a greater extent of political awareness and involvement than its poorer counterpart, having the incentive to participate politically in the preservation or promotion of its own interests.[13] Politicians also, acutely aware of the power of the middle-class vote and anxious to retain their status and influence, are unlikely to embrace and adopt social (and in particular penal) policy initiatives that do not have the potential acceptance of the majority of the electorate.

It is of interest to note that the majority of these democracies have, over the past two or three decades, developed increasingly punitive approaches towards crime and offenders, imprisoning more and more of those convicted and as a proportion of the overall population, for increasing periods of time. High rates of recidivism in many of these countries appear to have fuelled the belief among the public and politicians alike that preventive incarceration is the only logical approach to crime control, though the evidence to support such a contention is at the very least extremely speculative. In addition, declining belief in, or lip service paid to the concept of rehabilitation within the purposes of imprisonment has also resulted in the articulation of penal policies based predominantly upon the notions of retribution and deterrence.[14]

Increased and increasing resort to penal incarceration represents the most expensive and wasteful means of crime control imaginable. Institutional costs, both in terms of capital investment and logistical maintenance, are inevitability high, as is also the cost of employing custodial correctional employees on a daily round-the-clock basis. Increased use of imprisonment also leads to over-crowded correctional facilities, to restricted and impoverished regimes and ultimately to the risk of concerted disorder. Poor regimes result in a lack of purposeful and constructive activity for prison inmates, leading to boredom, frustration and more frequent incidences of rule-infracting behaviour and inter-personal violence. This degenerative situation within prisons has a spiralling effect beyond their confines, resulting in the eventual release back into the community of embittered, unrepentant and predatory individuals, many of whose levels of criminal sophistication have been enhanced by the experience of custody.

To make matters even worse, many ex-prisoners re-enter the community with diminished rather than improved prospects of legitimate and gainful employment, gravitating naturally towards the company of those similarly affected and whose life-styles are patterned by episodic resort to criminal activity committed as a means of survival (Box, 1987: 47-8). It therefore becomes somewhat in the nature of a self-

---

[13] Such, for instance, as low rates of taxation, eligibility for state provided benefits, and the implementation of measures to safeguard property and possessions.

[14] This contention is explained in considerably greater detail in the author's earlier work. See D. J. Cornwell (2006), op. cit., pp. 62-70.

fulfilling prophecy that rates of recorded recidivism rise in tandem with those of incarceration. The situation becomes the more questionable when all of this occurs as the almost inevitable outcome of deliberately contrived penal policies ostensibly designed to achieve crime reduction. Moreover, the situation occurs entirely because penal policies based upon the supposed effectiveness of retribution and deterrence place politicians and their advisers in a situation in which they inevitably have to punish more in order to uphold the apparent credibility of the law[15] (Blad, 2006a: 138-41).

This reveals both the stark complexity of the ultimate penological paradox and the nature of the political dilemma implicit within it. Indiscriminate punishment, or punishment *for its own sake alone* must, perforce, be retributive since it requites some notion of desert and reciprocity. In short, it repays a harm done with a harm imposed in contemporary circumstances and does so because the latter harm is deserved. If, however, punishment is designed primarily to deter, then when deterrence fails, resort to punishment becomes inevitable. Summarily, punishment becomes the price to be paid for failing to be deterred and the greater the emphasis placed upon deterrence, the more extensive the punishment must necessarily be. In either case, or both, little of substance is achieved beyond the inevitable imposition of punishment and in circumstances altogether unlikely to promote future law-abiding behaviour. To act thus represents the politics of despair.[16]

Now if punishment inflicted on the bases described above can be seen to achieve relatively little in promoting law-observance, it achieves even less in relation to the victims of crime, almost to the point of ignoring their situation altogether. But returning to Sidgwick's analysis presented earlier, we may note the insistence that the victims of crime have an axiomatic place in considerations relating to justice. Neither retributive nor deterrence-based punishment meets this essential need either in whole or in part, focussed as it becomes on the supposed need for offenders to be punished primarily for breaking the law rather than for causing harm to those offended against.[17] Yet again, the politics of contemporary punishment act in a strangely contrary manner with an evident lack of consideration for those law-abiding persons offended against, compounded largely by excluding them from considerations relating to the nature of appropriate punishment (Ashworth, 1993b: 505; Cavadino and Dignan, 1997b: 236-7).

---

[15] John Blad provides an excellent explanation of this situation in D. J. Cornwell (2006), op. cit., pp. 93-103.

[16] Norval Morris (1974) aptly described this situation as one of 'penal rudderlessness' in his most incisive work *The Future of Imprisonment*, London and Chicago: University of Chicago Free Press, p. 1. A broadly similar view is expressed by Hyman Gross (1979) in *A Theory of Criminal Justice*, New York: Oxford University Press, p. 5.

[17] This particular view is, however, far from universally accepted, particularly by judges and criminal lawyers, many of whom would insist that the primary focus of justice must be on maintaining the integrity of the law rather than, necessarily, on expressing concern for the victims of crime. Howard Zehr (2002a), op. cit., pp. 19-22, explains very clearly how the concept of restorative justice seeks to change this approach, perceiving crime as a violation of people and relationships to be of greater importance than the violation of the law and the state.

Those most immediately affected by criminal acts become 'victimised' when they have reason to feel that their situation is significantly disregarded within the processes of criminal justice. Respect for these processes is also diminished when they are seen to be preoccupied with primary outcomes other than the harm caused by crime. Moreover, as Rhodes pointed out over a quarter of a century ago:

Political interests formed by organizational roles and group behaviour establish the parameters of policy, objectives, standards, and even indicators as measures of success in goal fulfilment. Examples of such evaluation models that emerge from mind-sets are due-process models, administrative efficiency models, law-enforcement models and social-control models ...

One of the comprehensive goals of the criminal justice system most apt to be forgotten by the public and practitioners is protecting the citizen against being victimized ... To the extent that criminal justice policy analysis is to become comprehensive, it would do well to reduce its dependence on criminal law categories as reflected in arrests, reported crime, convictions and [social] control, and examine the impact policy has on reducing victimization ... The victim's suffering, as a measure of the success or failure of anti-crime policy, might be the key to comprehensive planning and evaluation in an area of public policy replete with contending problem definitions. (Rhodes, 1975: 21 and 26-8)

A reasoned argument has been made in former work[18] in favour of re-visiting the need for an inclusive theory of criminal punishment that might assist in resolving many of these conceptual and practical difficulties. The principal motivation for this lies in the unsatisfactory nature of the polarised discourse relating to what might be termed the 'retribution *versus* rehabilitation' conceptions of the aims of punishment. The *naissance* of restorative justice has provided an impetus and a rationale for resolving this hitherto intractable *impasse* and, more importantly, of enabling the conceptual divide between the retrospective and prospective purposes of punishment to be bridged satisfactorily.

The necessity for such an inquiry is both substantial and urgent, since continued failure to make both moral and operational sense of this central issue must extend the opportunities for political obfuscation and confusion in the deliberation of appropriate penal policies for this millennium. For as long as it remains possible and intellectually respectable for the punishment debate to oscillate in a haphazard pendulum-like manner between the fundamentally retributive and preponderantly rehabilitative approaches towards the purposes of criminal justice, the more ineffective and purposeless the processes of justice will become. From a political viewpoint also, it is necessary to re-shape the arena of justice to remove the potential for penal policies to be grounded in expediency and the outworn rhetoric of former decades. This implies the need to adopt a reasoned agenda for dealing more equitably with both the perpetrators and the victims of crime.

---

[18] Cornwell (2006), op. cit., pp. 62-70.

This work is about the manner in which the concept of restorative justice can, and in some instances already does, provide a framework for fairer and more effective justice. It aims to lessen significantly the potential for criminal justice systems to become political footballs and the instruments of purposeless punishment. To many observers of criminal justice in action, the notion of an integrated and inclusive concept of criminal punishment has a grail-like elusiveness that defies reasoned articulation. Such a view is not endorsed within these pages. In many respects the old discourse involving justice and punishment never changed because there was little or no incentive for it to do so. Today, for all manner of pressing reasons, not least amongst which are the humane and economic needs to reduce the use of prisons, there is a potentially positive incentive to do better justice.

THE MOTIVATION FOR CHANGE

Almost four decades ago Herbert Packer described a view of the law that was significantly different from that which had currency within the prevailing rhetoric of that era. His purpose was to advance a concept of law that encouraged law-abiding behaviour rather than merely punished infractions and one that was essentially inclusive rather than divisive. The following extract from his work provides a brief glimpse of the far-sightedness of his approach:

> Law, including the criminal law, must in a free society be judged ultimately on the basis of its success in promoting human autonomy and the capacity for individual human growth and development. The prevention of crime is an essential aspect of the environmental protection required if autonomy is to flourish. It is, however, a negative aspect and one which, pursued with single-minded zeal, may end up creating an environment in which all are safe but none is free ...
>
> The case for an essentially preventive view of the function of criminal law is unanswerable; anything else is the merest savagery. But a *purely* preventive view ... carries the danger that single-minded pursuit of the goal of crime prevention will slight and in the end defeat the ultimate goal of law in a free society, which is to liberate rather than restrain. Human autonomy is an illusion if we make it conditional on human perfection. As Holmes once observed, law, like other human contrivances, has to take some chances ... It is wrong to say that we should punish persons simply because they commit offences under circumstances that we can call blameworthy. It is right to say that we should *not* punish those who commit offences unless we can say that their conduct is blameworthy. (Packer, 1969: 65-6)[19] [Emphasis added]

Much of Packer's analysis has resonance within what has more recently been developed in formulating the concept of restorative justice. The various chapters within this work reflect not only the potential that restorative justice has to change existing penal dogmas, but also the liberating nature of its practical application in

---

[19] H. L. Packer (1969), 'Toward An Integrated Theory of Criminal Punishment', *The Limits of the Penal Sanction*, London: Oxford University Press, pp. 62-70.

relation both to offenders and victims of crime. Two particular issues, important for this discussion, emerge from his analysis.

One of the more pernicious of the prevailing penal dogmas is reflected in the contemporary trend within a number of Western European countries (and in particular the United Kingdom) to predicate penal policies on the basis of preserving public safety. By such means, the selection of particular groups of offenders for exemplary treatment within sentencing practices is 'legitimised' on the back of expressed public concern and media sensationalism in relation to specific forms of offending (Matravers and Hughes, 2003: 51-3).[20] Garland (2001) identifies a similar tendency in the United States to make public protection the dominant issue in penal policy deliberation.[21]

Taking chances is not a favoured option among those responsible for penal policy formulation, particularly in an era in which the immediacy of media attention can be brought to bear very forcefully upon the bizarre or inexplicable circumstances in which sensational crimes are committed. This is unfortunate in relation to the promotion of restorative justice principles that rely considerably upon reducing the use of custodial punishment and expansion of the use of community-based sanctions. It is, in fact, doubly unfortunate insofar as there is strong research evidence which indicates that the public in many countries considerably over-estimates the extent of crime and generally considers sentencing to be too lenient (Tonry, 2003: 5). This situation can be used to advantage by politicians anxious to pursue a 'tough on crime' agenda as a means of increasing the severity of sanctions, and of appearing to 'listen' to public concern and respond accordingly. I have referred to this elsewhere in this work as the politics of 'punitive instrumentalism'.[22]

Above all else, however, there is now an urgent need to free the thinking of politicians, penal policy-makers and those concerned with criminal justice administration from the shackles of the past, and in particular from the inevitability of punishment. If there is no foreseeable progress in this direction, then penal populations will continue in their inexorable growth and victims of crime will continue to be marginalised within the processes of criminal justice. Worse, however, is the prospect that offenders will be denied the opportunity to make practical amends for the harm caused to others, and remain largely unaffected or unchanged by the sanctions imposed upon them. None of these outcomes serves the interests either of crime control or crime reduction.

---

[20] In the United Kingdom, sexual offenders have been the target of specific legislative measures on the basis of their supposed dangerousness and repetitive offending which are not borne out either by rigorous research evidence or recorded reconviction rates. For a more detailed explanation see: A. Matravers, and G. V. Hughes, 'Unprincipled Sentencing?: The Policy Approach to Dangerous Sex Offenders' in M. Tonry (ed) (2003), *Confronting Crime: Crime Control Policy Under New Labour*, Devon: Willan Publishing, pp. 51-79.

[21] D. Garland (2001), *The Culture of Control*, Oxford: Oxford University Press, p. 12.

[22] See here, fn.19 at p24 and fn.24 at p. 29 *supra*. Also the account of Ronald Dworkin (1986), *Taking Rights Seriously*, Oxford: Clarendon Press, pp. 249-52.

On an entirely fiscal basis of consideration, the costs of criminal justice administration within most modern democracies represent the equivalent of multi-national businesses, consuming a significant portion of the gross national product. Recidivism rates provide an important indicator of the extent to which the existing structures of criminal justice are ineffective or inefficient. Moreover, when rates of re-offending are high and rates of incarceration are similarly high, the entire rationale for the punishment process is inevitably called into question. In fact, it would seem that little of substance has changed during the 25 years since Hyman Gross wrote the following assessment:

> At this point there are serious difficulties, for everywhere criminal justice is strangely uncertain in its goals. Sometimes it is said that the point is simply to pay the wicked for their wrongdoing; at other times, that correction of those who show themselves in need of it is the reason we determine criminal liability. One often hears the view that crimes are punished to show those who have broken the law and those who might be tempted to break it that the law has teeth that bite. And just as often one hears it suggested that the enterprise is carried on to make the community safer by identifying and then removing (or at least watching) those who have shown themselves to be dangerous ... This is distressing, for it is important to know what goal it is that causes this curious social pursuit to be carried on everywhere with such dedication ... A commercial enterprise similarly unenlightened could not long survive, and certainly would not prosper. (Gross, 1979: 5)[23]

If the principal goal of criminal justice in operation is the achievement of crime reduction, then high rates of recidivism indicate very strongly that the existing philosophies under-pinning the processes of criminal justice are inconsistent with delivering this purpose. More to the point, it must be evident that the prevailing modes of punishment fail in the essential task of deterring subsequent offending. Within many contemporary democracies this has clearly been the case over the past two or three decades.

Enlightened politicians and criminal justice practitioners, as well as the general public, must now be fully aware that existing policies for, and methods of dealing with crime, are seriously defective. They may not, however, be able or willing to contemplate the necessary philosophical and attitudinal shifts in thinking that are essential if the situation is to be changed significantly. Continuing simply to lock away increasing numbers of offenders at exorbitant operational cost and under existing conditions is certainly unlikely to provoke change other than for the worse, and this at least must be self-evident. At this stage, the law (as Packer has indicated) has, eventually and inevitably, to take some chances.

A central contention within this work is that restorative justice provides a window of opportunity for change and, given the resolve to do so, could be implemented within most criminal justice jurisdictions incrementally and without undue risk either to the quality of justice delivery or the safety of citizens. More than this, however, it holds out the very real prospect of delivering better justice, of

---

[23] H. Gross (1979), *A Theory of Criminal Justice*, New York: Oxford University Press.

reducing offending and of eventually enabling penal populations to be similarly reduced. Perhaps of equal importance, however, restorative justice gives due and appropriate consideration to the victims of crime, encourages offenders to take responsibility for their harmful behaviour and provides the opportunity for them to make some measure of reparation to those violated by their offences. These latter features of its fundamental philosophy are demonstrably not achieved under existing circumstances.

There is, however, a need to be clear about how the concept of what was formerly described as the 'rehabilitation' of offenders fits into any re-statement of criminal justice principles. The former rehabilitative construct of the 1960s and early 1970s became discredited for a wide variety of reasons, not the least of which were a *quasi*-medical notion of 'cure', and also the extent to which such a model invested discretion in the hands of criminal justice professionals (Hudson, 1987: 16-36; Bean, 1982: 44-6).[24] It is also interesting that what has widely been described as a 'neo-rehabilitative' revival occurred during the early 1980s when it became likely that the outcome of the 'nothing works'[25] analysis would signal an almost immediate return to retributive punishment (see, for example, Cullen and Gilbert, 1982; Hudson, 1987).

This, of course, was exactly what happened in Britain, America and elsewhere in Europe during the mid-1980s and onwards, and the rest, so to speak, is history. The 'justice model' was predominantly a product of the worldwide financial crisis of the late 1970s and early 1980s, the search for cost-reductions in criminal justice and also a reaction to the perceived 'excesses' of the rehabilitative model. Though of a 'minimalist' nature in its conception (the extent of punishment being strictly limited to desert (von Hirsch, 1976)), it sought to curb abuses of power and in particular, the use of punishment for other purposes—such as general deterrence. Had it been left to this purpose alone, the reductive effect on prison populations would have been potentially considerable.

The penal history of the late 1980s and early 1990s shows with clarity how the justice model became subverted from its original aspirations and was politically manipulated to meet the more punitive agendas of emergent 'law and order' initiatives. As Cullen and Gilbert pointed out:

> Justice model proponents have strongly advocated short sentences and the proliferation of alternatives to imprisonment, whereas conservatives have been convinced that longer prison sentences are integral to the reduction of the crime problem. In the end, one reality has thus become clear: the 'bare bones' of determinacy and desert are as easily adaptable to a program of 'getting tough on crime' as to one of 'doing justice'.
>
> (Cullen and Gilbert, 1982: 200; also quoted in Hudson, 1987: 59)

---

[24] But see also Philip Bean's interesting analysis concerning the relationship between proportionality and indeterminacy of sentencing where the rehabilitative model is pursued as the primary purpose of criminal punishment (Bean, 1981: 44-5).

[25] Of Robert Martinson (1974) which was, in fact, widely misinterpreted. See p. 22 and fn.16 *supra*.

The 'neo-justice model' that emerged in the 1990s almost excluded notions of rehabilitation from the criminal punishment discourse, focused as it became on retribution and deterrence. The outcome of this became a somewhat paradoxical situation: the political manipulation of the justice agenda resulted in increasing numbers of offenders being imprisoned, and these offenders were, predominantly, from the most socially and economically deprived sectors of society in both Britain and elsewhere. The original justice model sought, at least subconsciously, to safeguard the rights of all citizens equally within what had become, or had perhaps always been, socially unjust even though ostensibly democratic societies. Its successor succeeded in penalising even more of those already deprived, and with increased severity, while at the same time doing little, if anything at all, to remove the social problems that contributed to their relative deprivation.

The title of this book reflects the essence of the dilemma confronting democratic governments that urgently need to change the way in which their criminal justice systems approach the ultimate goal of crime reduction. Political decisions have to be made to initiate the processes of change and this is an inescapable fact.[26] Once there is a political will to change, the means of implementing change are available and can be progressively introduced. A number of nations throughout the world have begun this process to a limited extent, but they experience difficulty in moving restorative justice out of the margins and into the mainstream of criminal justice practice.

Implementing restorative justice philosophy and practice does not represent a 'soft option' for offenders, or imply either that serious and predatory criminals should not be sentenced to imprisonment. It does, however, propose that many lesser offenders presently sentenced to custody might be dealt with more effectively on a semi-custodial or non-custodial basis and ultimately with benefit to the community. It also advocates that prisons can be designed, built and operated (or converted) to deliver a reparative and restorative ethos, and that the victims of crime can be adequately considered, and will consequently feel less marginalised by the criminal justice process.

Ultimately, development of restorative justice philosophy as a central theme of a new penology might well result in a reduction in the present severity of sentencing and greater community involvement in the work of prisons. Indeed, prisons designed and operated to deliver restorative justice outcomes would not only be more purposeful, but they would also enable the earlier release of non-

---

[26] Here it should be noted that there is no intention to invoke a discussion based upon any particular form of political persuasion that might be found in many democracies. It matters not at all for the purposes of the argument within this work whether the prevailing political affiliations of governments are of any specific party-political orientation. The discussion is, more importantly, of a non-partisan nature, designed to stimulate contemplation of the perceived advantages of restorative justice principles, rather than the satisfaction of the ideological objectives of any specific political grouping.

dangerous offenders to supervised community-based programmes of direct benefit to the entire population.[27]

Even for those offenders whose crimes are so serious as to require many years of imprisonment as an appropriate sanction, there is no reason why regimes in custody cannot be designed to deliver a constructive and restorative ethos. Such regimes do much to preserve self-respect, provide purposeful activity, encourage self-examination and enhance the chances of eventual restoration and social reintegration.

THE CHALLENGE OF RESTORATIVE JUSTICE

Embracing restorative justice philosophy and practices requires political courage, far-sightedness and the will to do better justice for offenders, victims of crime and communities. It represents a challenge that might swiftly change the face of criminal justice for the better and deliver more humane, effective and considerate methods of dealing with all concerned in the commission of criminal offences.

This is no easy route to crime reduction, but adopting restorative principles must be infinitely preferable to continuing to do what we already do extremely unsatisfactorily and at excessive cost in both financial and human terms. Restorative justice gives the law a human face simply because it deals much more with *people* rather than *process*: with violated social relationships rather than breaches of criminal codes. Above all, perhaps, as Howard Zehr has so clearly indicated, restorative justice promotes the active engagement or participation of all those parties affected by crime and gives them significant roles in the justice process.[28] The essential emphasis of restorative justice is thus *inclusive* rather than *exclusive* and places an infinitely higher priority upon reconciliation than upon retribution.

There is no doubt that such a prescription sits uncomfortably alongside traditional concepts of punishment and criminal justice administration. Indeed, it threatens the clinical remoteness of existing processes and the theatrical manoeuvrings of the adversarial trial procedure. It does so because it seeks to reconcile offenders, victims and communities, rather than to emphasise the antagonistic situations occasioned by crime and the harm it causes. But restorative justice does insist that offenders take responsibility for the damage that they create and do something to repair the social relationships that are fractured by offences. This contributes much more to the effectiveness of justice than can be claimed for existing circumstances.

Unsurprisingly, there will always be those offenders who are remorseless, unrepentant and unwilling to accept responsibility for their actions. The essential nature of restorative justice makes no concessions whatsoever to such people.

---

[27] Insofar as programmes involving participants in purposeful work within the community are not only visible manifestations of justice in action, but are also evidently of practical benefit to communities which might otherwise be unable to fund or maintain them.

[28] This principle is explained in some detail in H. Zehr (2002a), op. cit., pp. 24-5.

Justice dictates that they continue to be dealt with under arrangements similar to those that presently exist, because they themselves make no concessions to the parties harmed by their wanton behaviour. Though this may, to some of a purist persuasion, be deemed objectionable in promoting a 'bifurcated' system of justice,[29] it also has the merit of enabling offenders who show genuine remorse for their offences to be dealt with either more leniently, or, as suggested here, within a restorative justice setting.

The reader will decide, as must politicians and criminal justice practitioners, where the greater merit lies in this compelling and important debate. It is, however, no accident that restorative justice has gained a foothold within many criminal justice systems worldwide, and continues to attract adherents among legal professionals, criminal justice practitioners and academic criminologists who recognise the necessity for a sea change in the way that justice is administered. That its application is presently limited predominantly to the areas of juvenile and minor offending within many jurisdictions is by no means unhelpful. It provides evidence that the concept is 'workable' and can readily be extended into the mainstream of criminal justice practice.

Criminal justice is in no sense delivered in a vacuum. Decisions relating to *how* it is delivered are as politically relevant as those that govern healthcare, education, policing and all other essential social services. This book is devoted to placing restorative justice on the political agenda for change, not least because in many contemporary democracies criminal justice systems are failing institutions. They fail because they reduce neither crime nor recidivism and become increasingly punitive as a frustrated response to this inability. They also fail because they persistently ignore the dynamic that inevitably exists between offenders, victims and communities when crimes are committed. Indifferent justice is ineffective justice, but it still comes at excessive cost that is ultimately borne by the citizen.

Politics is, above all else, about maximising the quality of life within nations through effective governance and use of resources. Inept and inappropriate criminal justice policies squander valuable national resources, in addition to being socially divisive and dysfunctional. Many countries urgently need a new vision of criminal justice to replace the outmoded practices of the past decades that have consistently failed to deliver effective outcomes. Restorative justice provides both a vision of justice and an opportunity to deliver better justice. This, at the least, now merits serious political consideration.

It is entirely understandable that many observers of restorative justice will view its principles as advancing what might be termed an 'alternative penology' that offers no proof of its actual ability to deliver better justice. Others will perceive it as

---

[29] The term 'bifurcation' relates to what might be described as a 'twin track' system of justice designed to deal differentially with offenders in relation to similar offences. It is widely attributed to Professor (later Sir) Anthony Bottoms who cited it in his inaugural lecture as Professor of Criminology in the University of Sheffield, UK, on 12 January 1977. The text of the lecture was subsequently printed in *The Howard Journal of Criminal Justice*, Vol. XVI, No.2, pp. 70—95.

a creator of unwanted tensions between traditional modes of justice administration and the apparatus of law-enforcement. Yet others will contend that to embrace its prescriptions fully requires too comprehensive a change to existing practices to be contemplated while penal systems are so heavily burdened with seemingly intractable problems of capacity, recidivism and widespread anti-social behaviour. All of these symptoms of social *malaise* constitute the realities of political life and cannot be ignored in terms of the pressures they place upon contemporary governments. However, when change becomes both necessary and unavoidable, short-term expediency seldom provides lasting solutions and a longer view becomes substantially more beneficial.

Restorative justice holds out no prospect of 'quick fixes', but rather represents a strategic prescription for a better quality of justice and, ultimately, lesser resort to the need to punish in the way in which sanctions are presently used. If the necessity to punish could be reduced, so also would be the inevitability of punishment with which many modern societies have become all too familiar. The compulsion to punish is both medieval and essentially retrospective: the motivation to restore is an outward and visible demonstration of faith in the capacity of most offenders to pursue law-abiding life-styles in the future and return to full citizenship. These are the key issues addressed within the subsequent chapters of this work.

Selection of the political slogan 'tough on crime and tough on the causes of crime' commits those who adopt it to two quite different social programmes: crime reduction and also the reduction of social inequality and lesser eligibility. Punishing harder does not inevitably result in less crime, but it does fill prisons: the contemporary penal crisis in Britain provides clear evidence of this fact.[30] Reducing social inequalities of access and outcome at least helps to reduce perceptions of discrimination. It has long been held that those most socially disadvantaged have the least incentive to be law-abiding, if for no other reason than that expressed so

---

[30] Here it is of significant interest to note that the average length of custodial sentences imposed at Crown Courts in England and Wales in 2004/5 as compared with 1998/9 reflected increases of considerably varying extent in relation to different forms of serious offending. These are summarised in the following table:

Offence	Average Sentence 1998/9	Average Sentence 2004/5
Robbery	36 months	42 months
Sexual Offences	41 months	44 months
Drug Offences	31 months	42 months
Violence Against Persons	22 months	25 months
Burglary	20 months	25 months

Source: Office for National Statistics (2006), *Social Trends* (No. 36), p. 142.

eloquently by Joe Sim in a different context: 'When you ain't got nothing, you got nothing to lose' (Sim, 1992).[31]

Such an analysis notwithstanding, there are encouraging signs that the more far-sighted elements of the British media are beginning to recognise this situation and attempt to shape public opinion in a more appropriate and less punitive manner. In a recent and sensitive newspaper article, Deborah Orr (2006: 16) has asserted that, essentially, the British government imprisons many offenders 'because it finds helping them too difficult.'[32] The same author points out that Britain has more people in its prisons serving life sentences than the whole of Western Europe put together.[33] It is, therefore, hardly surprising that the prison population has continued to increase, since the rate of admissions to custody considerably exceeds the rate of discharges from correctional facilities. To make matters worse, a considerable proportion of those held in prisons suffer from mental illness, drug addiction or alcoholism (Gibb and Ford (2006: 11); Riddell (2006: 24-5).[34] If the Lord Chief Justice of England and Wales can perceive the futility of the existing prisons situation and recommend greater use of community sanctions, there remains the possibility that politicians and their advisers may eventually, and however reluctantly, follow suit.

---

[31] Title of a conference paper first delivered at the British Criminology Conference at the University of York in July 1992. Subsequently published in K. Bottomley, T. Fowles and R. Reiner (eds) (1992), *Criminal Justice: Theory and Practice*, London: British Society of Criminology, pp. 273-300.

[32] D. Orr (2006), 'This Government Jails People Because it finds Helping Them too Difficult', *The Independent*, 14 October 2006, p. 16.

[33] *Ibid*. The return to widespread use of indeterminate sentences introduced within the Criminal Justice Act 2003 has resulted in one in every ten male prisoners in England and Wales serving life or indeterminate sentences, and the number of those serving life sentences has doubled since 1997. In addition, 55 *per cent* of all prisoners are serving sentences of four years or more.

[34] See F. Gibb and R. Ford (2006), 'Law Chief Attacks Longer Sentences', *The Times*, October 11, p. 11, and M. Riddell (2006), 'Yes, That's Me With the Spade: How Top Judge Turned Convict', *The Observer*, October 8, pp. 24-5. The latter article was based on an interview with Lord Phillips (LCJ) who had participated in a 'community pay-back' project in London for recidivist offenders sentenced to community orders.

CHAPTER 2

Making Justice Restorative: the Need for a New Penology

In his incisive and challenging contribution to the book that precedes this work,[1] John Blad has likened the state of many contemporary criminal justice systems to a hospital that has collected so many viruses as to make it pathogenic (Blad, 2006a: 93-103).[2] As he further points out, when demolition or entire refurbishment of such a structure becomes necessary, the patients are moved to another location because the process of attempting to make them well has to continue.

This analogy seems entirely appropriate in Britain as in many other countries at the present time, though it might, perhaps, be extended to suggest that it is also necessary to identify the viruses concerned with a view to their elimination or reduction to manageable proportions. Moreover, if pathogenic structures are allowed to remain virus infected, there is the additional hazard that infection will spread, with significant implications for the surrounding community.

STARTING TO THINK THE UNTHINKABLE

Many penal systems today are infected with a number of viruses, the most prevalent and resistant of which are what may be described as penal 'instrumentalism', ideological dogmatism and the influences of populist punitivism fostered by media attitudes towards crime and offenders. These viruses, in combination, become the more contagious because their resistance derives from their strong affinity and inter-dependence upon each other. Reduction of their potential to cause harm therefore relies upon all their pathogenic symptoms being addressed simultaneously.

The origins of most of the sources of contagion have been identified in the preceding chapter and thus do not require lengthy elaboration here. Increased and increasing resort to incarceration, misplaced confidence in the largely un-measurable effectiveness of punitive deterrence, the 'inevitability' of retributive approaches to sanctions and agendas to be 'tough on crime' at all costs, each contributes towards a severely infected contemporary penology. That the costs involved in human and financial terms are to an extent avoidable and certainly

---

[1] Cornwell (2006), op. cit.

[2] J. R. Blad (2006a), 'The Seductiveness of Punishment: A View From The Netherlands', in D. J. Cornwell, op. cit., pp. 93-103.

unaffordable makes the situation unsustainable in the longer term, if not the immediate future.

The challenge of restorative justice described in the concluding part of *Chapter 1* implies the need to re-appraise very critically the existing penology that forms the basis of contemporary criminal justice policies and practices. It is the contention here that such a re-appraisal has to be of a radical nature if it is to be effective. Indeed, the principles of restorative justice in themselves suggest the need for an entirely different penology (Zehr, 2002a: 19-41), without which the prescriptions that flow from them become inoperable. However unwelcome such a suggestion may be, the evidence in support of it is now beyond reasonable challenge.

Within this chapter, an attempt will be made to explain why this new penology has become necessary, its essential nature and the implications that follow from its adoption. In the course of the discussion it will also become clear why marginal 'tinkering' with the existing concepts and implementation of criminal justice in many 'Western-style' democracies cannot deliver an effective cure for current ills.

WHY A NEW PENOLOGY?

Standard dictionaries define penology as both the branch of the social sciences concerned with the punishment of crime and the science of prison management.[3] While this definition might suffice for general purposes, a more explicit definition may be helpful for the purposes here. Walsh and Poole (1983: 158-9) propose that penology has three main strands: the construction of penal codes; the sentencing of offenders; and the administration of penal sanctions.[4] This somewhat expanded account allows the conception of a *process* within which criminal offences are identified and punished when infracted, and considers how the punishment is carried out in practice.

Crime has, traditionally at least, been perceived in terms of violation of the laws of the state and, ultimately therefore, violation of the state. This is interesting if not somewhat anachronistic, since it is not actually the state that suffers directly the harm occasioned by crime, but rather those of its citizens against whom crimes are perpetrated. Though the state might reasonably be deemed to be harmed by acts of treason, certain forms of terrorism and the like, in the more general sense crime violates people (or their property) rather more than the state itself. Yet, to this time, it has been seen to be preferable to adopt the former definition and afford the victims of crime only a secondary (or incidental) status in relation to the outcomes of crime.

---

[3] See, for example, P. Hanks (ed.) (1983), *Collins Dictionary of the English Language*, London: Collins, p. 1085.

[4] D. Walsh and A. Poole (eds) (1983), *A Dictionary of Criminology*, London: Routledge & Kegan Paul, p. 158.

The logical straitjacket that such a definition of crime imposes is that when offences are committed, some person (or persons) is *guilty* of doing this and, in order to maintain the dignity and status of the law, has to be punished. Thus, the entire apparatus of the criminal justice system is designed to establish who offended, how blameworthy the offence was and, therefore, the extent to which punishment is necessary to mark its seriousness and discourage a recurrence. Once again, we perceive no directly expressed concern for the victims of crime.

In terms of its outcomes, this predominantly retributive conception of crime focuses primarily upon the offender and the need for the punishment to reflect the gravity of the offence in some or another sense of proportionality because it is *deserved*[5] (Mundle, 1954 and postscript 1968; Flew, 1954 and postscript 1967). This notion of desert relates primarily to the moral extent to which the law has been broken, rather more than to the degree of the harm done, while those who have suffered get, at best, only a residual consideration. The issue of proportionality has also proved a matter of considerable debate historically (see, for example, Hart, 1968; von Hirsch, 1976; Hudson, 1987), raising, as it inevitably must, questions about how possible it is to make penalties accurately reflect the harm caused by offences.[6] Each of these difficulties and many more besides, flow from adopting (and maintaining) a retributive approach to criminal punishment within what has come to be regarded as the 'classical tradition' of penology (Bottoms, 1977: 74).[7] It results, as Blad (2006a) reminds us, in both the inevitability of punishment and in 'penal instrumentalism'.[8]

---

[5] The notion of desert is extremely complex in a moral sense and has given rise to extensive debate within the literature on criminal punishment, particularly during the 1950s and 1960s in Europe. Professor C. W. K. Mundle (1954;1968) advances what seems to be the most precise analysis of the concept of desert in relation to retributive punishment in his essay 'Punishment and Desert' in H. B. Acton (ed) (1969), *The Philosophy of Punishment: A Collection of Papers*, London: Macmillan, pp. 65-82. But see also the utilitarian perspective discussed by A. G. N. Flew (1954) in the same volume pp. 83-104.

[6] I do not wish here to divert the reader's attention unnecessarily from the central argument proposed in this chapter. It is, however, important to indicate that the notions of *strict* and *commensurate* proportionality mean different things to different commentators within criminal jurisprudence. Most accept that, however desirable it is for sanctions to be directly relative to the gravity of offences, this is almost impossible to achieve with consistent accuracy. The idea of commensurate desert allows a more approximate approach, normally accompanied by the *caveat* that punishment should never be disproportionate—an argument that is inevitably somewhat circular. See H. L. A. Hart (1968), 'Prologomenon to the Principles of Punishment', in the re-printed *Punishment and Responsibility*, Oxford: Oxford University Press; A. von Hirsch (1976), *Doing Justice*, New York: Hill & Wang; and B. Hudson (1987), *Justice Through Punishment*, London: Macmillan.

[7] A. E. Bottoms (1977), 'Reflections on the Renaissance of Dangerousness', *Howard Journal of Criminal Justice*, Vol. XVI, no.2, p. 74.

[8] J. R. Blad (2006a), op. cit., pp. 139-40. This is so because, as Howard Zehr indicates, such a concept of justice requires the state to determine blame (guilt) and impose pain (punishment) as an invariable response to offences. See H. Zehr (2002a), *The Little Book of Restorative Justice*, Intercourse PA: Good Books, p. 21. Furthermore, as Blad notes, 'penal instrumentalism' is the process by which punished offenders become the means of achieving social and political objectives as a result of the sanctions imposed upon them.

The need for a new penology arises directly from the necessity of casting off the straitjacket described here. Retributive justice confines us to a view of offenders and offences that *compels* punishment and is not absolutely restricted by the principles of parsimony or proportionality—however vaguely or precisely these are defined. The former would urge us to punish to the *minimum* necessary extent, even in a retributive context: the latter insists that at the very least such punishment should be in no sense disproportionate. Offenders may be wicked or misguided, intentional or negligent, intelligent or intellectually limited, but offenders they are and punished they will be. Their punishment becomes a necessity and the retributive logic is largely impatient of extenuation or mitigation.

The rhetoric of retribution becomes the more objectionable when it is closely shackled to uncritical belief in the effectiveness of deterrence—whether of a general or specific nature.[9] For while intuition may inform us that some individuals can be deterred from offending as a result of seeing others punished, we simply have no idea how many they are, or for what particular reason. Similarly, it is as difficult to know how many offenders are deterred from further offending primarily as a result of being punished for former offences. Therefore, to use the concept of deterrence as a basis for decisions relating to the nature or extent of punishment is scarcely a moral way to proceed. The greater danger is that it also tends to lead to an escalation in the severity of sanctions and does so in a manner entirely disproportionate to the seriousness of offences (Hudson, 1987: 62-3).

Restorative justice principles offer a number of foundation stones upon which a new penology might be constructed for the future. These principles are clearly expressed, as set out by Howard Zehr (2002a) in the following comparison with 'traditional' justice:

Criminal Justice	Restorative Justice
Crime is a violation of the law and the state.	Crime is a violation of people and relationships.
Violations create guilt.	Violations create obligations.
Justice requires the state to determine blame (guilt) and and impose pain (punishment).	Justice involves victims, offenders and community members in an effort to put things right.
The central focus is on offenders getting what they deserve.	The central focus is on victim needs and offender responsibility for repairing harm.

(Zehr, 2002a: 21)

---

[9]   A situation discussed in some detail in earlier work, see Cornwell (2006), op. cit., in *Chapter 4*, pp. 52–65.

The importance of Zehr's comparison lies in the totally different conceptualisation of justice that it promotes and allows. First, it enables the traditional preoccupation with the state and the offender to be replaced with a socially more relevant consideration of the extent to which crime directly and adversely affects individuals and community relationships. Secondly, it extends the notion of guilt into a context in which the necessity to remedy harm becomes a categorical imperative. This suggests that the offence cannot be expiated fully unless, or until, the obligation to redress the harm is accepted and given practical effect. Thirdly, restorative justice demands that all parties to offences combine to restore the social equilibrium that is disrupted by criminal acts—albeit in different ways. And lastly, its central focus rests upon the legitimate needs of victims and the reparation they should receive from offenders.

Throughout the world today and in each of its continents, there is a growing belief that the time has come to abandon the 'traditional' model of justice that has served so indifferently in past decades. At the present time there is also an increasing conviction among many criminal justice practitioners, academics and others, that the principles of restorative justice at least provide the basis upon which a new penology might be established to replace the former model. The remaining part of this chapter is devoted to an analysis of the implications of such a change and, in particular, of the demands that it might make of offenders, communities and legal systems.

THE NEED FOR A NEW CONCEPT OF REHABILITATION

Restorative justice does not deny the need for people who commit offences to expect that sanctions will result from their actions and neither does it deny that these sanctions will be to some extent retributive. What is important is that these sanctions, when imposed, are not *entirely* retributive, but have the primary purposes of restoring or 'putting wrongs right', taking victims into consideration and enabling offenders to resume a law-abiding lifestyle within their communities. This can only be done by making sanctions constructive and by enabling offenders to take responsibility for offences and make reparation for them.

Though the latter process might seem somewhat close to what has historically been termed the concept of rehabilitation, within a restorative justice setting it takes on a rather different meaning. The reasons for this need to be understood if the new penology offered by restorative justice is to have a greater social usefulness than that presently delivered within existing concepts of crime and punishment.

Rehabilitation, traditionally viewed, has focussed almost exclusively on offenders and primarily on offenders in the custodial penal setting. In spite of an intensive and long-running debate extending back into the mid-1970s, there has never been a consensus about the effectiveness of efforts to 'rehabilitate' people in prisons, or, indeed, how best to do so.[10] There are several strands to this debate and the more important of these have become entwined in a somewhat confused web of reasoning that has much more to do with objections to medical analogies of 'treatment and cure', sentencing indeterminacy, excessive professional discretion and the like, than the measurable outcomes of particular programmes[11] (Hudson, 1987: 28-36; Tonry, 2003: 190-1; Cavadino and Dignan, 1997a: 36-7).

The inherent weakness in rehabilitative programmes operated within prisons resides in what might be termed the generic, 'one size fits all' approach to delivery. This is admirably summarised by Hudson in the following terms:

> More or better rehabilitation schemes in prison, the right rather than privilege of rehabilitation programmes—Cullen and Gilbert's (1982) state obligated rehabilitation is not, however, the answer. The prison not only *is* an ineffective arena for rehabilitation, it must inevitably be so. For the prison is a reformist institution, whose principle and mode is pedagogic. As in the school, the ideal pedagogic institution, the pedagogic mode of operation stresses common characteristics in order to cope with people in large numbers ...
>
> The prison, too, operates on this principle. Inmates are grouped according to common characteristics: age, gender, security classification. Reformism is essentially a curriculum with elements of learning included to inculcate a common achievement, namely adherence to the work ethic and the necessary personal, social and vocational skills to implement the commitment to legitimate work ...
>
> Treatment, on the other hand, with its psychoanalytic/medical mode, is based on people's differences, rather than their commonalities. The therapeutic endeavour engages with the ways in which individuals are diverging from normal behaviour, normal personality and then attempts to work with their individuality, their singular pattern of departure from the normal. Treatment should be prescribed for the individual and ideally it should be individually administered. A large-scale institution cannot function on the basis of emphasising people's individuality and thus rehabilitation and the prison are quite incompatible.
>
> (Hudson, 1987: 34-5)

To this criticism must also be added the fact that 'treatment programmes' currently delivered in British prisons (and elsewhere) are predominantly of a

---

[10] This debate originates in the now famous 'Nothing Works' scenario attributed to Robert Martinson (1974), which was widely misunderstood at the time and subsequently. Martinson suggested that in relation to the outcomes of treatment programmes, there was little reliable evaluative evidence to prove that any particular approach worked better than any other in reducing recidivism. In fairness, however, the claim related to comparative research which sought to establish universal measures of effectiveness among a wide range of treatment programmes that were, in the main, not strictly comparable in the circumstances in which they were carried out, or the variables used. See R. Martinson (1974), 'What Works?—Questions and Answers About Prison Reform', *The Public Interest*, No. 35 (Spring) and references p. 22, fn.16 and p. 49, fn.25 *supra*.

[11] Barbara Hudson provides an extensive and helpful critique of this situation in B. Hudson (1987), *Justice Through Punishment*, London: Macmillan, pp. 28-36.

'generic' nature, designed to 'target' particular forms of offending (sexual, aggressive, anti-social, etc.), as though the individuals assigned to them displayed significantly common characteristics beyond the generic 'label'. This is unfortunate because while it can be claimed that such programmes are available and delivered, the delivery focuses primarily upon the nature of the offending rather than the individual pathology of the people involved.

These 'structural' difficulties apart, it has to be questionable whether focus entirely upon the generic offender has much rehabilitative merit at all. Failure to deal with individual pathology also implies failure to address the nature of the harm that is specific to the victim(s) of particular offences and thus largely to ignore this important dimension of offending. The same criticism can and indeed should, be extended to consideration of the impact of offending upon the communities (or social groupings) within which crimes are committed. Recently, serious doubts have been expressed in relation to the effectiveness of a number of these programmes in terms of their effect upon recidivism (Civitas, 2005: 5-6; Rose, 2003; Friendship *et al.*, 2002; Friendship *et al*, 2003).

Many people who commit serious crime become isolated or alienated from their families and close friends because of the nature of their offences and the effect that these can have upon the immediate communities in which their families live. It is thus the case that the need for 'restoration' is far from confined to individual offenders and must, essentially, be viewed in a broader social context (Van Ness, 2005: 3). It is in its agenda to address all these dimensions and effects of offending that restorative justice seeks to re-state fundamentally the traditional concept of rehabilitation.

How, then, can we best arrive at a new concept of rehabilitation? Possibly by proposing that rehabilitation is a process with a social rather than a *quasi*-medical purpose: designed to restore offenders to a full place within their communities after they have acknowledged the harm of their wrongful acts, taken responsibility for these and made reparation for their offences. Such a re-conception may also be helpful in a different respect since it allows us to separate, from a criminal justice viewpoint, those individuals who are prepared to engage with reparative and restorative processes from those who decline to do so. This differentiation has some significance for the discussion that will follow in *Chapters 4, 5* and *6*. After all, it appears somewhat nonsensical to speak of rehabilitating the recalcitrant and impenitent offender who is unprepared to accept the consequences of his or her wrongdoing, even though such people must normally, at some stage, be released back into society.

THE DEMANDS OF RESTORATIVE JUSTICE ON OFFENDERS

The first point to be made here is that a new penology grounded in the principles of restorative justice would not dismantle the concept of retribution within the purposes of criminal punishment, though it would place limitations upon its nature and extent. There is nothing immoral in the idea that violation of people (victims) and communities is intrinsically wrong and that when it occurs it should, at least, have unpleasant consequences for the perpetrator(s) (Walgrave, 2003; Kaptein, 2004). This much stated, however, if there were to be a consensus that it is desirable to punish to the *minimum* extent consistent with securing a just outcome for those offended against, then the process of criminal justice might be perceived in a more favourable light.[12]

One of the main criticisms levelled against contemporary criminal justice systems is that in present circumstances the use (and indeed, widely, the over-use) of imprisonment represents a 'negative' sanction. By this is implied that the custodial process demands no necessary response from those committed to custody other than to 'do the time for the crime' and neither does it positively discriminate in any meaningful way in favour of those who demonstrate remorse and wish to make reparation for their offences.[13]

As will become evident in *Chapter 6*, there are ways of overcoming these difficulties, particularly in the custodial sector of corrections, though in order to do so a radically different strategy for the use of prisons has to be envisaged and adopted. It is important to stress again at this stage, however, that both custodial and non-custodial sanctions operated on restorative justice principles represent no 'soft option' for offenders. Indeed, it is necessary to assert the contention (subsequently elaborated in *Chapter 5*) that restoration becomes contingent upon reparation within an entirely new conception of what has, traditionally, been described as the process of rehabilitation. This means, in effect, that offenders face an absolute requirement to acknowledge the harm caused by their offences, where appropriate make sincere apology for them and also do something purposeful to make reparation to victims.

The requirement to take responsibility for offences and recognise the situation of the victim(s) opens the door to a situation in which, at present,

---

[12] James Dignan discusses the issue of consensus within the body of restorative justice advocates very helpfully in his contribution to Lode Walgrave's edited volume on restorative justice and the law. See J. Dignan, 'Restorative Justice and the Law: The Case for an Integrated Systemic Approach'. In L. Walgrave (ed.) (2002), *Restorative Justice and the Law*, Devon, UK: Willan Publishing, pp. 168-190 and in particular, pp. 171-2 and 175-6.

[13] This issue is addressed in some detail in *Chapter 6* and is not pursued in depth at this point in the discussion. Supporters of the 'traditional' model would, however, perhaps contend that parole systems contribute to the recognition of remorse and are capable of responding to it appropriately.

opinions among proponents of restorative justice are to an extent divided.[14] This concerns the extent to which reconciliation between offenders and victims can realistically be facilitated in practice, particularly in cases in which victims are traumatised mentally and/or physically by perpetrators of crime. This stated, however, there remains no reason why offenders who are willing to engage with restorative sanctions should not be obliged to address (with appropriate support and counselling) the nature and effect of their offences. It might logically be insisted that such a process should precede any reparative activity, or, at the least, take place simultaneously with it.

Strategies also have to be devised to identify and deal appropriately with offenders who attempt to subvert the principles of restorative justice by insincere demonstrations of apparent remorse, in attempts to evade or reduce the effects of reasonable punishment. This suggests the need for rigorous and intensive assessment processes conducted over a period of sufficient duration to permit underlying attitudes and motivations to be thoroughly examined (Dignan, 2002: 180; McElrea, 2005: 9).[15]

On occasions, some (normally serious) offenders indicate an apparent wish to be permitted to contact their victims, ostensibly to apologise for their crimes. They do so not from remorse or concern to right a wrong, but from other motivations that may include a wish to make the victim suffer as a result of their own punishment. Once again, great care has to be taken to ensure that this form of sadistic behaviour is unsuccessful in creating further harm. It is for this reason that the initial contact with victims is normally made by accredited intermediaries whose first task is to ascertain whether the victim is prepared to enter into the process of reconciliation and under what circumstances. This situation is discussed further in *Chapter 3*.

Offender–victim mediation and reconciliation can also be extremely stressful and disturbing for offenders, particularly in cases where abusive or violent behaviour is a major characteristic of offences. The process involves the offender in having to review and analyse his or her own motivations and conduct in addition to risking the reactions of disgust, anger or hurt evident in the reactions of the victim. Prisons are sometimes not the most suitable venues for mediation or reconciliation because victims may find the custodial atmosphere oppressive, intimidating, or one in which they are incapable of relaxing sufficiently to release

---

[14] During the course of the preparation of this book, the author has had extensive discussion and correspondence with a number of eminent criminal justice practitioners worldwide relating to offender–victim mediation and reconciliation. While all of these professionals endorse the general principle and its desirability, a number of them express considerable reservations as to the extent to which contact between victims and offenders should be of a direct nature. I return to this discussion in a later part of this chapter.

[15] Here see F. W. M. McElrea (Judge Fred McElrea) (2005), 'The New Zealand Experience of Restorative Justice Legislation', paper presented to the 11th Annual Restorative Justice Conference, Fresno Pacific University, California 23-24 September, 2005.

their own anxiety. For these and a number of other reasons, the process of mediation may best be left until the offender is released from custody.

From the foregoing discussion, it should be apparent that restorative justice is certainly more demanding of offenders than is the case with conventional sanctions. There is no doubt that it has greater potential for dealing successfully with lesser forms of offending that do not result in the offender being imprisoned or removed from the wider community. This to some extent explains why most of the initiatives to implement restorative justice principles and practices have been community-based and facilitated by using healing circles, family group conference (FGC) processes and the like (McElrea, 2006; Cormier, 2006; Marshall, 2001).[16]

There is, however, an increasing volume of literature that describes the movement towards the development of restorative justice practices in prisons across the world (Van Ness, 2005; VOMA, 2005).[17] This is encouraging because it indicates that attention is being turned towards more serious offenders and also there is a growing recognition that there is an urgent need to change the 'culture' of prisons within many jurisdictions. This transformation becomes the focus of discussion in *Chapter 6*.

THE DEMANDS OF RESTORATIVE JUSTICE ON VICTIMS AND COMMUNITIES

The perspective of the victim of any crime, whether violent or otherwise, is a very personal matter, much depending on the personality and attitudes of the individual concerned. Reactions to becoming a victim of crime cover a spectrum of emotions that includes anger, seeking revenge, disgust, humiliation, trauma, pain—both physical and mental, social withdrawal, bitterness and even, sometimes, hopelessness and despair. Each of these emotions is an indicator of the harm caused by the crime and this, like any other damage, takes time and effort to repair. In the case of certain crimes such as murder, manslaughter, unlawful killing, rape, certain forms of sexual abuse and the use of gross violence, the damage may be so extensive as to be irreparable.

Because restorative justice perceives crime as a violation of individuals and communities more than of the law and the state, victims of crime occupy a central place in considerations relating to the way offenders are dealt with. In many

---

16 These processes are described in some detail in the contributions of McElrea and Cormier in Cornwell (2006), op, cit., at *Chapters 9* and *11* respectively. See also C. D. Marshall (2001), *Beyond Retribution: A New Testament Vision for Justice, Crime and Punishment*, Grand Rapids, Michigan: W. B. Eerdmans Publishing Company.

17 See D. W. Van Ness (2005), 'Restorative Justice in Prisons', Paper to the Symposium on Restorative Justice and Peace, Columbia CA, 9-12 February 2005. The Victim Offender Mediation Service (VOMA) also publishes a worldwide Restorative Justice Bibliography, continuously updated at http: //www.voma.org/bibliography

respects, the nature and extent of the harm suffered by victims should dictate the form of sanctions imposed on offenders, but this is not the primary focus of the 'traditional' model of criminal justice. This means that victims of crime are presently afforded less than reasonable access to the criminal justice process and many therefore feel marginalised to a considerable extent as a result.

It is also evident that the more serious the harm suffered by victims, the less easy it is for them to consider extending forgiveness to those who have violated them. Restorative justice seeks to reconcile victims and offenders where possible as part of the healing process of the former and the eventual restoration of the latter within society, but in many respects this demands more of victims than of offenders. In present circumstances, the criminal law is not particularly concerned whether victims forgive offenders, or even whether offenders show any remorse towards victims. This is the difficulty that occurs when crime is perceived primarily as a violation of the law rather than of people.

In contrast with traditional models of criminal justice, restorative justice actively promotes the participation of victims and communities, but since justice should seek to 'put things right', its first concern is for victims and thereafter all others concerned in the equation (Zehr, 2002a: 32). This shift of emphasis invites all the stakeholders within the criminal justice process (professionals, victims, offenders, community members) to enter into a collaborative process—to the extent possible— with the purpose of identifying the harms, needs and obligations resulting from offending. Such an approach may be relatively straightforward in cases of minor offending, but is much more difficult and demanding in relation to serious crime. It goes almost without saying, however, that the excessive or unnecessary use of custodial sentences clearly mitigates against the potential to resolve differences between victims, offenders and communities through mediation which is best attempted in a non-custodial environment.

The extent to which communities can become involved in the processes of mediation and reconciliation between victims and offenders is also a matter of some debate. As will become clear in *Chapter 5*, there is an evident need to make prisons more amenable to community involvement, but this is only a part of the process of restoring offenders to full community status. Moreover, as Mark Umbreit so perceptively indicates in the *Foreword* to this book, the spontaneous and focussed effects of small, community-based programmes devoted to reconciliation are possibly less prone to errors than those operated at the macro-level of states and their institutions. We shall return to this discussion in *Chapter 6*.

THE DEMANDS OF RESTORATIVE JUSTICE ON LEGAL SYSTEMS

This fact brings us to the core of the problem and the challenge that restorative justice faces in relation to the existing structures of criminal justice in most (if not all) modern democracies. There are many people (practitioners, politicians and public alike) who hold on, tenaciously and sincerely, to the belief that by comparison with present concepts of jurisprudence, restorative justice is unrealistic, unnecessarily intrusive and over-inclusive. This is to a considerable extent understandable, though it might be suggested that the objections arise more from 'conservatism' and resistance to change, than from sound reasoning. It is evidently necessary to address each of these reservations briefly to ascertain their validity.

Restorative justice principles may be considered unrealistic because they challenge the traditional views of crime, guilt and punishment and seek to change the central focus of the criminal justice process. The concept proposes that victim needs and offender responsibility for repairing harm are more important in relation to distributive justice than offenders 'getting what they *deserve'*. The question that this raises is whether such an approach delivers *better (and fairer) justice*, or, rather, whether the predisposition to punish for its own sake outweighs a wider moral and social responsibility. However difficult and unpalatable the prospect of such a change might be, if the more desirable imperative resides within the former, then restorative justice cannot reasonably be considered unrealistic. Challenging it may be; uncomfortable it may also be; but unrealistic it is not.

Restorative justice, others might argue, would cloud the relatively straightforward process of establishing guilt, allocating blame and imposing punishment. It would do so by introducing other and extraneous considerations of 'obligations', remorse, willingness to make reparation and the like and by involvement of mediation professionals and conciliation initiatives that 'dilute' the concept of 'swift and certain' justice. This form of objection has some force if the sole (or dominant) aim of criminal justice is to punish due to the compulsion to do so (see, for example, Blad, 2006a and b, op. cit.). If, however, the continued use of 'negative' sanctions, increasing severity of sentencing and the resultant escalation of prison populations are to be avoided, then alternative strategies deserve consideration. Restorative justice provides a potential for impact upon each of these socially dysfunctional realities.

Implementation of restorative justice principles would, some people might insist, result in the administration of justice becoming more complicated, more time-consuming and involving more stakeholders in the process of reaching reasonable decisions. Once again, the concept proposes that there are wider (and equally legitimate) interests involved than solely the determination of guilt and infliction of punishment. It contends that the interests of justice would be better served by giving greater consideration to victims of crime,[18] and by involving offenders, victims and others in a concerted attempt to 'put wrongs right'. Above all else, however, restorative justice demands more of offenders in accepting responsibility,

---

[18] Though not necessarily to the extent of allowing 'victim allocution' or participation in the deliberations concerned with sentencing decisions. See, for example, M. Cavadino and J. Dignan (1977), 'Reparation, Retribution and Rights', *International Review of Victimology*, 4, pp. 233-53 and particularly pp. 236-7.

addressing their behaviour and making practical reparation to victims. There are encouraging signs that each of these can result in the reduction of recidivism (McElrea, 2005: 12; Hanson, 2001; Harris and Hanson, 2004).[19]

These arguments and objections notwithstanding, there is no doubt whatsoever that the prescriptions of restorative justice require criminal justice systems in general and legal processes in particular to undergo significant change over time. It is not suggested here that this change should be immediate or precipitate, but rather that, as in Canada, New Zealand and Australia as particular examples, principles encouraging restorative practices should be incorporated successively within national legislation. This form of initiative has already been endorsed by the Economic and Social Council of the United Nations in July 2002,[20] and by the European Union Council in its Framework Decision of 15 March 2001.[21]

The difficulty that all this suggests is that although there is now an almost worldwide acceptance that adoption of restorative justice principles has the potential to change the face of criminal justice and a number of other forms of mediation or conciliation practices for the better, resistance to such change remains considerable. It is difficult to escape from the conclusion that this reluctance has its origins in a complex of monolithic governmental and *quasi*-governmental structures whose vested interests lie in the perpetuation of the *status quo*. Moreover, because the inter-connectedness of the various elements that form traditional criminal justice 'systems' is so limited in many countries and professional interest-groups are generally so self-conscious, each will pursue its own agenda for limiting the impact of change-seeking initiatives.

Legal systems almost universally, and particularly those within what might be termed the 'Anglo-Saxon' tradition, have traditionally proved to be among the most obdurate of change-resistant structures, due primarily to their guiding motivation to preserve judicial independence (see, for example, Cavadino and Dignan, 1997a: 86-88; McKittrick and Rex, 2003: 150-52;[22] Hudson, 1987: 62-3; Dworkin, 1986: 10). This obduracy can be construed as a strength and as a weakness, depending upon the particular context in which it has an immediate effect. Judicial independence is often perceived as a virtue in circumstances in which judges evidently conspire to resist the implementation of measures designed by the executive branches of government to pursue policy initiatives with an overtly political bias.[23] Conversely,

---

[19] As recorded in the contributions of these authors in Cornwell (2006). op. cit., at *Chapters 9* and *11*.

[20] In its adoption of the Commission on Crime Prevention and Criminal Justice's recommendations — see J. Eaton and F. W. M. McElrea (J) (2003a), 'Restorative Justice — An Explanation', in *Sentencing: The New Dimensions*, New Zealand Law Society Seminar (March), at p. 12.

[21] *Ibid.* The European Union direction required each member state to 'put in place laws, regulations and administrative provisions' to promote the use of restorative justice in appropriate cases within their national law by March 2006.

[22] In M. Tonry (ed) (2003, op. cit.), pp. 140-155.

[23] In so doing, it has been argued by some observers that judges themselves behave in a 'political' manner, but this is disputable. See, for example, J. A. G. Griffiths (1991), *The Politics of the Judiciary*, Manchester: Manchester University Press and R. Dworkin (1986), *A Matter of Principle*, Oxford: Clarendon Press, pp. 9-10.

it is viewed as a weakness where these officials deliberately depart from legislative provisions and exhortations designed specifically to deliver socially desirable outcomes such as a decreased dependence upon custodial punishment.

Such observations apart, it is clear that the prescriptions of restorative justice do not sit comfortably alongside the 'traditional' concepts of crime and punishment, particularly in relation to the manner in which its re-definition of crime and guilt are concerned. Both of these reappraisals lead to outcomes that presently lie beyond the established concepts of operational justice. Furthermore, the suggestion that justice involves victims, offenders and community members in working together not only potentially transfers a measure of authority away from the courts, but also widens the range of acknowledged 'stakeholders' within the central area of justice administration.

One of the main objections to the incorporation of restorative practices into court procedures lies in the claim that this would disturb the principle of sentencing uniformity, or dealing with like cases similarly and different cases individually (Umbreit *et al.*, 2005a and b; O'Hear, 2005: 306). However, as O'Hear so eloquently points out (2005: 305-25), much depends upon how the term 'uniformity' is interpreted and what benefits are supposed to flow from insistence upon it. Within a concept of mandatory minimum sentences for serious offences, there arises a considerably greater tension between restorative justice and sentencing uniformity than is the case where sentencing *maxima* only are the guiding factors. The main reason for this tension is the imperative within restorative justice to provide an incentive for the reconciliation of offenders and victims, encourage the making of reparation and, where these become possible, to punish to the *least* extent, consistent with the seriousness of offences and the harm occasioned (see also Braithwaite and Petit, 1990; Braithwaite, 1991 and 2001; Blad, 2006a).

As O'Hear further points out, the vision of restorative justice for a transformed criminal justice system holds considerable appeal, if only because the conventional system seems such a dismal failure and manages to alienate *both* offenders and victims (O'Hear, 2005: 305). It does not, however, necessarily imply sentencing leniency, other than where genuine remorse, acceptance of responsibility for harm done and willingness to make reparation, enable lesser penalties to be imposed than would be appropriate in the absence of such contrition. In this particular respect, sentencing *minima* are less helpful since these perpetuate an essentially retributive ethos, rather than encourage genuinely restorative outcomes.

For all these reasons, restorative justice places demands on existing legal systems that many may consider unreasonable, yet these demands, if pursued, might result in a better quality of justice delivery. In many respects it represents a 'participative' model within a 'distributive' framework and thus is also a more democratic formulation of a process within which autocracy has hitherto been jealously preserved. Herein reside its potential strengths, although its vulnerability to resistance and obfuscation are also readily apparent.

UNLOCKING THE DOOR TO A NEW PENOLOGY

From all that has been suggested in the foregoing sections of this chapter, it will be apparent that restorative justice poses a number of very real challenges to the way in which most penal systems operate within 'traditional' models of criminal justice. There would seem to be two important dimensions to this particular situation. First, restorative justice does not necessarily seek to replace traditional justice in a radical sense, but rather to modify the way in which it is perceived and administered in a more humane manner that has relevance for contemporary societies. The second dimension is one of language and interpretation: it focuses on how, whether and to what extent the guiding principles of restorative justice can be accommodated within the present framework in which criminal justice operates.

Because in a restorative context it becomes necessary to re-frame definitions of crime, guilt and justice, it might easily be argued that only a new penology can realistically deliver the guiding purposes of restorative justice. This stated, however, there remain aspects of continuity in relation to traditional conceptions of justice that cannot be overlooked. Though restorative justice perceives retribution somewhat differently, there is no doubt that in many senses punishment of criminal offences is and must remain, essentially retributive. In addition, both the traditional and the restorative models discussed here propose what might be described as a 'rehabilitative' ethic, though in very different forms and extent.

Insofar as retributive philosophy is concerned, one of the principal difficulties to be overcome is that of discarding what might be described as its primarily *theological* justification in favour of a strictly *ethical* conceptualisation. This would better enable it to be said that because a violation has occurred, putting it right must, inevitably, involve unpleasant consequences for the perpetrator. The extent to which this unpleasantness is imposed must also be directly related to the harm occasioned, but not be either disproportionate or arbitrarily increased in pursuit of secondary or subsidiary objectives.[24]

The concept of rehabilitation presents an altogether different situation. For all the reasons discussed here, it must be considered very doubtful whether the idea is any longer of a sustainable nature. Put another way, perhaps, nothing much would be lost if rehabilitation were to be deleted from the lexicon of penology, particularly because it is replaceable with the more constructive concept of restoration. Whether or not in relation to custodial sanctions it makes any theoretical or operational sense to retain the rehabilitative discourse will remain a moot point, but from a practical viewpoint the concept has largely lapsed into desuetude. The argument for restoration through self-examination,

---

[24] Such, for instance, as general deterrence, or by use of indeterminate sentencing.

acceptance of responsibility and reparation has an infinitely more positive potential, as will become evident in *Chapters 4, 5* and *6*.

Within the foregoing sections of this chapter, we have examined in some detail the different demands that adoption of restorative justice principles would place on offenders, victims, communities and legal systems respectively. The central purpose of this discussion has been to identify ways in which a new approach to justice administration would, through the incorporation of such a penal philosophy, become both more positive and restorative. One of the main purposes of such a development would be the reduction of what have been termed 'negative sanctions' which require little response from offenders other than compliance with the requirement to pass time—particularly in custody.

It also became evident that the use of prisons has to change significantly if reparative and restorative practices are to become a central purpose of custodial regimes. This aspect is explored in more depth in *Chapter 6*. There does, however, have to be a coherent strategy for dealing with those who are reluctant (or indeed unwilling) to enter into reparative regimes, to ensure that they do not disrupt the custodial lives of others. Though this inevitably leads to a measure of what has been described as 'bifurcation', the difficulty is far from insurmountable.

What does become clear is that restorative practices (whether custodial or non-custodial in nature), offer no 'soft option' for offenders. Though there are potential pitfalls in the operation of victim–offender mediation schemes, particularly in the prison setting, sufficiently robust safeguards can be set in place to prevent these being subverted by predatory offenders. If such mediation results in some measure of vindication for victims and also a route to restoration for offenders, this would represent a significant advance by comparison with present practices.

In the concluding section of this chapter we have examined the ways in which legal systems would have to change in order to promote restorative justice principles. Some of the more obvious objections to such change have been identified and discussed, although it has been recognised that this is a particular area of potential difficulty and resistance. Two of the most formidable barriers to be overcome are evident in the independence of judiciaries and the diverse structural composition of criminal justice 'systems' themselves. In the former situation, judges as a professional body have traditionally insisted upon maintaining the freedom to act in a manner that is ultimately more consistent with preserving the traditional concepts of law and its precedents, than of inevitable compliance with legislative provisions—particularly in relation to sentencing guidelines. In many respects this has proved to be more of a virtue than a defect, but it does raise the question of accountability in the relationship between judiciaries and executive functions of government.

Implementation of restorative justice principles would significantly alter the present manner in which courts undertake their role and to some extent would lead to a degree of 'democratisation' within legal processes which, many people would insist, is long overdue. It would also require judges to re-conceive the essential nature of criminal justice as Zehr (and others) have proposed.[25] However, as McElrea (2005 and 2006) has so clearly pointed out, neither of these problems has proved insurmountable within the New Zealand experience.[26]

The structure of criminal justice 'systems' presents a more daunting prospect altogether. Many modern democracies have opted for the ministry of justice model of operation, which brings under one roof all the disparate agencies involved in contributing to the administration of criminal justice. These are generally held to comprise police, prosecution services, prisons, probation, courts, parole bodies and, in some instances, judiciaries themselves. Centralisation has the potential benefit of ensuring that all concerned receive and interpret criminal justice policies similarly, irrespective of differing professional agendas and operational roles. In practice, however, the potential benefits are seldom realised, largely because the disparities of professional orientation dictate otherwise and some degree of compromise almost invariably results.

There is no particular reason to suppose that adoption of a restorative approach to criminal justice would necessarily alter this situation significantly, though it certainly has the potential to do so. The discussion within *Chapter 7* will focus on this particular issue. What is more important for present purposes is the essential nature of the central philosophy that guides the determination of criminal justice policies and the near inevitability that these policies will suffer the inconsistencies associated with the ideological preferences of political parties within legislatures.

Restorative justice proposes an altogether different approach to dealing with crime, punishment, offenders, victims and communities. In many respects, its singular virtue lies in an apolitical stance and its more reasoned prescriptions for making justice systems work in a socially more cohesive way for the ultimate benefit of all concerned. Within this chapter, a range of issues touching upon this approach have been discussed in some depth, each of them suggesting the need to rethink the ways in which better justice might be delivered. Taken together, these issues somewhat inexorably point to the necessity of rethinking contemporary penology itself. If it were possible to accommodate the principles and practices required by the restorative justice philosophy within a modified version of existing penology, the situation would be considerably different. Unfortunately, or rather perhaps fortunately, such an accommodation is evidently unrealistic and this is what makes the challenge of restorative justice both real and exciting.

---

[25] See pp. 43-46 *supra*.
[26] McElrea's analysis is particularly focused on the Youth Court legislation in New Zealand subsequent to the Children, Young Persons and their Families Act 1989 and later provisions— particularly the Sentencing Act 2002 in that country.

All of this contributes to a most interesting contemporary situation. The British government, like many others, is a signatory to Articles 10 and 17 of the European Union Council Framework Agreement Decision of 15 March 2001 and the United Nations Basic Principles on the Use of Restorative Justice Programmes in Criminal Justice Matters (2002). The former agreement, in particular, requires each member state to put in place 'laws, regulations and administrative provisions' to promote the use of restorative justice where appropriate within their national legislation by March 2006 (McElrea, 2002b: 1). In July 2003, the British Government published its strategy document for the implementation of restorative justice (Home Office, 2003b), which, among other statements of intent, committed it to 'maximise the use of restorative justice in the criminal justice system (CJS) as it works well at both addressing the needs of the victim and in reducing offending' (Home Office, 2006a: 1).[27]

The same document indicated the intention of the government to 'build in high quality restorative justice at all stages of the criminal justice system' and to the development of policy on 'key issues about mainstreaming restorative justice in the criminal justice system' (*ibid.*: 1-2). At first sight these statements appeared promising in the extreme, but it will be noted that more than three years have elapsed since the strategy document was published and that in the meantime, a volume of criminal justice legislation has been enacted, little of which makes any specific reference to the implementation of restorative justice principles within mainstream criminal justice in Britain.

In *Chapter 3*, we shall examine the ways in which a penology grounded in restorative justice would enable the needs and concerns of crime victims to be met more effectively. During recent years considerable attention has been focussed on the legitimate expectations of victims on a worldwide basis and, as will become evident, the research literature is extensive. The majority of this work emanates from the North American continent, Australia and New Zealand and to a much lesser extent from Northern Europe, though with the notable exception of Scandinavia (Miers, 2001; Morris, 2004; VOMA, 2005). It is also of interest that the tradition of victim–offender mediation is strongest in areas of the world that still preserve the cultures and traditions of their indigenous peoples, among whom the instinct for reconciliation is stronger than that for retribution. Societies that do not have or preserve such a legacy may well find the demands of restorative justice much more challenging to meet.

---

[27] Home Office (2006a), 'Working Offenders', *Restorative Justice: The Government's Strategy*, [Briefing Document] www.crimereduction.gov.uk/working offenders42.htm.

CHAPTER 3

Victims' Voices: The Place of Victims in a Restorative Justice Setting

The title of this chapter is deliberately phrased in a contextual framework that is in many ways analogous with the notion of a table prepared for a meal or for a similarly organized gathering, at which it is anticipated that a number of participants will attend. Within such an analogy it might be suggested that those attending do so either because they have been invited to partake, or because due to their 'status' they have what might be described as a 'right' to participate. In the latter sense, the 'right' need not necessarily derive from some formally stated prescription, but might depend upon a consensual view that attendance was necessary, desirable, or otherwise of an indispensable nature.

SOME PRELIMINARY OBSERVATIONS

In recent years it has become increasingly fashionable to describe participants in such a context as 'stakeholders'—an expression commonly associated with having a legitimate interest in the conduct, deliberations and outcomes of a process or enterprise. Insofar as here we are concerned specifically with the promotion of restorative justice as a means of achieving what might be considered to be 'better justice', it becomes necessary to identify those who should have stakeholder status in that particular endeavour.

In setting out their 'fundamental principles of restorative justice', Howard Zehr and Harry Mika (1998) identified victims, offenders and the affected communities as the key stakeholders in justice (Zehr and Mika, 1998; Zehr, 2002a: 64-69). [1] While endorsing this approach, I retain some reservation as to its completeness and after due consideration believe that the state has to be added to the list. My reasons for this suggestion are explained in the first section of this chapter, though I believe that I understand why these two eminent writers deliberately made the omission.

As will also become clear later, there are divergent views on the extent to which victims of crime (and their personal circumstances) should be included within the processes of trial and sentencing. Some proponents of restorative justice practices suggest involvement to the point of permitting 'allocution' in the

---

[1] Here, see H. Zehr and H. Mika (1998), 'Fundamental Principles of Restorative Justice', in *The Contemporary Justice Review*, Vol.1, No.1, pp. 47-55. A concise summary of this discussion is to be found in H. Zehr, 2002a, op. cit., at Appendix 1, pp. 64-69.

courts, while others are strongly opposed to going this far, though they might accept the admission of Victim Impact Statements (VISs) or similar forms of submission by, or on behalf of victims, (Cavadino and Dignan, 1997b: 237-8 and footnotes thereto; Ashworth, 1992b: 8). In England and Wales since October 2001, Victim Personal Statements (VPSs) have been admissible in the courts and must, if lodged, be considered prior to the sentencing of offenders. We shall return to the implications of this initiative later in this chapter. [2, 3]

It is necessary to be clear at the outset of a discussion of this nature who can, and should, be included within a general definition of victims of crime. Evidently, some offences (such as assault or rape) are committed against individuals on a very direct, inter-personal basis, while others (such as criminal damage, fraud and certain forms of arson) cause a wider concept of harm that extends to local communities within which the offences are committed. In addition, it may be the case that the primary harm caused to individuals such as the victim of rape actually extends (in a secondary sense) to immediate family, friends, or others who feel outraged and hurt by the aggression, or whose lives are materially affected by fear of a similar event involving themselves. [4] In this sense, a concept of primary, secondary and subsidiary victims may prove positively helpful, since when it becomes appropriate to discuss issues of reparation, compensation and mediation, there may be necessary limits to who can and should become directly involved.

CRIME AS THE CREATOR OF OBLIGATIONS

Within the framework of restorative justice, commission of offences places an obligation upon the offender who wishes to resume full citizenship to act in a

---

[2] There is, however, some suggestion that such practices relate strongly to a retributive model of punishment, and that sentencing in fact becomes harsher in the event that victims' views or submissions are given significant consideration in the deliberation of sanctions (Cavadino and Dignan, 1997b: .250, fn.12; Cooper, 1991: 197-222). For evident reasons within this work, there is no support for a notion of restorative justice closely aligned to primarily retributive modes or models of punishment.

[3] In this regard it should be noted that in October 2001, the Lord Chief Justice of England and Wales issued a Practice Direction on Victim Personal Statements which affected all criminal cases in which a victim could be identified. Under the Practice Direction, when a police officer takes a statement, the victim is given an opportunity to say how a crime has affected him/her, and the chance to make a Victim Personal Statement (VPS). This statement can be made or updated at any time up to the disposal of the case in court. If the court is presented with a VPS, it must be taken into account by the court prior to passing sentence. A VPS must also be served on the defendant or his/her legal representative prior to the sentencing hearing. Practice Direction (Crime: Victim Personal Statements) [2001] 4 All ER 640 : III. 28.

[4] In circumstances in which, for example, a vicious and predatory rapist commits a number of offences within a limited geographic area without being brought to justice, it is likely that many young women may be caused to avoid entering the locality completely until the offender is apprehended. Such avoidance measures might, in turn, affect the revenue of local traders who could themselves be considered to have been victimised.

positive and substantial manner to put right the harm he or she has done (Zehr, 2002a: 23). This fact alone creates a further set of obligations: on the state to provide the means by which offenders are enabled to make reparation to victims; on offenders to undertake action of a reparative nature; and on communities to accept the restoration of ex-offenders once reparative action has been carried out. Here it will be noted that there is no necessary obligation on the victims of crime to forgive those who offend against them, although where this is possible and appropriate, the mediation role of restorative justice will encourage and even facilitate such reconciliation.[5]

It will be noted that in the foregoing paragraph, the first of the further obligations identified was that of the state to provide the means by which offenders can make reparation. This might be achieved in the custodial sector by transforming the role of prisons from a predominantly retributive mode of custody to a reparative and restorative one as discussed in *Chapter 6*. Alternatively, non-custodial sanctions can be expanded and strengthened to create reparative opportunities within the community as indicated in *Chapter 7*. Either way, it is a duty of the state to make this provision, and to ensure that it is adequately resourced. This is the reason for my earlier contention that the state should, and must, be seen to be a stakeholder within restorative corrections. It seems likely that its omission from Zehr and Mika's analysis was due to their redefinition of crime as a violation of people and relationships, rather than of the law and the state: a re-statement entirely endorsed within this work.

The second further obligation follows naturally from the first. Once the state has made adequate provision for reparation, it must fall to the offender to accept the opportunity to make reparation through productive and purposeful work that earns the revenue for victim restitution. This obligation has two important implications: the first is the concept of voluntarism on the part of offenders; and the second is the existence of means by which victims receive reparation and how far the extent of it is assessed. However, before addressing these, there is one additional aspect of state obligation that should be noted.

This concerns the legislative framework within which provisions are made to allow for offenders at the trial stage to accept guilt and opt to make reparation whatever the sanction imposed by the court, and how those who do not adopt this option are dealt with differently. For if the overall objective is to move towards a more reparative and restorative mode of criminal justice, giving

---

[5] Here it should be noted that there is a considerable divergence of view among proponents of restorative justice and criminal justice practitioners as to the extent to which it is either appropriate or realistic in the case of serious inter-personal offences for victims and offenders to become involved in direct contact, and as to the management of such confrontations. The author has consulted widely on this issue, and noted the considerable reservations expressed by a number of correspondents in relation to this practice. There is, however, almost universal agreement that where an offender desires to make apology (either oral or written), it is appropriate for the victim to be approached to ascertain, initially, whether such an apology would be welcomed or acceptable.

victims of crime adequate consideration, there is an obligation of some importance to facilitate this through legislation. This inevitably leads to the need to re-assess the desirability of differential sentencing for similar offences, without removing the necessary *maximum* retributive element marking the seriousness of the offence(s) and the culpability of the offender.[6]

Without such a re-assessment, it becomes likely that offenders will have no positive incentive to opt for reparative sanctions, victims will continue to receive inadequate consideration and restorative justice will be deprived of its essential 'cutting edge'. In addition, it is probable that the present excessive use of custodial punishment in many jurisdictions will continue unabated and that prison populations will continue to spiral upwards. Each of these dysfunctional aspects of existing criminal justice can be avoided if the principle of differential sentencing can be accommodated and included within legislative provisions.

Voluntarism within restorative justice becomes a central issue of crucial significance. Without it the present toleration of 'negative sanctions' will continue relatively unchallenged, particularly in relation to the use of imprisonment.[7] Voluntarism also becomes important in circumstances in which victim–offender mediation occurs only in the period subsequent to expiry of the sanction. Some observers of restorative justice consider post-sentence mediation to be preferable and possibly of greater genuineness than at earlier stages of the sanction period. It may also mean more to victims, since it will be evident that the offender has completed the requirements of the sentence and is still prepared to enter into the process of reconciliation subsequently.

The manner in which victims of crime receive reparation is clearly a pivotal issue for the restorative justice agenda. Evidently it is unrealistic to imagine a situation in which individual offenders make reparation *directly* to their victims, since only in cases where offenders opted to make reparation would victims be compensated and others would be entirely neglected. The issue also arises as to how the appropriate extent of reparation is assessed prior to the deliberation of sentences and expressed either as a total financial sum or in terms of *per diem* rates within the sentence period.[8] Either way, it would be essential that the

---

6 This issue of what has been termed 'bifurcation' (see Bottoms, 1977: 88-90 and p. 52, fn. 29 *supra*) emerges at a number of points in this work, and in particular in *Chapter 6* in relation to custodial punishment. It is also closely allied to the notion of parsimony in sentencing which envisages punishing *to the minimum extent* consistent with the seriousness of offences and without other extraneous or ulterior motivations (such as the supposed effectiveness of general or specific deterrence). See, Cornwell (2006, op. cit.), particularly at *Chapter 4*.

7 The term 'negative sanctions' implies forms of punishment or sentence that do not require anything of offenders other than to 'serve the time for the crime'. Thus the requirements for self-examination through analysis of offending behaviour, and the action of making reparation to victims, are at best optional and at worst absent from the operational outcomes of sanctions.

8 The notion of *per diem* rates suggests that a fixed daily 'victim reparation' sum can be determined within the wage structure of offenders, which is automatically credited to a centrally administered fund for victim compensation. Though this is practically difficult without significant

process adopted was capable of being directly related to productive work done by offenders (either in custody or in the community), and that the mechanisms for accounting were both reliable and auditable in the public interest.

It seems important at this stage to draw a distinction between the ideas of *reparation* and *compensation* in relation to victims of crime. The obligation that crime imposes on offenders in this conception of justice is that of reparation—or, in other words, doing something positive to 'put things right'. There is no suggestion that offenders can fully compensate victims for the harm done to them, or even that in the majority of cases, it would be possible to determine what extent of compensation (financial or otherwise) would precisely—or even perhaps approximately—meet the needs and reasonable expectations of victims. In this sense reparation, as a financial concept, is strictly limited in its potential, though it forms an indispensable element of restoration. This distinction is discussed further in following chapters and need not detain us here. Where compensation of victims is necessary and appropriate, this should better be a state prerogative and operate outside the confines of the criminal justice system.

CRIME VIOLATES VICTIMS AND COMMUNITIES

While it is clear that the immediate victims of crime are those most directly affected by wrongful acts, and that these victims may suffer damage in a number of different ways (physical, emotional, psychological, financial), it is far from evident what, and how much, can and should be done to alleviate their situations. It is also frequently alleged that victims have 'rights', though rarely do these extend in any significantly prescriptive way to enable such supposed 'rights' to be sustained within criminal justice.[9] We shall return to this issue in due course.

The proposition (initially advanced by Zehr (2002a) and others) that crime violates communities is similarly problematic.[10] The term 'community', in a sociological sense at least, means widely different things depending upon the context in which it occurs. Crime as a social phenomenon damages entire societies due to its impact on the daily lives of citizens, the cost of law-enforcement that, ideally, might be diverted to other social priorities and, ultimately, the expenses incurred in maintaining the entire criminal justice

---

'administrative' cost and, one might suspect, additional bureaucracy, the concept is essentially workable.

[9] Here, it is necessary to distinguish between the notion of 'rights' in a criminal justice sense, and the civil law conception of damages to which claimants have recourse within the framework of litigation designed to consider aspects of compensation. This dichotomy has led some observers of restorative justice to suggest that its ultimate merit may only lie in resolving situations at the margins of either process that are 'resolvable' by mediation and diversion from one system to the other (see, for example, J. Dignan (2002) pp. 176-7).

[10] H. Zehr (2002a: op. cit.,) pp. 27-8.

system.[11] In this sense, the term 'community' is synonymous with that of 'society'.

Crime can also affect communities in a more direct and selective manner, as becomes the case when, for example, a particular neighbourhood becomes the target for specific forms of offence—such as car theft or burglary. Not only do such offences cause personal loss to the individuals offended against, but also the local areas themselves become residentially undesirable, property values become diminished and the inhabitants live their lives in a constant state of anxiety.

In yet another sense also, there are 'communities' of people identifiable by common characteristics such as ethnicity, religion, political persuasion and the like, that become victims of homogenic offences specifically intended to cause them misery or provoke migration. Though the individuals with membership of such groups may not be concentrated in particular geographic areas and may, indeed, be widely dispersed, they become the victims of offences designed to harm them collectively.

Lastly, there are 'communities' represented by extended family ties and close friendships that are also affected significantly when one or more of their members become the victims of serious criminal acts. These micro-communities, as secondary victims, can have an important role to play in restorative practices, particularly where offender–victim mediation and family group conferencing become the preferred means of resolving the harm done by criminal acts (McElrea, 2005: 10). They also have a potentially valuable contribution to make in the structuring of plans for serious offenders to return to their areas of domicile on release from custody (Van Ness, 2005: 3).

The particular emphasis that restorative justice places on the concept of community participation in the processes of criminal justice stems from its evidently different view of the nature of criminal offences. For while it is clear that crime is an infraction of the law and such cannot be denied, this is not the *primary* consideration if restorative outcomes of the criminal justice process are preferable to those that have traditionally resulted from the imposition of criminal punishment. This particular proposition, it might be suggested, lies at the core of the difficulty of moving restorative justice from the margins and into the mainstream of contemporary criminal justice practice.

From a philosophical viewpoint, perceiving crime as a violation of victims and communities *to a greater extent than* of the law and the state enables socially more desirable outcomes to flow naturally from the criminal justice process. There are a number of reasons for this that deserve brief elaboration here. First, such an approach widens participation within the justice process to include the real actors affected by crime—offenders, victims and those who can assist in

---

[11] This includes the additional cost of compensation schemes for victims of crime. In the UK in 2005, financial payments to victims of crime exceeded £200m in addition to the £30m allocated by government to Victim Support. Source: Government Consultation Paper (Home Office, 2005b), *Rebuilding Lives—Supporting Victims of Crime*, Cm. 6705, London: HMSO (December).

putting matters right. For though the state retains a role in ensuring that just outcomes are arrived at, the primary emphasis is moved away from the concept of the state *versus* the offender and towards a more inclusive agenda for confronting offences.

Secondly, the inclusion of victims and offenders of both a primary and secondary nature offers the potential for mediation to take place between the parties either directly or indirectly. It enables offenders to make apology and agree to make reparation *in advance of* being appropriately sentenced and thus, in some degree, to ameliorate the harm caused to victims—even in relation to relatively serious offences. The third reason derives logically from the preceding one, since where sincere apology and reparation are forthcoming, victims perceive themselves as being to some extent vindicated and that their situation is, at least, afforded appropriate consideration in decisions relating to the sanctioning of offenders.

Fourthly, and in some respects, perhaps, most important of all, the potential for mediation enables punishment to be limited strictly to the extent of the harm caused by offences and mitigated to an appropriate degree consistent with the contrition of the offender and his or her willingness to make reparation. To many observers of contemporary criminal justice, a return to the principle of parsimony in the use of sanctions is long overdue. Since the infliction of punishment inevitably causes pain, our moral intuition compels that the pain be limited to the necessary minimum. All else becomes arbitrary and vicarious.

THE MYTHICAL NATURE OF VICTIMS' RIGHTS

To many people concerned with the administration of criminal justice, it seems almost incomprehensible that until the present time and the advent of restorative justice, the status of victims of crime within criminal proceedings has remained largely undefined. It is true that in recent years there has emerged a greater awareness of the needs of victims within many jurisdictions, but it might be suggested that this awareness is located more within what might be termed the 'culture of compensation' than in concern to include victims within the processes of justice.

It is also true that within many countries worldwide, there has been a discernible pattern of activity within criminal justice policy development devoted to the support of victims of crime, particularly the protection and support of victims as potential witnesses within criminal proceedings (Jung, 2003; Garland, 2002; Home Office, 2005a).[12] Indeed, the *naissance* of victimology as a branch of criminology has been notable in many European countries, North

---

[12] Here, see for instance H. Jung (2003), 'The Renaissance of the Victim in Criminal Policy', in L. Zedner and A. Ashworth (eds) (2003), *The Criminological Foundations of Penal Policy*, [Essays in Honour of Roger Hood], Oxford: Oxford University Press, pp. 443-62. Also, D. Garland (2002), *The Culture of Control*, Oxford: Oxford University Press, pp. 121-2.

America and elsewhere. The emphasis of research has, however, been predominantly on the procedural aspects of victim representation and protection, rather than in pursuit of the wider specification of victims' rights as such. As Jung points out:

> The development of criminal justice is closely linked to the state or, we should rather say, to the emergence of central powers acting in the public interest. Consequently, criminal law has traditionally been defined by the formula 'the State vs. the Accused' or the 'State vs. the Offender'. This preoccupation has led to a certain 'neutralisation' of the victim whose distinct interests were integrated into and deformed by the paternalism of an administrative system which increasingly acquired traits of self-perpetuating bureaucracy. 'Public interest' took over, disregarding to a large extent the personal impact of such conflicts. The personal aspects, losses, emotions, and suffering of victims, as well as suspects and offenders, were downplayed in a process of rationalization. Of course, such rationalization is an indicator of an advanced 'civilised' system of criminal justice which requires some form of conflict resolution. However, the acceptance of criminal justice as a state-bound activity may mean that victims are not being taken seriously 'in their own right' and that they are being discarded as 'flat characters' in the plot. (Jung, 2003: 446-7)

The issue of concern that emerges from the foregoing analysis is that it might be suggested that victims are not so much being 'discarded', but may, rather, be the subjects of deliberate political manipulation within a contemporary 'populist' penology. Though such a suggestion may, at first sight, appear somewhat extreme, there are a number of evident trends within many countries of the world that would seem to support such an assertion. The recent development of increasingly punitive penal policies, usually accompanied by 'sound-bite' slogans such as 'prison works', 'tough on crime—and tough on the causes of crime', 'three strikes', 'austere prisons', 'zero-tolerance' and the like, are designed to evidence substantive governmental responses towards what is frequently asserted by media sources as the widespread public 'fear of crime'. Moreover, these policies, when accompanied by reduced use of parole release and increased measures for community surveillance of ex-offenders, display a marked preference for what has come to be termed 'punitive segregation'.[13]

There is no doubt also, that the use of terms such as 'Megan's Law',[14] and more recently, in Britain, the media urging of a 'Sarah's Law',[15] is a visible

---

[13] For a more detailed analysis of this situation, see D. Garland (2002, op. cit.), pp. 142-4.

[14] 'Megan's Law' relates to the case of Megan Kanka, aged seven, who was brutally raped and murdered in New Jersey, USA in 1995 by an offender who lived opposite her home and who had a previous history of child molestation. At the time the police were prohibited from publicly disclosing his presence or previous convictions. As a result of the trial, what came to be known as 'Megan's Law' permitted such disclosure as a matter of legislation.

[15] Sarah Payne, aged eight, disappeared while playing in fields close to the home of her grandparents in West Sussex, UK in 2000. Roy Whiting, previously convicted of child molestation and abduction in 1995, was subsequently charged with her murder. Whiting had been released from prison after serving two years of a four-year sentence in 1997. He was convicted and sentenced to life imprisonment, with a recommendation that he never be released. The case was sensationally

manifestation of victims of high-profile violent crime being used to underpin the political resort to 'populist punitivism' and the proclamation of what Garland has described as 'retaliatory legislation passed for public display and political advantage' (Garland, 2002: 143). Indeed, the now increasingly frequent practice of interviewing victims of crime in televised news broadcasts provides both a regular reminder of the prevalence of violent crime and an apparent justification for increasingly punitive criminal justice legislation.

Bearing in mind the Practice Direction issued by the Lord Chief Justice of England and Wales in October 2001 in relation to the admissibility of VPSs,[16] it might be argued that a trend has been established towards granting victims 'rights' within the legal process. A VPS may be made (or updated) at any stage up to the sentencing hearing and courts are obliged to consider such statements in deciding upon sanctions. Indeed, the court will pass what it deems to be an appropriate sentence having regard to the circumstances of the offence and of the offender, taking into account, insofar as it seems appropriate, the consequences of the offence upon the victim. However, no opinion of the victim, or the close relatives of the victim, about what a relevant sentence should be can be taken into account by the court.

This raises an important issue. As a number of criminal lawyers have noted, one of the key principles of sentencing is that similar penalties should be imposed in like cases and, where VPSs are considered, there is the possibility that two persons could be convicted of identical offences, but one victim might decide to make a VPS and the other might not. This could lead to a court passing a harsher sentence in the former instance than in the latter and introduces an element of arbitrariness into the criminal justice system that might be perceived as infringing that most basic principle of justice—equality before the law.

The same form of inequality might also be said to have a potential to affect victims themselves. Those who are less articulate or less willing to make a statement might be disadvantaged by comparison with others more able and willing to do so. It is further a matter of some interest that both the rules of natural justice and human rights obligations require courts to give reasons for their decisions and this might be deemed to include the requirement to indicate the extent to which a VPS influenced the court in reaching its sentencing decision.

Within this context, there has occurred in Britain during 2005 what might be termed a sudden flurry of governmental activity in relation to 'victims' rights'.

---

highlighted in the British press, in a campaign to change the law to permit serious sexual offenders to be detained indefinitely. However, in a subsequent White Paper (Home Office (2002a), *Justice For All*, CM 5563, London: HMSO, p. 95), the British government put forward proposals for the indeterminate detention of serious sexual and other offenders 'until the Parole Board were *completely satisfied* that the risk they posed to the public was sufficiently diminished' to permit their release. A plan to introduce a modified form of Sarah's law by way of pilot projects in some areas of the UK was announced by the Home Office in April 2007.

[16] See footnotes 2 and 3 above.

At the political level, the decision has been made to replace the Victims' Charter[17] originally published in 1990, with what is advertised as a Code of Practice for Victims of Crime,[18] following a consultation process spanning, in its entirety, the period between February 2001 and October 2005. The latter document includes (in its second part) the draft of a proposed new charter that places obligations, in their dealings with victims and witnesses, on the 12 different departments (or agencies) of state that together comprise the criminal justice system.[19] Accompanying this initiative, the Home Office and its Office for Criminal Justice Reform (Victims and Confidence Unit) have severally issued statements relating to the proposed new code of practice under the banner headline of 'Victims' Rights', indicating the intention that it will 'become law' in April 2006.[20]

The interesting point that emerges from all this much publicised governmental activity is the stated intention that, to quote from the documents concerned: 'We're reforming the justice system so that the needs and rights of victims and witnesses are placed at the heart of what we do.'[21] Close examination of the documents concerned, however, reveals that these 'rights' are shrouded in somewhat oblique terms that relate to the responsibilities of the police when crimes are reported, the entitlement of victims to free confidential advice from the charity Victim Support and further, equally equivocal references to individual privacy in relation to criminal investigations by the police and the release of offenders from custody.

What, then, do these much-publicised 'rights' of victims actually amount to? To the cynically disposed, there is very little of substance that amounts to any form of absolute right, though the various documents contain a plethora of intentions and behavioural obligations which the proposed Code of Practice for Victims of Crime would impose on the various constituent elements of the criminal justice system in relation to victims and witnesses. The closest that any of the proposals within the code comes to assigning definitive 'rights' lies within five particular areas:

---

[17] The Victims' Charter was first published in 1990 and revised in 1996, but remained a document without legal force. In February 2001, the Home Office issued a Consultation Paper entitled 'Review of the Victims' Charter', inviting comment by interested parties by June 2001. In July 2003, the government launched what was termed a 'national strategy for victims and witnesses' under the title: Home Office (2003b), *A New Deal for Victims and Witnesses: National Strategy to Deliver Improved Services* (July), see www.cjsonline.gov.uk/home.

[18] See: Home Office (2005c), *The Code of Practice for Victims of Crime*, London: HMSO (October) which can be viewed at http://www.homeoffice.gov.uk/documents/victims-code-of-practice.

[19] Specifically, these include: the Criminal Cases Review Commission, the Criminal Injuries Compensation Authority, the Criminal Injuries Compensation Appeals Panel, the Crown Prosecution Service (CPS), Her Majesty's Courts Service, the Joint Police/ CPS Witness Care Units, all police forces of England and Wales, the British Transport Police, the Ministry of Defence Police, the Parole Board, the Prison Service, the Probation Service, and Youth Offending Teams.

[20] These statements may be viewed on the Home Office web-site (www.homeoffice.gov.uk) under the title 'Victims' Rights' and 'The Code of Practice for Victims of Crime' respectively.

[21] Home Office (2005d), 'Victims' Rights' – http: //www.homeoffice.gov.uk/crime-victims at p. 1.

- the 'right' of victims to information about their crime within specific time scales, including the 'right' to be notified of any arrests and court cases;
- the 'right' to clear information from the Criminal Injuries Compensation Authority (CICA) on eligibility for compensation under the Scheme;
- the 'right' of victims to be informed if they are required as witnesses;
- the 'entitlement' to free, confidential advice from the charity Victim Support which should aim to contact victims within four working days of reporting a crime; and
- the 'right' to be informed (in cases in which an offender is imprisoned for longer than one year) of his or her release from custody.

It will further be noted that even the so-called 'right' of victims to privacy is hedged around with provisions permitting the police 'for the purposes of investigating an offence or crime prevention, to release the details of a victim's case to the media.'[22]

All in all, there is not much in the raft of papers and proposals surveyed in the foregoing discussion that could not be described as other than a reasonable expectation that any victim of crime might have of the state, or its criminal justice system. More specifically, there is no reference to any right to have the post-crime circumstances of victims considered in the sentencing process,[23] or to any intention to implement any form of victim–offender mediation. The issue of victim access to the court process (either directly—other than as a witness—or indirectly) is left evidently unconsidered, as is the entire concept of offender reparation to victims of crime.

In all the circumstances described here, it would seem that the publicity attaching to what has been so grandly heralded as 'victims' rights' is, in a strict sense, scarcely less than a rather cynical political manoeuvre to focus public attention on victims of crime as a means of pursuing more punitive strategies against the perpetrators of crime and, in particular, violent and sexual offenders. Indeed the omissions from the discussion process indicate very clearly that what might be termed the pivotal issues of restorative justice have no place in the present or projected strategies for either crime control or crime reduction. The extent of the so-called 'victims' rights' hardly exceeds what might be termed 'normative expectations' and leaves the true concept of victims' rights more in a state of myth than of material existence.

---

[22] The document *Victims' Rights* (Home Office, 2005d) makes the explicit additional proviso that a victim's right to privacy and the media's right to freedom of expression are both set out under the Human Rights Act 1988.

[23] Through, for instance, an absolute requirement of those passing sentence to consider any submission made by a victim in the form of a VIS or similar document.

OBLIGATIONS INVOLVE 'PUTTING THINGS RIGHT'

In the absence of substantive initiatives within the United Kingdom and many other jurisdictions to afford victims of crime reasonable statutory rights within existing criminal justice processes, it becomes necessary to consider how, within a restorative concept of justice, this might all be done somewhat better. We have noted, earlier in this chapter, the proposition that crime creates obligations and that these obligations fall directly to both the state (as a stake-holder) and to offenders to discharge. Here it might be suggested that if, in fact, victims of crime have any absolute 'right', then that right is upheld only when both forms of obligations are met as substantially as possible.

The obligation for offenders to make reparation to victims of crime appears to be widely accepted in theory, but largely ignored in practice. Few prisons throughout the world run primarily reparative regimes and within the range of community-based sanctions, work-related reparative activities for offenders require levels of organization and supervision that are seldom attractive to local authorities and offender management services due to the alleged cost involved in maintaining them. The simple fact is that neither of these deficits is either insurmountable or reasonable, given the resources and the will to overcome them. This situation forms the basis of the discussion in *Chapters 6* and *7*, and it suffices at this stage to indicate only the principles involved.

The prevailing ideology of corrections is essentially punitive rather than restorative almost universally. The same ideology is largely disconnected from any intrinsic concept of victim awareness because the welfare of victims of crime is almost invariably the business of other functions of state and of voluntary organizations that may, or may not be state-funded in part, or entirely. Moreover, the primary focus of punitive custodial correctional ideology is on the warehousing of offenders in appropriate conditions (or levels) of security for periods of time specified by the courts, rather than on the inculcation of socially constructive and law-abiding behaviour. In short, since the organizational ethos of contemporary corrections is predominantly victim-unconscious there is no innate sense of obligation to demonstrate concern for victims of crime. It is also to a considerable extent a matter of indifference to the punitive correctional ideology whether or not subsequent re-offending occurs, simply because correctional authorities have no control over the behaviour of ex-offenders who have 'paid the price' for their offences.

This much stated, however, it is also a matter of choice for each individual offender to decide whether to make constructive use of correctional sanctions, or to decline to do so. The punitive correctional ideology may encourage positive behaviour and self-improvement on the part of offenders, but can neither compel this nor rely upon it. Even when it does promote such responses, this may be done more in the interests of institutional control than of social readjustment. In such circumstances, the dominant obligation of the punitive ideology is to itself and its effectiveness in ensuring the social incapacitation of offenders.

Garland (2002: 142-5) suggests that the contemporary strategies of 'punitive segregation' appear to consider victims of crime, while cynically pursuing entirely different objectives:

The third feature of this strategy is that it purports to give a privileged place to victims, though in fact that place is occupied by a projected, politicised image of 'the victim' rather than by the interests and opinions of victims themselves. When introducing new measures of punitive segregation, elected officials now routinely invoke the feelings of 'the victim' as a source of support and legitimacy. The need to reduce the present or future suffering of victims functions today as an all-purpose justification for measures of penal repression, and the political imperative of being responsive to victims' feelings now serves to reinforce the retributive sentiments that increasingly inform penal legislation.

> If victims were once the forgotten, hidden casualties of criminal behaviour, they have now returned with a vengeance, brought back into full public view by politicians and media executives who routinely exploit the victim's experience for their own purposes. The sanctified persona of the suffering victim has become a valued commodity in the circuits of political and media exchange; real individuals are now placed in front of the cameras and invited to play this role—often becoming media celebrities or victims' movement activists in the process. (Garland, 2002: 143)

If this is true and the plight of victims is to some or another extent exploited for ulterior purposes, then such behaviour is reprehensible to say the least. It also calls into question the extent to which restorative approaches to criminal justice can expect a dispassionate hearing within the echelons of government that exercise control over the formulation of contemporary penal policies— particularly in countries such as the United Kingdom.

On the other hand, since the 1980s there has arisen an international interest in the situation of victims of crime, pursued by organizations like the World Society of Victimology and subsequently by the United Nations and the Council of Europe.[24] Though this movement grew initially out of a widespread desire to see victims more adequately compensated financially, there has been an increasing focus on the needs of victims for practical and emotional support, and the range of services necessary to promote this (Shapland, *et al.*, 1985; Maguire and Corbett, 1987; Joutsen, 1987).[25]

The missing piece of the jigsaw is, of course, readily apparent from the foregoing discussion: the obligation on the part of offenders to 'put things right' is conspicuously absent from contemporary penal policies in most jurisdictions

---

[24] See Heike Jung's account of this development in 'The Renaissance of the Victim in Criminal Policy', in L. Zedner and A. Ashworth (eds) (2003), pp. 454-8. See also *Chapter 2, supra*, at p. 64 and fn. 17 thereto. The *International Review of Victimology* is also a valuable source of research and reference material in relation to victims of crime, and victim-centred research worldwide.

[25] Cited in H. Jung (2003) at p. 455 and fn. 49-52.

and thus from the way in which sanctions are designed, approved and implemented in practice. As we shall see in subsequent chapters of this work, a reparative and restorative approach to criminal sanctions absolutely relies upon affirmative action to afford victims greater consideration and encourage offenders to accept responsibility for their offences.

VICTIM PARTICIPATION IN CRIMINAL JUSTICE PROCESSES

In recent years there has been a considerable debate concerning the extent to which it is reasonable and appropriate for victims to participate in the various elements of the legal processes that originate in an offence and terminate in the imposition of sanctions on the perpetrators of crime. The emergence of restorative justice has made this debate more vivid, particularly insofar as it insists that victims are stakeholders in the criminal justice process if for no other reason than that they have legitimate expectations that should be met by that process. This contention raises a number of issues that extend beyond a concept of 'moral' rights and into the realm of what might be termed 'procedural' rights and the question of how such 'rights' should properly be specified and safeguarded.

The question is, undoubtedly, a difficult one and particularly so in circumstances in which the 'state *versus* the offender' paradigm of justice delivery dominates the procedural landscape. To many criminal lawyers, the legitimate expectations of victims exist to no greater extent than that they may be assured that offenders are punished and punished in a manner that adequately reflects the seriousness of their offences. Moreover, in the event that financial compensation is appropriate, then the remedy for the wrong done should be pursued through litigation in the civil courts and not cloud the deliberations of the criminal courts. Of course, victims may be material witnesses within the trial process and in this respect have the right to adequate protection, but beyond this, according to such a view, victims should 'be seen and not heard' as the old proverb suggests.

It is the case, however, that within some jurisdictions the criminal courts have the power to award financial compensation to victims of crime, but this is not, altogether, the main point at issue within the conventional perception of the justice process. Far more important, in the sense of traditional justice, is the *extent* to which victims should be permitted to influence the outcomes of the trial process[26] (see, for example, Ashworth, 1992a: 8; and 1993b: 505; Cavadino and

---

[26] Through, for instance, submission of VISs to be considered at the sentencing stage of trials, or even through what has come to be known as 'victim allocution' — a process which permits the victim to address the court in person.

Dignan, 1997b: 233-5). The same argument affects also the extent to which the views of the victim should be considered in decisions made as to whether to prosecute in the first instance.

Proponents of restorative justice perceive the argument entirely differently. Because, in their view of the situation, crime primarily violates individuals and communities and also creates an obligation on offenders to 'put things right', there arises an inevitable relationship between offenders and victims that cannot be ignored and has to be addressed. There cannot exist an obligation to 'put things right' without some opportunity being available to facilitate such action and therefore, logically, some element of victim–offender mediation and considerations relating to reparation becomes a constituent aspect of the justice process. Furthermore, within such an approach towards justice, mediation may prove to be an essential means of enabling offenders to take responsibility for the harm caused to victims.

Taken one stage further, restorative justice proposes different outcomes for offenders prepared to take responsibility and make reparation, from those who decline to do so. In this respect, also, mediation has a key role to play in deciding the extent to which offenders have demonstrated contrition for the harm caused to victims and their willingness to make amends for this. There are, of course, many observers of and practitioners within criminal justice who would resist, from a desert-based approach to punishment, any suggestion of differential sentencing. These same critics would perceive a necessity to treat like cases similarly, since the harm done cannot be undone and the punishment is, therefore, deserved. Viewed another way, however, this reliance on desert can render the argument vulnerable to the counter-assertion that even within the traditional model of punishment, desert has usually been tempered by the mitigating aspects of remorse and contrition (Smart, 1969: 217-19; Dworkin, 1986: 11-15).[27]

Here, it must be admitted, restorative justice, and its approach to the punishment of criminal offences, does not sit comfortably alongside concepts of strict proportionality. In fact, it argues a case for *proportionately less* punishment in instances where offenders are prepared to take responsibility and make reparation. Thus, for those (Ashworth, 1993a; von Hirsch, 1993; and others) for whom proportionality is a primary consideration, its prescriptions will, inevitably, prove problematic. This does not, however, make its case invalid, particularly since restorative justice seeks to distance 'justice model'

---

[27] Interestingly, Ronald Dworkin (1986), in his seminal work: *A Matter of Principle*, Oxford: Oxford University Press, draws a clear distinction between what he terms 'Rule-Book Rights' and 'moral rights'. The former are identified as codified rights set down in legislation, or other binding provisions, that demand strict compliance as a matter of substantive justice. Moral rights, as perceived by Dworkin, are those that exist other than, or prior to, those afforded (or circumscribed) by legislation, but in relation to which there may be no clear consensus within communities. Thus, in the context identified here, the 'right' of offenders to have their remorse or contrition considered in sentencing decisions may be more of a 'moral' than of a 'Rule-Book' nature.

considerations from its agenda, in its search for a more democratic and less overtly punitive approach to the delivery of justice.[28]

It is, of course, this 'democratisation' of the criminal justice process that poses the main threat to the *status quo* and makes restorative justice, with its emphasis on the desirability of reparation rather than punishment, such a challenging proposition. To suggest, in addition, that victims of crime have a stake in the justice process to the extent of active participation, is bound, for some, to seem excessively 'imaginative'. Yet there are soundly based reasons for such an approach, providing that these are sensibly limited to the extent that enhances rather than detracts from the quality of outcomes of the justice process.

Offender–victim mediation can produce positive outcomes in a number of different respects that are largely neglected within traditional approaches to criminal justice. Mediation, where it is possible and acceptable to the parties directly involved, can result in victims feeling to some extent vindicated and their situation acknowledged. It can also make offenders aware of the harm done to direct and indirect victims and persuade them of the appropriateness of making reparation to those offended against. Equally importantly, perhaps, mediation can cause perpetrators of crime to analyse the reasons for their offending, and then seek help and support to avoid further future offending.

Many proponents of restorative justice agree, however, that 'full-blown' access to victim allocution[29] at the sentencing stage of criminal cases is entirely unreasonable, particularly where it might adversely affect the outcome of the overall trial process or the extent of sanctions. Such a view is broadly endorsed within this work. Similar reservations are expressed by some criminal justice practitioners as to the desirability of admitting VISs to be considered by the court before sentencing takes place. Though such a practice may, on the face of it, appear to be much less objectionable, there is a danger that it may result in harsher sentencing practices than are strictly necessary, particularly where offenders are reluctant to make reparation[30] (Cooper, 1991: 197-222, cited in Cavadino and Dignan, 1997b: 249-250, fn.12).

---

[28] Cavadino and Dignan (1997b) discuss this issue in some detail in their analysis 'Reparation, Retribution and Rights', in *International Review of Victimology*, 4, pp. 233-53.

[29] This term implies the opportunity for a victim to address the court orally prior to the determination of sentence to express a view on the harm caused by the offence(s), or the extent of punishment considered appropriate. The same view is held by some commentators (such as Ashworth) in relation to the acceptability of VISs. See, for example, A. Ashworth (1993b), 'Victim Impact Statements and Sentencing', *Criminal Law Review*, pp. 498-509.

[30] In most criminal cases, the extent of the harm occasioned to victims becomes a matter of evidence, and reflects, to some extent, the gravity of the offence. The potential difficulty with VISs lies in the fact that these may promote harsher sentencing practices both for offenders prepared to make reparation, and, in particular, for those reluctant to do so.

SUMMARY - WHY VICTIMS MATTER

Within this chapter, the focus of attention has been placed on the extent to which victims of crime presently occupy a considered place within the criminal justice processes of many contemporary jurisdictions. All the evidence points to the conclusion that although appearances might indicate an almost universal trend towards increased awareness of the needs of victims, these needs are significantly under-met in practice. Though much has been said about the present situation in the United Kingdom in particular, it seems evident from surveying the international literature that broadly similar scenarios are to be found within many of the developed democracies of the world today.

Even more evident, perhaps, is the fact that the concept of restorative justice poses a substantial challenge to the *status quo* because it fundamentally questions the entire rationale sustaining the punitive ideology that dominates so many contemporary jurisdictions. It does so by making victims of crime stakeholders within the processes of criminal justice and by proposing an entirely different relationship between crime and its outcomes within societies. Moreover, by altering the prevailing conception of crime as a violation of the law and the state to one of being a violation of people and communities, restorative justice creates a clear relationship between offenders and victims.

Victims matter not only because they suffer primarily from offences, but also because recognition of this fact has far-reaching consequences for the *quality* of justice. In many respects, victims—when appropriately considered—become the catalysts through which an entirely more constructive use of criminal sanctions might easily be envisaged. For while there seems to be a consensus that victims deserve reparation for the harm done to them, little is done to enable this to happen, beyond the provision of limited financial compensation. To make matters worse, almost universally little is actually required of offenders by way of 'putting things right'. Thus and for reasons of political preference, the punitive ideology is sustained in a largely unchallenged manner.

In many respects also, within a restorative justice concept, the relationship between victims and offenders—although of an indirect nature—becomes a critical feature of the future for both parties to offences. For when mediation between these parties can be set in place, the potential for positive outcomes is considerable. Victims feel less marginalised because they receive greater consideration and offenders are offered a practical way of accepting responsibility for their actions and of making reparation for the harm they have done. As will become evident in the chapters that follow, reparation becomes the route to eventual restoration of offenders and the means by which they can become reconciled with the wider community.

This much stated, however, the obligation to make reparation cannot be left to offenders alone. The state has a duty to make available the means by which reparative work can be undertaken, within both prisons and centres for community corrections. Significantly, this means that prisons have to be given a reparative ethos and the means of doing this are discussed in *Chapter 6*. Similarly, the hoped-for expansion of community corrections that might result from adoption of penal policies grounded in restorative justice would need the same realignment; the potential for this is indicated in *Chapter 7*. In addition, it might be anticipated that the scope for victim–offender mediation and reconciliation would be greater within the field of community-based corrections and form a core aspect of community sanctions.

From the discussion within the later part of this chapter, it is clear that the extent of the active participation of victims within the processes of criminal justice is a matter of legitimate debate. While it is important for courts to be aware of the extent to which victims and those close to them have suffered from the commission of offences, the matter of victim allocution and admission of VISs or VPSs prior to sentencing will remain a controversial issue and understandably so. Ultimately, it will be necessary to arrive at clearly stated definitions of the rights of victims in these circumstances and a restorative penology would insist upon this being given some priority.

Finally, within this chapter much of the discussion has been concerned with the need for victims to receive adequate reparation for the harm done to them. In the chapters that follow, we shall examine how such an apparently lofty ideal might be put into practice both in theory and in the custodial and non-custodial sectors of corrections respectively. It has been suggested already that it may be necessary for offenders willing to make reparation to be dealt with differently from those unwilling to do so. Though this may appear to be an entirely logical outcome of the restorative justice agenda, it is one not without attendant dilemmas and difficulties, as will become apparent in *Chapter 6*.

CHAPTER 4

Penal Politics, Reparation and Restoration: Towards a Pragmatic Position

THE CONTEMPORARY POLITICS OF CRIMINAL JUSTICE

The politicisation of crime and of its punishment has become an enduring feature of most so-called modern democracies. It has also historically been, to a marked, though somewhat different extent, a dominant characteristic of nation states of a non-democratic or totalitarian nature. The apparent justification for this situation appears, in both cases, to be based on a form of presumptive logic that insists that crime exists because laws are broken and that laws properly exist because states enact them in legislative criminal codes. The circularity of these propositions has a persuasive quality that frequently passes unchallenged, other than occasionally by lawyers and criminologists.[1]

The 'politicisation' of crime may be described as the process of using the universal nature of crime for political and electoral advantage. It is a deliberate and strategic policy agenda pursued by many governments with the primary purpose of maintaining the incidence and anti-social nature of crime in the forefront of the national consciousness and it has a number of outcomes that are important within this analysis. First, it enables national crime control policies to be presented as 'the war on crime' that is, axiomatically, a 'just' war and the measures used to wage it apparently, therefore, require little further moral or operational justification.

Second, the 'war on crime' is conducted against a readily identifiable sub-class of the population (criminal offenders) with a view to controlling the nature and extent of their anti-social behaviour, but not necessarily the socially dysfunctional factors that encourage crime (Box, 1987: 150-2). Third, the 'war' envisages few necessary limitations or restrictions on the extent of its responses to crime, or the requirement for strict proportionality of punishment imposed for crime committed. Finally, the 'rules of engagement' are ideologically anchored in

---

[1] The argument is, in fact, perverse, since it fails to account for instances in which 'bad' laws are enacted, or in which deliberately restrictive measures are set in place for political purposes that become essentially 'unjust' or discriminatory. The 'apartheid' laws enacted in pre-1994 South Africa provide an excellent example of such situations. While there is no doubt that such were 'laws' enacted by the processes of the state, their purpose was both inhumane and designed to criminalise legitimate opposition to the practice of racial segregation.

uncritical belief in general deterrence which can be used to 'augment' the extent of punishment imposed beyond the limits of strict proportionality.

The latter point seems to be to be an important one, since it suggests that the necessity for punishment derives from convicted breaches of the law in a way that leaves little scope for deliberations relating to the appropriateness of sanctions. Worse, perhaps, it reduces, very considerably, the exercise of discretion in relation to the modes of punishment most likely to redress and repair the social harm occasioned by offending. Indeed, this situation is compounded when the immediate victims of crime are largely excluded from considerations within the legal process. In short, we punish for the sake of punishment rather than for its supposedly beneficial effects, or predominantly as a means of restoring some concept of social cohesion. Moreover, as Blom-Cooper and Drewry indicated some 30 years ago now:

> As long, therefore, as we have not dispensed with the belief that punishment is a necessary concomitant of a criminal conviction, we are stuck with a choice of penal aims that are often antipathetic. In selecting the penal sanction we will inevitably have to acknowledge social and moral limitations. But moral considerations should never precede the ascertainment of social factors. Moral judgements about social action or inaction, when made without the basis of such information, proceed upon social assumptions that may turn out to be invalid.
>
> (Blom-Cooper and Drewry, 1976: 65)

I shall propose in this chapter that what has been termed the 'instrumentalism' of punishment,[2] that is to say its use as a means of achieving political ends, forms the principal barrier to contemporary socio-legal progress. More than this, however, it subverts the achievement of true justice by pursuing purposes that are far removed from any rational concept of distributive justice[3] and social reconciliation. Here, in particular, I agree with John Blad in his contention that our contemporary concepts of criminal justice effectively compel us to punish simply because reliance upon deterrence places the integrity of the legal process at risk if we fail to do so (Blad, 2003: 130-41).

---

[2] The term 'instrumentalism' is used here in the sense that Dworkin (1986: 249-52) suggests, insofar as punishment is used for purposes other than the immediate one(s) that might be anticipated to flow from it. Dworkin differentiates between what he terms 'strong' and 'weak' forms of instrumentalism in relation to the extent and nature of the outcomes intended from its use. In the sense of its use here, a more ulterior purpose is suggested, insofar as the use of retributive and deterrent punishment may be perceived as being deliberately intended to secure an inhibiting effect on human behaviour through its disproportionate use (see D. J. Cornwell, 1989: 65; R. Baxter and C. Nuttall, 1978: 221-6; F. E. Zimring and G. Hawkins, 1973).

[3] In the sense of its use within this chapter, the term 'distributive justice' is intended to indicate its fairness of application to all classes of people in a strictly utilitarian sense. The concept is discussed by Dworkin in some detail, though in an economic sense, in *A Matter of Principle* (1986 op. cit.), pp. 204 and 256 *et seq.*

It will become evident that in common with a number of other present day academic commentators on criminal justice within what are termed the 'Western' democracies (see, for example, Zehr, 2002a and b; McElrea, 2002a; Blad, 2003; Dignan, 2002), my preference is for a significant shift in criminological thinking if better justice is to be delivered in a twenty-first century context. This shift would enable us to move away from the reactive and traditionalist concepts of punishment that have served so indifferently in the past, towards a more 'participative' form of justice embracing a reparative ethos.[4] As will become clear, however, it is the reactionary nature of penal politics that provides the major obstacle in the path of such necessary and evolutionary change.

POLITICS, POWER AND PENOLOGICAL RHETORIC

The seductive dogmas of contemporary approaches to criminal punishment focus attention within the legal process almost exclusively upon the state and the offender (or alleged offender). Stated bluntly (the argument proceeds), it is the state's law that has been infracted, the perpetrator of crime who has committed the infraction and the latter therefore deserves punishment. How much punishment and in what form become dependent issues, but punishment must be seen to be administered and in a manner assumed likely to deter others from similar offending. The extent of the punishment imposed need not necessarily bear a direct relationship (or proportionality) to the harm occasioned by the offence(s), but must be evidently supposed to be sufficient to persuade other 'would-be' offenders to refrain from similar actions. This is, in essence, the politics of contemporary strategic crime reduction.[5]

There is no doubt that crime reduction occupies a prominent position within the social policy agendas of most Western democracies (Stenson and Sullivan, 2000; Garland, 2002). It has become commonplace for politicians to speak of 'the war against crime' in an emotive manner designed to convince the voters who

---

[4] I am concerned here to draw a distinction between what are subsequently described as 'reparative' and 'restorative' forms of justice respectively. The reason for this is that in the prevailing political circumstances of most democracies, acceptance of 'restorative' justice to the full extent of its proposition by Zehr (2002a) and others may be at best reluctant due to its necessary demands for radical change and the implications of these demands. The case for 'reparative' justice is somewhat more persuasive, though it adheres to the same fundamental principles. As will be noted subsequently I propose the latter as a transitional stage towards the former, more as a matter of pragmatism than of essential difference.

[5] The principle of proportionality within criminal punishment as articulated by Hart (1960) and others is not disputed. What is challenged is the prevailing tendency to use disproportionate punishment in a manner deriving from 'justice model' adherence, predominantly for the supposedly beneficial purposes of general deterrence. Most contemporary crime reduction strategies continue to be predicated to a greater or lesser extent upon belief in the efficacy of deterrence, in spite of clear evidence within recidivism statistics that its effects are, at best, uncertain.

maintain them in power that they are 'tough on crime and tough on the causes of crime'. Specific forms of prevalent offending that cause alarm or discontent within the public domain are frequently targeted for exemplary policing, since these, if reducible, serve to convince the populace that the 'war' is being 'fought' in a substantial manner. Escalating prison populations also provide apparently positive, though frequently misleading evidence that the 'war' is being won. This is the politics of power-retention.

Political power-retention is a precarious business. Fundamentally it requires that dominant social issues are maintained in a prominent position within the overall social policy agenda, are continuously addressed and are apparently resolved. Crime has traditionally assumed a high profile within the collective consciousness since it is universally deplored for its dysfunctional social effects, and the perpetrators of crime can be 'demonised' without any fear of political backlash. The process of 'demonisation' has a socially cathartic effect which serves to reinforce the essential 'rightness' of the criminal justice process and thus the higher the number of incarcerated 'demons', the more visibly effective the waging of the 'war' is deemed to be. This is the contemporary politics of penology.

Criminal punishment is the ammunition used in the 'war on crime'. As is the case in all conflicts, it becomes largely irrelevant and unnecessary to be concerned with how much ammunition is expended, but much more important to be confident about its lethality. Large calibre weapons have generally a wider spread effect and penetration than those of lesser size, though the collateral damage that the former cause is greater. Within the calibre scale of sanctions, imprisonment may be described as the artillery of punishment, used to secure the optimum tactical advantage combined with effective neutralisation of the target. The target is crime in general and the criminal in particular and the overall aim is 'containment' or incapacitation, rather necessarily than crime reduction[6] (Garland, 2002: 140-1). This strategy represents the politics of punishment in its early twenty-first century context.

But above all of this, perhaps, there arches a more sinister and concerning rhetoric that reifies the agenda of criminal punishment as an indispensable social

---

[6] Increasing use of custodial punishment measured in both the size of prison populations and sentencing severity suggests that incapacitation of criminals is the over-riding priority of criminal justice administration in many areas of the world. There is also strong evidence that political parties with criminal justice orientations towards either the extreme left or extreme right differ only marginally in their contemporary approaches to crime control. The single factor that characterises both approaches is the need to retain political credibility in the 'war against crime'. The use of slogans such as 'prison works' (as attributed to Michael Howard, Tory Home Secretary,1993) and 'tough on crime and tough on the causes of crime' (British Labour Party election manifesto, 1996) provide excellent examples. As Barbara Hudson has suggested, 'the justice model may have been dreamed up by liberals, but it expresses a conservative consciousness' (Hudson, 1987 op. cit.: 162). A similar analysis is provided by F. Cullen and K. Gilbert (1982), *Reaffirming Rehabilitation*, Cincinnati: Anderson, p. 200.

necessity requiring a permanent and visible presence within modern societies. This rhetoric is the product of frustration with the apparent failure of crime control measures, combined with an inability on the part of politicians to accept the illusory nature of deterrence in practical operation. Deterrence has become the 'sacred cow' and cornerstone of present-day punishment philosophy, sustained by uncritical belief in the apparently self-evident and protected by its own fundamentalist logic. Its demotion to a lesser status within the supposed aims of punishment represents an unthinkable political risk tantamount to a diminished fervour to win the 'war against crime'. Moreover, since deterrence has a potentially universal application with relatively low directly attributable cost, it remains a favoured (even if unquantifiable) weapon within the political arsenal.

Such is not to suggest that some potential offenders may not be deflected from their purpose by the prospect of detection and punishment; it is, however, to insist that there is no means of knowing how many and why such persons were dissuaded. From an essentially pragmatic viewpoint, however, recidivism statistics within most developed democracies suggest that increasingly large numbers are not so inhibited and consider the risk–gain calculus to weigh in their favour. The generally rising extent and nature of reported and unreported crime combined with relatively low police 'clear-up' rates would tend to support their contention.

The picture that emerges as a result of this analysis represents every politician's worst nightmare. To prosecute the 'war' less fervently is perceived as a 'soft on crime' approach and politically suicidal, while to adopt a more combative law and order agenda incurs both fiscal and social policy penalties that lead to the denigration of other public welfare imperatives and priorities. From this apparent 'no win' situation, there might seem to be few attractive avenues of retreat. Of those that do remain open, however, one in particular might be considered to be significantly less disadvantageous than the remainder from both a political and a penological perspective.

Any perspective of criminal justice that is to hope to compete effectively against the contemporary *impasse* evidently has to minimise political risk and maximise social cohesiveness. It has also to be capable of persuading both politicians and the body politic that it will result in a form of justice that is not only better, but also fairer in principle as well as in practice. While this may appear to involve the search for some form of criminological 'grail', the resulting imperative may be to punish differently rather than necessarily to punish less (Blad, 2006a and b). It may also be necessary to punish for different reasons than at present, but only when this is essential and with different outcomes in mind for all those who become involved.[7] Better justice in this context does not,

---

[7] As was, for example, decided in 1998 by the Canadian Parliamentary Justice Committee in relation to the purposes of sentencing. In re-framing the existing criteria for sentencing, the committee placed primary importance on holding offenders accountable for offences, acknowledging the

therefore, necessarily imply increased leniency but it does, and must, imply greater distributive fairness and transparency in its motivations. In short, it must move us away from the necessity for punishment and towards the appropriateness of punishment.

RETRIBUTION AND REPARATION: PENETRATING THE LINGUISTIC MAZE

One of the principal problems invariably encountered in explanations of the supposed purposes of criminal punishment is the apparent inevitability that retribution has to be considered as a prerequisite rather than a subordinate imperative. The centrality of retribution within the punishment debate is of such ancient origin and its appeal to moral righteousness so deep-rooted as to make it almost immutable within the penological lexicon (Armstrong, 1961; Mabbott, 1939; Bean, 1981: 22-3). This situation suggests, or indeed insists, that there is an essential moral 'rightness' about the visitation of pain or unpleasantness upon guilty offenders, almost to the point that without it, the entire concept of punishment becomes devoid of meaning.

However closely or loosely the notions of retribution and vengeance become entwined within explanations of the morality of punishment, the apparent necessity for retribution remains to a considerable extent unchallenged and also in the minds of many scholars and jurists largely indisputable and inseparable. I shall briefly explain why I believe it to be right to challenge this widely endorsed assumption concerning the inevitability of retribution and in a more particular sense, its centrality within considerations relating to criminal punishment. My purpose in doing so is not to dismiss retributive considerations as entirely irrelevant, but to suggest that these become largely anachronistic within a context of justice that is reparative rather than essentially punitive.

The idea of retributive justice is, I should like to suggest, an inevitable outcome of perceiving crime predominantly as a violation of state laws rather than as the violation of reasonable individual and collective social expectations. It places the primary focus of attention upon the extent to which the law has been broken and the adjudged seriousness of the act(s) in question in breaching the authority of the state. Viewed thus, wrongful acts place the perpetrator in a position of confrontation with the authority of the state and the logical response of the state is to re-assert its authority through the imposition of punishment. The nature of this punishment is essentially (some would insist necessarily) reciprocal and retributive, since it is designed primarily to redress the extent of the harm done to the authority of the state.

---

harm caused by these offences, and recognising any attempts by offenders to make reparation to victims (Roberts and Roach, 2003: 245; Blad, 2006b: 117).

Such a view of criminal acts can easily be reinforced by appeals to the moral 'wrongness' of the offence(s) committed, its seriousness according to some measure of the harm occasioned and thus of the extent to which the perpetrator is deemed to be culpable and therefore 'deserves' punishment. These considerations are, however, of a secondary or subsidiary nature, serving to justify the *extent* of punishment rather than its *necessity*. The essential point remains, that within such a construct of justice, the state rather than the victim(s) of crime becomes the injured party. The corollary of this situation is that retributive punishment becomes not only justifiable but also inevitable. Moreover, its inevitability derives from the notion of deservedness which, at the least, implies some element of equivalence in relation to the harm done. Thus, within the retributive account of punishment, desert becomes inseparable from a formal system of penalties that must be exacted as a response to crime. This, as Honderich (1976: 26-33) has indicated, leads to a situation of some ambiguity. Interestingly, however, as Bean most perceptively points out:

> Retribution is unable to provide clear guidelines as to what equivalence should mean in practice. (It) refuses to take adequate account of the consequences of punishment or to consider anything other than the direct relationship between punishment and the crime; no consideration is given to the nature of the law or rules ... Although retributivists insist on treating the offender as a moral agent, there is no proof that treatment of a person as a moral agent leads to retributive punishment. To say that punishment is an end or a good in itself can only be established by intuition, or be seen as self-evident. (Bean, 1981: 29)

This situation is made worse in circumstances in which considerations relating to deterrence (either general or specific) encourage excessive use of punishment in a manner disproportionate to the harm done. Difficult though it may be to conceive of a mechanism that makes punishment strictly or even approximately proportionate to harm, the imposition of exemplary (or additional) punishment in the pursuit of deterrence makes the process vindictive. Vindictive punishment is the antithesis of fairness, since the aggregate penalty becomes entirely disproportionate to the seriousness of the offence(s). It also constitutes what in many respects might be termed an abuse of state power, using the individual offender as a means to the end of deterring others who might offend similarly.

So why do criminal justice systems cling so desperately to such unworthy concepts of punishment? We have already noted the perceived need of politicians to retain credibility in the 'war against crime', but this credibility becomes very fragile when criminal punishment is used in the purely retributive manner previously described, or for this and the purposes of deterrence. The question that arises from the discussion is that of whether this difficult concept can be approached more appropriately by adopting a different perspective. I shall attempt to provide at least an outline suggestion of how such a task might be envisaged.

A growing number of criminological scholars and legal professionals concerned with criminal justice administration have, over recent years, concerned themselves with the search for a more equitable, transparent and morally justifiable rationale of punishment that would overcome the conceptual difficulties previously described. Though this movement has led to the development of the concept of restorative justice which now attracts many adherents worldwide, this is not precisely the approach that I would wish to adopt here, albeit many of the principles it proposes are almost identical.[8] The main reason for this is that I wish to argue the case for a fairer and more humanistic approach to criminal justice administration from first principles rather than from any preconceptions about its moral, ethical and social desirability alone.

Central to this case is the notion that in terms of true justice, a wrong or offence is not requited unless or until some action is taken to make good the harm done to the victim(s) and that the responsibility for this lies firmly with the person(s) occasioning the offence. My concern is thus for the development of a concept of justice that places the parties injured by crime, rather than necessarily the state, at the centre of judicial considerations and ensures, insofar as it is possible to do so, that they receive a just measure of reparation for the harm done to them. Further, that where this reparation is made in full by the perpetrators of crime (whether directly or indirectly), any other considerations of punishment become a tangential or secondary issue. The reasoning for this approach requires some elaboration, since such a view is strongly opposed by eminent scholars such as Ashworth (1992a and 1993a), Von Hirsch (1993) and a number of others.

It should be stated at the outset that it is not suggested here that the role of the state should be changed in relation to the trial of criminal offences. Although some adjustment to the traditional methods of trials might well become necessary to ensure that the circumstances of victims are adequately considered, such would not justify major change to the role of the courts or judiciary. Neither do I propose that a full-blown model of 'victim allocution' would significantly enhance the cause of justice, or indeed of victims themselves. I do, however, perceive the matter of Victim Impact Statements (VISs) somewhat differently and discuss this subsequently.

What I do wish to suggest here is that if the operational concept of reparation were to become a more central and indispensable part of the criminal justice process, then a number of advantageous developments might flow from such a

---

[8] Reparative justice should, it might be suggested, be perceived as a transitional form of restorative justice—see fn 4 *supra*. However, I believe that the case for reparative justice has the philosophical advantage in the present circumstances of critical penology of offering a step-wise approach to necessary reform which is arguable from first principles rather than from a predominantly anti-retributive position. As will be seen later, there is a potential to view reparative justice and retribution as not being the antithesis one of the other. My concern is to move from a backward-looking concept of criminal sanctions towards one that has a prospective orientation.

change of emphasis in relation to criminal punishment. The first of these is the potential to speak more of sanctions than of punishment, the second is that sanctions might become reparative rather than retributive and the third is that both the victims and the perpetrators of crime would feel more fairly treated. A further advantage of such a development might accrue to the genuine rehabilitation of offenders,[9] and to the confidence of the general public in the effectiveness of criminal justice delivery.

The term 'reparation' carries with it an explicit intention of making amends or of 'putting matters right' where it is possible to do so. The concept of reparative justice requires the perpetrator of an offence to take responsibility for its commission, to understand the nature and extent of the harm caused by the offence and to be willing to recompense the victim of the offence in a practical manner. In such a context, reparation must be viewed quite differently from notions of restitution normally associated with financial compensation, since evidently in the case of certain serious offences (such as murder, rape, etc.) financial compensation might be incalculable and largely inappropriate. Thus reparation has a wider meaning that has a potentially 'empowering' effect on both offenders and victims and this may be seen in stark contrast with the 'disempowering' effects of retributive justice.

One of the frequently encountered objections to propositions of this nature is that reparative and restorative models of justice may deal adequately with minor (anti-social) offending and offences committed by young people, but are much less appropriate in relation to serious offences that normally attract custodial sentences. Another objection is that such models approach criminal justice from a 'reductionist' viewpoint, seeking more the limitation of and diversion from imprisonment, than the imposition of adequately retributive penalties. Neither of these objections is, in my view, necessarily valid, though it has to be admitted that in most countries that have initiated restorative justice projects, these have tended to be tried initially in the youth justice sector and in relation to minor offending. As to the second objection, there is no reason why prisons and custodial regimes cannot be designed to deliver a reparative ethos, though the concept has met with some resistance in many contemporary democracies. I shall return to this particular discussion in *Chapter 5.*

The traditional language of criminal justice is, without doubt, its most powerful and influential proponent, even within those democracies that recognise the shackles that it imposes upon progressive criminological thinking (McElrea, 2006). Thus to suggest that significant (and possibly long overdue) changes to the linguistics of criminal punishment might ultimately be

---

[9] The term rehabilitation continues to suffer linguistically from its untimely demise in the justice-model era and from the difficulties associated with its implementation in the custodial context. Reintegration seems to provide a preferable descriptive account of the need for and process by which, offenders should be accepted back into full social status following the imposition of criminal sanctions.

advantageous is regarded in many 'establishment' sectors as heresy in its most extreme form. The term 'retribution' conveys a powerful symbolic message with a direct appeal to the moral sentiments, but remains essentially vindictive in the strictest sense. 'Deterrence', with its own seductive logic, is a persuasive notion with little, if any, measurable authenticity. 'Reform' as a supposed aim of punishment has lapsed almost into desuetude as a pious hope belied by recidivism statistics. 'Rehabilitation', as we shall shortly see, has entirely different meanings depending upon the context in which it is used or abused and may better be considered as a process of reintegration. The implications of replacing the word 'punishment' by 'sanctions' are far-reaching and potentially useful, but invoke near-apoplexy in many judicial circles. And perhaps most significant of all, talking seriously about restorative or reparative justice requires all of these linguistic changes and a number of others besides. It is no small wonder that the *naissance* of this compelling innovation has proved so problematic.

REPARATION, RESTORATION AND REINTEGRATION: MAKING A VIRTUE OUT OF NECESSITY

It must be considered to be in many ways unfortunate that the concept of rehabilitation became the principal casualty of the emergence of the so-called 'justice' model of punishment during the 1970s, and largely for all the wrong reasons.[10] For while there were many objectionable aspects of the rehabilitative model of the 1960s, it retained the important virtue of focussing the attention of both offenders and criminal justice professionals on the future rather than the past. It also provided the processes of criminal punishment with a social purpose distinctly removed from retributive motivations. That the model was too hastily discarded is a matter of criminological history and yet the rehabilitative ethic still retains a strong foothold within ethical considerations of punishment, however pejoratively it may be viewed within the politics of contemporary penology.

The difficulties posed by the rehabilitative model lay principally in its appeal to indeterminacy, the largely unfettered discretionary power it invested in criminal justice professionals and the problems of measuring its effectiveness (or otherwise) (Hudson, 1987: 43-48). Politically it was a time bomb with a slow-burning fuse, waiting to explode an era of rising violent crime rates and evidently high rates of recidivism—particularly in relation to those offenders released from custodial sentences. The latter problem served very effectively to

---

[10] Chiefly because of the wide, and in some respects deliberate, misunderstanding of Martinson's (1974) analysis of the effectiveness of treatment programmes and the subsequent publication of the collaborative study by Lipton, Martinson and Wilks in the following year (1975).

fuel the fires of doubt as to the efficacy of parole systems and also of pre-release schemes operated within prison establishments.

The demise of the rehabilitative ideal and uncritical adoption of the justice model during the 1980s certainly opened the floodgates for a return to harsher determinate sentencing based predominantly upon retribution and deterrence (Hudson, 1987: 163-5). It also brought in its wake significant increases in the prison populations of almost every Western-style democracy. These in turn led to crises of over-crowding, prison unrest and ultimately of confidence in the forces of law and order so clearly articulated by Cavadino and Dignan (1997a) and earlier by Evans (1980), Thomas and Pooley (1980), Adams (1992), Fleisher (1989) and a number of others in both Britain and North America. Worse, perhaps, there arose what Cavadino and Dignan have so aptly described as a 'crisis of legitimacy' in relation to the entire functioning of criminal justice systems (Cavadino and Dignan, 1997a: 27-31).

In such conditions of ideological trauma, there also arose a hardening of antipathetic public and political attitudes towards prisons and prisoners upon which politicians were not slow to capitalise. During the 1990s in particular, the rhetoric of the 'law and order' debate became increasingly harsh, political utterances more strident[11] and prisoners themselves increasingly intransigent. As the decade wore on, increasing numbers of prison places were provided, and, as was only to be expected, increasing numbers of offenders filled them. The rhetoric of 'just deserts' quickly replaced any last vestiges of rehabilitative fervour and the penological climate change was accomplished. Though a small number of offence-related programmes remained in operation, principally for sexual, violent and drug-addicted offenders, any meaningful pretence to rehabilitate offenders in custody was effectively abandoned.

Viewed with the benefit of hindsight, these developments may yet be seen to have unwittingly cleared the way for others of an infinitely more positive nature. The simple fact is that criminal justice within most of the Western democracies has manoeuvred itself onto the rocks upon which it will eventually founder unless it adopts a profoundly different approach in this millennium. Each and all of the traditionally espoused punishment philosophies, and combinations of these, have been tried and found to fail. Moreover, these have been found to fail at almost catastrophic fiscal and social cost that is not sustainable into the future.[12] The more progressive and alert nations of the democratic world have already perceived the need for radical change and have begun to set this in

---

[11] See here the pronouncement of Michael Howard in October 1993 (fn.6 *supra*) and the comprehensive analysis of Cavadino and Dignan (1997a), particularly pp. 8-31.

[12] Cormier (2006) and Cayley (1998) present a very clear description of the Canadian experience in this situation and of the deliberate measures set in place to reduce the prison population of that country during the late 1990s. But see also Blad's (2006a) account of the entirely different approach adopted by the Netherlands government in the closing years of the 1980s and the early 1990s.

place.[13] Others will follow in due course, however reluctantly, because they have no viable alternative but to do so.

Reparative justice provides both an ethical and moral rationale as well as the operational methodology for enabling a radical change in criminal justice administration to take place within the foreseeable future. Paradoxically it may be the demise of rehabilitation that will facilitate this change, since reparative justice does not rely upon rehabilitation as it has previously been perceived and concentrates instead on the more pragmatic task of social reintegration.[14] Reparative justice recognises the inevitability of the fact that the vast proportion of offenders and particularly those imprisoned, either occupy a place within the community, or will return to it upon release from custody. Acceptance of offenders within or on return to the community will depend entirely upon it becoming evident that they have made a substantial attempt to make practical amends for the harm done by their offending. This can only be achieved by offenders engaging in work or activities that result in the direct or indirect reparation or compensation of the victims of crime.

All of this provides the potential for a new era of criminal justice that would place victims of crime in a more considered situation in relation to the effects of criminal offending. For while there is no absolute necessity for offenders to make reparation to the victims of their offences directly, it might be possible for them to do so in particular instances. Of equal importance, however, is the need for all citizens to be able to identify themselves with a system of justice that has a visible social purpose and makes constructive rather than destructive use of penal sanctions. Moreover, because victims of crime would receive appropriate recognition and reparation, the perpetrators of crime would also be perceived as having 'paid their debt to society' in a manner that might make social reintegration somewhat easier.

The process of social restoration and reintegration evidently consists in two essential ingredients, whether the sanction imposed is of a custodial or a non-custodial nature. The first of these is the need for offenders to accept responsibility for their wrongful actions and the harm that these cause both to victims and the wider society. The second component is the willingness to make amends for the harm in a practical way by undertaking to work in a manner that will provide reparation to the victims of crime. Both of these purposes can be met within a custodial setting or within the community under appropriate direction and supervision. If, as a result, use of custody eventually became a genuine strategy of last resort, significant reductions in present prison populations might easily be realised. The use of imprisonment would, however, always remain

---

[13] For example, see the commentary by McElrea (2002a and b; 2006) of the implementation of restorative justice principles in New Zealand.

[14] See fn.7 *supra*. There is also a view, widely espoused by proponents of restorative justice, that through the processes of offence recognition, acceptance of responsibility and reparation, the offender in fact rehabilitates himself or herself and thus has a right to full social reintegration.

necessary for the most serious offences, though the time spent in reparative custody would be more constructively used.

The question that always returns to be answered is that of how offenders who indicate no remorse, deny responsibility, or decline to enter into a reparative process should be dealt with. These situations raise the spectre of what have been criticised as 'birfurcated' (or twin-track) penal policies, dealing differentially with identifiable groups of persons for particular reasons, even though their offences might be identical or significantly similar (see Bottoms, 1977: 88-90; Cavadino and Dignan, 1997a: 23 and 26-8). It is undeniably the case that bifurcated penal policies give rise to moral and ethical dilemmas both from a sentencing viewpoint and also operationally. This admitted, however, I am not sure that in the context of our present deliberations, the potential problem is either indefensible or insurmountable.[15] This particular issue does, however, arise on a number of occasions in the later chapters of this work.

The underlying reason for this contention is somewhat complex, though capable of relatively brief explanation providing that one starts from the perspective of reparative justice becoming the normative mode of operating criminal sanctions. The trial process for all offenders could be conducted on an identical basis for *all* alleged offenders, up to and including a finding of guilt or innocence and (in the cases of those found guilty) of subsequent deliberation of sentence. At that point the convicted offender might be afforded the opportunity of accepting one or other of two options. The first option would be a tariff-based sentence for the offence(s) with prevailing remission provision and the second option would be a reparative sentence, providing that he/she indicated in mitigation that responsibility for the offence(s) is accepted, some degree of remorse and a willingness to enter the reparative process.

In the case of the former, the offender would serve a sentence (whether custodial or non-custodial) in much the same manner as at present, and, where such custodial provisions exist, would attract remission of sentence for reasonable and constructive conduct. He or she would not be obliged to make any reparative contribution to victims of crime and would be released on expiry of sentence under existing arrangements. In the case of non-custodial sentences or orders, the offender would be required to satisfy the provisions of the sanction in full, with arrangements for breach of conditions being the same as those currently in force.[16]

---

[15] Such is to imply that in the circumstances described here, a measure of bifurcation may amount to the lesser of several evils, even though in an ideal world it should clearly be avoided whenever possible. If reparative justice is to establish credibility, some means has to be devised of dealing with offenders who decline to enter into the reparative process. On balance, there seems to be some merit in making the reparative option preferable, while not penalising those who decline in any greater measure than at present.

[16] In many jurisdictions breach of the conditions of non-custodial sanctions makes the offender liable to the immediate imposition of a custodial sentence or a more stringent variation of the non-custodial penalty. In the case of the former, it would not seem inappropriate for such a sentence to

For those offenders opting to serve a reparative sentence it would seem appropriate that the submission made by the defence in mitigation of sentence should include an agreed package of conditions under which the term would be served. This would include details of the reparation to be made either directly or indirectly to victim(s) and how, any apology to be made and the offender might also be obliged to sign a binding agreement to meet the conditions in full. Once the court was satisfied as to the conditions agreed, it might then decide upon the extent of the sentence to be imposed. This is broadly the New Zealand model described by McElrea (2006). In such circumstances it would seem entirely reasonable for the sentence passed to be of a reduced nature, though breach of the agreed conditions should carry with it provision for a non-reparative sentence to be substituted immediately by the court adjudicating the breach proceedings. It would therefore be necessary for the court imposing the original reparative sentence to specify what non-reparative sentence would have been imposed in the circumstances of the offence(s) tried and convicted.

Though arrangements such as those described briefly above might seem appropriate in the vast majority of the less serious offences tried by courts, it is obvious that very serious offences (including those that attract mandatory or discretionary life or equivalent sentences) need to be viewed somewhat differently. One means of doing so might be to limit reparative sentences to terms of (say) ten years or less in duration, thus automatically excluding more serious offences from consideration. Alternatively and if it were considered desirable to extend the principle of reparative sentencing to *all* offences, the concept of indeterminate life sentences would have to discarded and replaced by determinate provisions.[17] My preference would be for the latter, since it seems wrong in principle to increase the present element of bifurcation by arbitrarily excluding the most serious offences from the potential benefits of reparative sentencing arrangements.

---

be of a reparative nature, even if it were imposed for breach of the conditions of a non-custodial sanction.

[17] The continued existence of the mandatory and discretionary provisions for indeterminate life sentences in Britain and elsewhere presents a serious difficulty for the inclusion of serious offenders within a reparative sentencing structure. Yet it remains desirable that those serving life sentences should not become the victims of discrimination if, in every other respect, they might be enabled to make some amends for their offences (however heinous) in a reparative manner. Since it is normal practice for the judiciary to express an opinion on the sentence tariff period (presently deemed necessary to meet the requirements of retribution and deterrence), it should logically follow that the case for the retention of indeterminate sentences is not immutable.

REPARATION AND RESTORATION: A BRIDGE TOO FAR?

My purpose in this chapter has been to make a substantive case for a sea-change in the way in which criminal justice is administered in most countries that embrace a Western-style approach to criminal punishment. This case is set forward because it seems evident that the present circumstances in which criminal justice systems operate are based upon a set of out-worn linguistic constructs that have scant relevance for contemporary society and are in imminent danger of causing more harm than good. The danger of further penal crises is a direct product of both an archaic and excessive approach to the use of custodial punishment and a failure to explore in any substantial way the challenging opportunities that hold out the possibility of genuine progress in the future.

I have attempted to sketch, however much in outline, the extent to which it is evident that the politics of criminal justice administration contribute to the stagnating situation. The sheer cost and escalation of the proportion of national economic resources allocated to crime control bear witness to the fact that criminal justice has become a *mega*-business for most democracies, diverting much-needed fiscal resources from other and infinitely more desirable social policy priorities. And yet, the reluctance of most politicians to discard outmoded and in some cases discredited theories concerning crime and justice, or to embrace the possibilities offered by radical re-appraisal of them, continues to prevent real progress from becoming a reality.

Within this chapter I have focussed on what has been termed 'reparative justice' and mentioned restorative justice only occasionally; there is an important reason for this. Admirable as the concept of restorative justice may be and however much reparative justice may represent only a significant aspect of it, I remain bleakly and reluctantly unconfident that either the socio-political nor the criminological world is presently able or willing to accept restorative justice as an *operational* concept — other than in a strictly limited sense. This is an unfortunate, though I believe, honest assessment of the contemporary situation. The main problem, it seems, resides not so much in the reparative but in the restorative challenge implicit in these new approaches to the delivery of true justice.[18]

---

[18] One of the main aspects of objection or reservation encountered in discussion of restorative justice principles with criminal justice professionals is that of offender–victim reconciliation processes. Many professionals have considerable reservations concerning direct contact between offenders and victims, particularly those victims who have been traumatised by serious violent or sexually motivated offences. Restorative justice makes no specific distinction in relation to the nature of offences in its general prescriptions and might be perceived as somewhat ambivalent in this particular area. Considered more closely however, the situation is not as unclear as might be supposed. Zehr (2002a: 38-9) is signally clear that the question that should be asked is: 'What is the *appropriate* process to involve stakeholders in an effort to put things right?' Thus, in some cases of domestic violence, rape, child molestation, etc., victim–offender encounters should not be considered appropriate when there is any possibility that further harm might result.

The notion of offenders being 'restored' to full citizenship as a result of having penal sanctions imposed upon them, and having complied with the requirements of these, is morally valid and entirely appropriate. For all manner of structural and social reasons, however, former offenders do not attract the status of 'having the slate wiped clean' and neither is the fact that they may be considered to have 'paid their debt to society' a matter of forgiveness within the social structure. In many respects quite the opposite becomes the case and ex-offenders become the recipients of actual discrimination in terms of employment, economic status, social surveillance and the like. There is presently no evidence to suggest that within modern democracies there is any particular willingness to redress this situation: if anything, the prevailing mood is contrary both officially and socially.

Blad (2006a) has suggested that if it were possible to discard the term 'punishment' and replace it by 'sanctions', then the way might eventually become open for a greater extent of genuine forgiveness of former offenders within developed societies. He so proposes on the basis that the idea of sanctions necessarily implies a measure of social disapprobation, whereas the term punishment is the self-fulfilling outcome of penal policies grounded in retribution and deterrence. We continue to punish in the way that we do as a matter of necessity and entirely because not to punish would render such policies incredible. Punishment thus becomes more a matter of judicial than of social censure. If, alternatively, the term sanction were to be more widely embraced, the general public might perceive itself as having a greater stake within the process of justice and more able to adopt ideas of forgiveness and restoration.

Blad's proposition is, I believe, subtle rather than semantic and one in which many criminologists and moral philosophers may find common cause. It contains echoes of John Dryden's poetical assertion that 'forgiveness to the injured doth belong'[19] and there seems an ever-present danger of overlooking the fact that it is principally society rather than the state that is harmed by criminal offending. As Zehr (2002a: 22) also reminds us: 'Restorative justice understands crime first of all as harm done to people and communities. Our legal system, with its focus on rules and laws, often loses sight of this reality'.

The title of this chapter deliberately addresses the issue of politics and penology for the very reason that Zehr so succinctly criticises within the foregoing quotation. But it is not only our legal systems that lose sight of the reality that the primary harm occasioned by crime directly affects society, victims and offenders themselves. The nature and tenor of the political discourse within most modern democracies are deliberately shaped to perpetuate the belief that it is the state that occupies the moral high ground in the 'war against crime' and

---

[19] John Dryden, *The Conquest of Grenada*, Part I, i.

that only the state can become the repository of the moral conscience. The corollary of such arrogance is that only the state can *do justice* and that its subservient populations must be satisfied with *justice being done to them*.

Both reparative and restorative justice perceive this relationship altogether differently, the former comprising a necessary, though interim, stepping stone to the much more desirable goal represented by the latter. Moreover, if it is the case that within the political climate of most contemporary democracies the transition to restorative justice is, in fact, a bridge too far at present, then the more achievable purposes of reparative justice provide a very substantial and credible foundation.

REINTEGRATION: THE NEED FOR MORE CREDIBLE SANCTIONS?

The view has been expressed earlier in this analysis that rehabilitation as a purpose of, or justification for criminal punishment became terminally affected in the late 1970s and subsequently never recovered. Curiously, however, it seems to have obstinately retained a notional and vestigial currency that is still evident within contemporary penology (Hazell, 1980: 2-8). With the benefit of hindsight, it seems reasonable to suggest that although the 'treatment model' of punishment may have been abandoned and replaced by the so-called 'justice model' of the late 1980s and 1990s, there remained a perceived need to provide the process of punishment with a prospective purpose, however vaguely defined (Hudson, 1987: 170-6; Palmer, 1975: 135). Since any ideas that punishment, particularly of a custodial nature, would reform offenders had largely been abandoned, the term rehabilitation was all that remained available to provide retributive punishment with the necessary prospective respectability.

Seen in such a light, custodial rehabilitation in Britain was strictly confined during the 1990s to the generation of a number of programmes that were designed to address offending behaviour of various forms and in a general sense. Little pretence was, however, made to deal with the majority of offenders in an individual manner, or to focus on their social deficits, particularly within prisons. In any case, the constantly increasing size of the prison population made any such intervention difficult and in many prisons, impossible to attempt.

Nevertheless, there has always existed a need to prepare offenders held in custody, particularly those serving sentences measured in years, for the transition to liberty and freedom of choice. Many of them become deeply institutionalised, routine dependent, introspective and self-centred. In many cases also, relationships with close others will have changed, deteriorated, or even been abandoned. A significant proportion of those discharged from prisons will experience unemployment and be tempted back to crime or the 'alternative economy' as a means of making a livelihood. It is therefore difficult to envisage how, other than within graduated release schemes, prisons can effectively 'rehabilitate' offenders within an institutional setting.

Graduated release schemes are unpopular with politicians, criminal justice professionals and the general public because they carry an inevitable social risk. A proportion of offenders will inevitably re-offend under parole, 'work-out'[20] and temporary release[21] conditions, and this normally attracts considerable adverse media attention.[22] In many cases, however, graduated release represents a safer option than unconditional or conditional release on expiry of the sentence period. The more enlightened jurisdictions have developed 'hostel-type' semi-custodial facilities as annexes to prisons, to which offenders return at the end of each working day, in order to operate temporary release or 'work-out' schemes (Kessler, 2002: 21).[23] Though such facilities incur capital and operational cost, this is invariably less *per capita* than that of retaining inmates in prison custody.

The central issue here is that the effective reintegration of offenders back into full citizenship carries with it not only a public risk of re-offending, but also the private (or individual) risks of rejection, discrimination and marginalisation. Many people fall prey to the temptations of re-offending because they return to the same areas and criminal associates, find regular employment difficult to obtain and have no constructive ways of occupying their time. Others are affected by homelessness, broken relationships and a feeling of hopelessness in the face of all the challenges confronting them. Some, in particular sexual offenders, find themselves subject to significant stigmatisation and restrictions on their employability due to the nature of their offences,[24] and cannot return to their former employment. All of these factors and a number of others, make those released from custody vulnerable to the risks of recidivism (Box, 1971: 240-2).

Ex-offenders frequently become socially and financially marginalised due to their restricted ability to earn and thus find that their financial credit ratings preclude the obtaining of loans, mortgages, bank credit, hire purchase facilities and the like. These factors tend to dictate not only their financial situations, but also where they live, their standards of living and their freedom of movement. Social

---

[20] 'Work-out' or sometimes 'working-out' schemes normally involve day release from prison but return to custody during the night hours.

[21] Temporary release is most frequently granted for a number of consecutive days, with a requirement to return to custody on the expiry of the release period. It can also be operated on a day-by-day basis.

[22] See, for example, J. Doward (2006b), 'Violence Fears Grow As Offenders Go Unchecked', *The Observer*, 29 January [News], p. 7 and D. Foggo and J. Grimston (2006), 'Tagged Criminals Shun Curfews and Run Amok', *The Sunday Times*, 29 January, pp. 1 and 4.

[23] An admirable example of this is the Mecklenburg County Work Release and Restitution Centre adjacent to the County Jail in Charlotte, North Carolina, USA, in which inmate residents pay for their own accommodation and expenses while taking part in reparative and restorative programmes within the local community.

[24] Provisions such as automatic placement on sexual offender registers normally preclude re-employment in professions such as teaching, childcare or other occupations involving routine contact with children or young persons.

attitudes towards ex-offenders can also be such as to add to the feelings of exclusion, discrimination and lesser eligibility. In some respects it becomes unremarkable that ex-offenders seek refuge in the company of those enduring similar social circumstances and restrictions. Though technically they may have 'repaid their debt to society', many ex-offenders find themselves subject to a range of secondary (or subsidiary) sanctions that effectively diminish their subsequent life chances (Hudson, 1987: 100-102; Box, 1987: 46-8; Thornberry and Christenson, 1984: 398-411).

In some countries within which significant levels of unemployment are endemically persistent and many honest citizens find themselves at the margins of the social structure, it becomes difficult to propose or justify measures of positive discrimination in favour of ex-offenders. Indeed, to do so might serve to harden socially negative attitudes towards this group into outright antipathy. This stated, however, when the costs of high rates of recidivism are weighed against those of providing some measure of structural support for ex-offenders, the desirability of the latter becomes much less marginal. There seems also to be an evident relationship between the overuse of imprisonment and high rates of subsequent recidivism. As Rutherford (1986) points out in an assessment of three national studies[25] into the use of imprisonment:

> Indeed, the adverse effects are not limited to loss of liberty during confinement; imprisonment affects prisoners' social life after release, an aftermath from which their families are not exempt. Moreover, incarceration, particularly over a long period of time, weakens the ability of offenders to adapt themselves to society following release and destroys the foundation of free community life experience indispensable to reintegration into society. This in turn strongly enhances the likelihood that they will recidivate. It should also be stressed that indiscriminate and widespread use of imprisonment as a sanction against criminal conduct that is not truly serious not only imposes an un-needed burden on the community, but also dilutes the deterrent impact of imprisonment generally in potential criminals and thus may promote rather than hinder the commission of heinous or serious offences. (Rutherford, 1986: 145)

If, for all the reasons discussed here, the correlation between overuse of imprisonment and recidivism is strongly significant, then the case is made either for lesser use of custody, or for enhanced measures to assist ex-offenders. In ideal circumstances it might be suggested that both are desirable, if not essential.

Moreover, if the reintegration of offenders back into society is to have meaning, then the necessity for reconciliation extends much more widely than has hitherto been appreciated. Political reconciliation involves governments in ensuring that the dysfunctional effects of secondary (or subsidiary) sanctions are mitigated to an extent that is not actually discriminative. It also involves governments in providing reparative facilities and programmes, both in prisons and the community, that enable meaningful reparation to be made. This implies legislative change in

---

[25] These studies related to the use of imprisonment during the early 1980s in England, the Netherlands and Japan. See A. Rutherford (1986), op. cit., pp. 121-51.

addition to the radical restructuring of penal resources and regimes. It also implies the desirability of making lesser use of custodial punishment and restricting its use to situations in which no other sanction is appropriate and necessary.

Social reconciliation requires a change in public attitudes towards offenders and in particular towards those who make reparation for their offences. To some extent this also involves governmental leadership in making plain the fact that reparative sanctions represent no 'soft option' for offenders and that these sanctions are both ideologically and practically preferable to traditional approaches. The increased use of community-based reparative sanctions should, in time, lead to a wider understanding and recognition that true justice is being delivered and that the benefits of this extend to victims, communities and offenders in similar measure.

Individual reconciliation of offenders, victims and communities can only flow from an acceptance that offenders have done something positive and socially useful to put right the harm done by their wrongful actions. This means that victims need to feel vindicated *in addition to* the law being upheld (Eaton and McElrea, 2003b: 15-16; Zehr, 2002b: 28-9; Biggar, 2004: 20). Once it is evident that sanctions can make this a reality in a truly constructive manner, then victims and communities may become more forgiving of offenders and less antagonistic towards them. Prevailing public attitudes towards imprisonment are at best ambivalent and at worst hypercritical simply because prisons are perceived as serving no real social purpose beyond the temporary incapacitation of offenders. High rates of recidivism serve to reinforce this prejudice and fuel the argument for increased rather than decreased use of custodial punishment.

TOWARDS A NEW IMAGE OF CORRECTIONS

I have sought within the scope of this chapter to propose that the processes of reparation, restoration and reintegration of offenders have a sequential effect within the new image of restorative justice. Each of these ideas is essential to the notion of forgiveness and they are, to a very considerable extent, contingent one upon another. Viewed together, these concepts have much to do with what was formerly described as the expiative function of criminal sanctions and incorporate the 'right of every offender to exercise every available opportunity to make reparation for his offence' (Doyle, 1967: 164-5).[26]

It may be considered by some that such an approach is over-precise and that the separation is somewhat arbitrary in effect. My reasoning for it is, however, rather more than a semantic consideration and derives from the imperative to indicate that restorative justice, far from being a new concept, has a clear relationship with former explanations of the purposes of criminal punishment. That

---

[26] See also A. C. Ewing (1929), *The Morality of Punishment*, London: Kegan Paul, Trench and Trubner, p. 30.

it has different purposes is beyond dispute, but it does not seek to discard altogether the notion of retribution within its nobler aims of making amends or 'putting wrongs right'.

The willingness (or otherwise) of offenders to take responsibility for the harm caused and to make reparation for this insofar as it is possible to do so, seems an entirely reasonable starting point for deliberations about sanctions. It is, however, conditional upon viewing the essential nature of offences as violations of persons and relationships rather than necessarily of the state and its laws. Within such a conception of justice, even notions of strict desert might become capable of revision and some extent of bifurcation come to be viewed as both desirable and useful. More importantly, perhaps, it would remove the absolute necessity for punishment predicated by reliance upon retribution and deterrence.

The act of making reparation provides both vindication for the victims of crime in a positive sense and the potential for the offender to 'restore his reputation and status within the legal community' (Doyle, 1967: *ibid.*). Restoration of offenders to full citizenship must, therefore, logically be viewed as a consequence of reparation having been made. The 'legal community' envisaged by Doyle is that constituency of law-abiding persons who, in addition to the victims of crime, are violated by the commission of offences. In the absence of reparation and subsequent restoration, the reintegration of offenders within the community becomes problematic and largely meaningless.

Our contemporary conceptions of justice effectively preclude this sequential process, with a number of dysfunctional outcomes inevitably resulting. The circumstances of victims are largely disregarded (or are at the least given minimal consideration) largely because reparative provisions are not a central aspect of either the implementation of sanctions or of judicial considerations. Victims themselves are denied vindication simply because offenders are largely precluded from making reparation and thus of attracting forgiveness. The capacity to exercise or withhold forgiveness is the prerogative of and ultimately the vindication of victims and is normally (and logically) contingent upon contrition and some measure of reparation having been made. Restoration becomes incomplete without reparation and forgiveness providing the potential for some extent of reconciliation between victims and offenders, allowing the latter to resume their place within the community.

I have suggested formerly[27] that the concept of restorative justice may be a 'bridge too far' for politicians and penal policy makers to accept readily in the contemporary context of criminology. Its prescriptions, as McElrea (2002a and b; 2006) and others have pointed out, require a shift in penological thinking and in the practices of criminal justice. This shift might, after all, not need to be quite as extensive or radical as may at first be imagined, particularly if restorative justice were to be approached in the sequential manner described here. There is no doubt, however, that it proposes a different and more humane form of justice than that

---

[27] D. J. Cornwell (2006), op. cit., pp. 9-10.

presently delivered in the majority of modern democracies. If it were to be successful in reducing the perceived necessity for punishment and replacing this with a concept of sanctions (Blad 2006a), justice might display a more humane and considerate face within the foreseeable future.

There is, it might be insisted, no good reason why restorative justice should continue, as at present, to occupy a place at the margins of criminal jurisprudence, merely because it proposes the need for change that is probably long overdue. It is also no accident that its worldwide acceptance and impetus have emerged from the work of academics and criminal justice practitioners, rather than from politicians and their governmental advisors. This account and the many others to which it makes reference represent an attempt to move restorative justice with its essentially reparative rather than retributive ethic, out of the margins and into the mainstream of criminal justice. How this might take effect in both the custodial and non-custodial sectors of corrections becomes the focus of discussion within the chapters that follow.

The principles that restorative justice sets in place are evidently clear. Andrew Coyle provides an illuminating and cogent summary of these in the following words:

> The debate about law and order in this country [the UK] and the attempt by some commentators to produce simple, quick-fire solutions to eternal problems of human nature underline the need for a new statement about the principles on which criminal justice is based. The principles remain as valid as they ever were. But they have to be articulated in a language which can be understood today, rather than in tired and outworn clichés. This should take us beyond the notion of retribution, suffering and the infliction of pain and on to the concept of repairing the damage which has been done, to restoring the balance between victim and offender, to bringing the offender to the realisation of the harm which has been done and of the need to make amends. It will give victims the satisfaction of knowing that the pain and the hurt which they have suffered is understood and regretted. (Coyle, 2001: 3)

CHAPTER 5

Making Prisons Reparative and Restorative: Designing for Outcomes in Custodial Corrections

The existing literature dealing with reparative and restorative prison regimes could scarcely be described as extensive. Though much has, in former years, been written about rehabilitation in prisons, the rehabilitative ideal has progressively faded from the discourse and operational aspirations of contemporary penal practice almost universally (Fitzgerald and Sim, 1982: 28-9; Roberts and Smith, 2003: 190-1; Cavadino and Dignan, 1997a: 36-7). Restorative justice seeks to reverse this situation, not primarily from the viewpoint of providing a neo-rehabilitative agenda or rationale for imprisonment, but rather because prisons can serve the dual purposes of victim reparation and offender restoration. This may, at first sight, seem somewhat like 'rehabilitation re-branded', but that is far from the intention within this chapter.

A VERY UNCERTAIN STARTING POINT

Some 20 years ago now, as the 'justice model' of criminal punishment was gaining its momentum, I proposed the following analysis of the demise of rehabilitation while then a serving prison governor:

> In just the same way as empirical measurement of the efficacy of deterrence within penal practice is difficult, fraught with operational problems and therefore largely speculative, the concept of rehabilitation is a somewhat crude amalgam of ethical perceptions and perspectives equally entitled to consideration and evaluation within the overall idea of punishment ... Though certain aspects of the terms 'treatment' and 'coercion' are both ethically and morally objectionable, these in themselves do not negate the principle or notion of a restorative rather than a 'curative' mode of corrections.
>
> If the practice of imprisonment is to have a socially useful purpose beyond that merely of isolating the criminally obnoxious element of the population, there has to be an acceptable and explicit ethos within the custodial sanction beyond the external facility that it affords society and to which it gives operational effect. It is insufficient for this internal motivation to remain implicit within the range of assumptions relevant to imprisonment, because if it is so left, then the implementation of the most severe socio-legal penalty becomes an interpretative matter exacerbated by the dysfunctional effects of arbitrariness and inequity. (Cornwell, 1985b: 6).[1]

---

[1] The journal article cited here was written as a response to the (then) emerging concept of 'humane containment' first described in the British government's White Paper: *People in Prison* (Home Office, Cmnd. 4214, 1969) as the primary task of the Prison Service. This White Paper may be seen

Viewed today and within the context of this work, there are aspects of this discussion that provoke a certain sense of *déja vu*. The contemporary linguistics of penology, now largely stripped of a rehabilitative motivation, urgently require an explicit social ethos or sense of vision and it has emerged that restorative justice can, potentially, provide this. The difficulty lies in overcoming the 'exploitable imprecisions' of the rehabilitative era and, at the same time, providing the process of custodial corrections with a prospective purpose.

The title of this chapter suggests that prisons can be made to serve reparative and restorative agendas and that there is a necessary distinction between these two concepts. Indeed, it will be insisted later that the ideas of reparation and restoration are not only inter-dependent, but also that even more importantly, restoration is consequent upon reparation. Coyle has proposed that:

> A truly restorative regime in a prison would, on a daily basis, present prisoners with a series of duties, challenges and learning opportunities. It would invest trust in the prisoners' capacity to take responsibility for performing tasks, for meeting challenges and for using learning opportunities. (Coyle, 2001b: 6)

There is much within this proposition with which to agree and Coyle has more to say about the nature of regimes that enable inmates to make restitution to both victims and the wider society. It does not, however, make the explicit distinction between reparation and restoration that forms the core of the discussion here.

Both Coyle (2001b) and Newell (2002), as experienced former prison governors in Britain, suggest a wider application of restorative practices within prisons, particularly in areas of regimes in which conflict resolution strategies can be brought to bear upon prison management and the conduct of the daily regime programme.[2] The same general approach has been adopted in Belgium during the past decade and with some considerable benefit to prison regimes and the behaviour of inmates (Biermans, 2002: 161-4). While acknowledging the potential for these developments, the primary focus of this chapter is on the more specific application of restorative justice principles within the inmate regime and sentence management sectors of custodial corrections. It is, however, important to indicate that developments in such areas of prison management contribute to an overall set of values and principles upon which more enlightened governance of prisons should properly be based (DiIulio, 1987: 11-13; Lewis, 1977).[3]

---

with hindsight to presage a retreat from the rehabilitative ethic that subsequently occurred in the mid-1970s and onwards.

[2] These areas include disciplinary hearings, anti-bullying strategies, race relations, requests and complaints procedures, and the like. Conflict resolution processes can also be applied within industrial relations dispute negotiation between prison management and accredited trade or professional unions (Coyle, 2001b: 6-7; Newell, 2002: 8).

[3] Here see also the recent publication by Kimmett Edgar and Tim Newell (2006), *Restorative Justice in Prisons: Making it Happen*, Winchester: Waterside Press. Their work expands the prospective use of restorative processes in a considerably wider context of prison regime management than is suggested in this analysis.

THE LEGACY OF THE PENITENTIARY

As an encyclopaedia article on prison architecture compiled in 1826 made clear:

> Prison buildings offer an effectual method of exciting the imagination to a most desirable point of abhorrence. Persons, in general, refer their horror of prisons to an instinctive feeling rather than to any accurate knowledge of the privations or inflictions therein endured ... The exterior of a prison should, therefore, be formed in the heavy and sombre style which most frequently impresses the spectator with gloom and terror. (Cited in Johnston, 1973: 26-7)[4]

In many countries of the world, prisons have traditionally been designed and built on a 'fortress' basis intended primarily to keep inmates within the perimeter and the public outside it (Fitzgerald and Sim, 1982: 160-1; Johnston, *ibid.*). Such designs are typified by the erection of walls or high fences with cladding affixed to them to prevent external observation of the interior, thus sealing the facility as a place of exclusion from the immediate neighbourhood in which it is situated. The secluded nature of most prisons serves as a visible indication to the wider population both of the realities of incarceration and of the exclusive nature of the custodial process. Most prisons thus historically become introspective islands housing communities of unwilling detainees whose removal from society becomes absolute for a greater or lesser period of time (Ignatieff, 1978; Fitzgerald and Sim, 1982: 161-3). Nagel captures this situation precisely in the following words:

> The prison experience too often corrodes those who guard and those who are guarded. This reality is not essentially the product of good or bad prison architecture. It is the inevitable product of a process that holds troubled people together in a closed and limited space, depriving them of their freedom, their families and their humanity.
> (Nagel, 1977: 154-5)

These somewhat obvious and inevitable aspects of prisons stated, there is a disingenuous triteness about the claim that the extent of punishment incurred in imprisonment relates only to the deprivation of liberty (Treverton-Jones, 1989: 25; Fowles, 1989: xv) and that an offender is imprisoned *as* punishment and not *for* punishment (CIO, 1978: 39; Rutherford, 1986: 90).[5] Any person who has served a prison sentence or worked as a correctional official is more than aware that the loss of liberty is but one of the many privations and restrictions inherent in custodial punishment. Imprisonment therefore becomes predominantly a process of passing time in isolation from the wider community and in conditions that are at the least uncongenial, often over-crowded and in most present

---

[4] Quoted in M. Fitzgerald and J. Sim (1982), *British Prisons* (Second Edition), Oxford: Basil Blackwell, p. 161.

[5] Cited in a Report of the Church of England General Synod Board for Social Responsibility (1978), *Prisons and Prisoners in England Today*, London: CIO Publishing, p. 39.

circumstances, considerably worse (King and McDermott, 1989; Rutherford, 1986: 90-118).

Ever since the decline of the rehabilitative ideal and the emergence of 'justice' models of criminal punishment, the declared purposes of sanctions have become confused and uncertain.[6] This uncertainty has markedly affected the operation of prisons in several national jurisdictions because it has reduced the emphasis formerly placed on provision of skills training and educative programmes in preparation for release. Indeed, in many prisons in Britain and elsewhere, escalating inmate populations, often to the point of exceeding normal operating capacities, have placed excessive pressure upon such regime resources as were originally provided. This, in its turn, makes it difficult to provide prison inmates with constructive daily routines of work, or, indeed, the opportunity to improve their prospects of gainful employment upon release.

The difficulties associated with providing appropriate and regular employment for prison inmates frequently result in them spending considerable periods of time in conditions of boredom and relative inactivity. As a result, such prison wages that they can earn are meagre, days are passed in a largely unproductive and seemingly pointless manner and the entire experience of custody becomes tediously negative and devoid of any constructive purpose. In such circumstances it becomes all the more likely that prisoners will adopt bitter, resentful and negative attitudes towards the prison authorities whose task it becomes to contain them in such conditions.

Worse still, perhaps, the wider community tends to receive back on the expiry of prison sentences concerning numbers of predominantly young, disaffected and in many instances, unemployable people, largely unchanged (other, perhaps, than for the worse) by the experience of custody (Nagel, 1977: 154-5; Hoskison, 1998[7]; Ramsbotham, 2003). In many cases also, association with more experienced offenders enhances the criminal sophistication of individuals exposed to prison life (Fleisher, 1989: 143-96; Irwin, 1985; Foucault 1977: 265-6). As a result, the likelihood of further and more extensive offending becomes a serious reality. The statistics associated with recidivism tend to confirm this contention in many countries of the world at present.

This is the unfortunate legacy of penal systems used to deliver the purposes of retribution and deterrence, particularly over the past three decades. It is also the outcome of instrumental punishment that derives from the perceived compulsion to punish with increasing severity because laws are broken with increasing frequency and offenders are evidently not deterred. The result is a spiralling effect, sending more and more offenders to prison, for longer terms in

---

6   See the analysis by Hyman Gross (1979) quoted p. 48 *supra*.
7   John Hoskison's commentary on the experience of living as an inmate within prisons in England is remarkable for its clarity and honesty. A professional man of blameless record before being involved in a manslaughter incident while driving his car, his candid and penetrating book: *Inside: One Man's Experience of Prison* (1998) provides a true insight into the nature of inmate sub-cultures and the attitudes of prison staff towards deviant institutional behaviour.

custody and in crowded conditions that diminish regimes and increase boredom. Such situations are only alleviated by increasing prison capacity (at immense public cost), or by resort to early executive release, or by fundamentally reappraising the entire rationale of criminal punishment (Orr, 2006: 16).

Ironically and particularly in Britain which has endured a chronic penal crisis since the mid-1980s, the preferred option of successive governments has been to increase prison capacity *and* at intervals to pursue the option of executive release by one device or another.[8] The courts have repeatedly ignored the periodic pleas of governments to use custodial sentencing more sparingly, and the average daily prison population of England and Wales has escalated almost continuously over the past 25 years. At a record level of over 80,300 in March 2007, it has risen by more than 90.7 *per cent* since 1980.[9] The prison authorities in England and Wales currently house 147 people *per* 100,000 of the population and broadly similar, if not worse situations are evident in the USA, Russia, South Africa, China, Spain, Canada, Australia, New Zealand and Italy, in which rates of incarceration exceed 100 *per* 100,000 of the population (Mauer, 2003: 15; Millie *et al.*, 2003; Dunning, 2006).[10]

More to the point, however, is the fact that within most contemporary jurisdictions, the use of imprisonment represents a negative sanction under existing circumstances. This implies that it requires no necessary response from offenders other than to undergo the imposition of the sentence and provides no specific incentive to those who might otherwise respond in an appropriate manner in relation to the harm caused by their offence(s). Given this situation, it is difficult to perceive the entire process of criminal punishment as other than essentially retributive, though there are some who would still contend that deterrence remains a significant consideration within sentencing philosophy. When rates of recidivism are taken into account, however and the difficulties of quantifying deterrence are acknowledged, the evidence for such a claim is at the least speculative.

---

[8] The release dates of prisoners in custody can be advanced either by altering the proportion of the total sentence that must be served in prison before discharge to community supervision can be considered, or by increasing the amount of sentence remission that can be earned by remaining free of disciplinary offences (or both).

[9] In April 1980 the average daily prison population in England and Wales was 42,109 with certified normal accommodation for 38,930 inmates in 116 prison establishments. By October 2006 the prison population exceeded 79,000 for the first time, very close to the operational capacity of the 140 prisons identified as 80,300. The Certified Normal Accommodation (CNA) figure in June 2006 was 70,949 with overall occupancy at 111.6 per cent. Source: London: International Centre for Prison Studies, King's College.

[10] Worldwide international statistics for incarceration rates can be found at http://www.sentencingproject.org/pdfs/pub9036.pdf and similar web-sites providing internet information on prison statistics. A detailed international study presented in June 2003 to the US Commission on Human Rights is to be found in M. Mauer (2003), *Comparative International Rates of Incarceration: An Evaluation of Causes and Trends*, at the same web-site. More recent comparative global statistics can be found in map format with data selection at www,kcl.ac.uk/depsta/rel/icps/worldbrief/world_brief.html (A. Dunning (ed) (2006)).

In considerations relating to the present and future uses of imprisonment within developed societies, it becomes inevitable that the main questions that have to be answered are those concerning how much longer more and more people must continue to be incarcerated; whether this is strictly necessary and affordable; and whether there are not more effective and useful ways of using prisons. Within this chapter, the discussion will focus on the extent to which implementation of restorative justice principles and practices might enable these questions to be answered in a more constructive manner than is possible at the present time.

CHANGING THE ETHOS AND SOCIAL PURPOSE OF PRISONS

Given the range of dysfunctional characteristics of prisons within many contemporary jurisdictions that have been noted briefly in the foregoing paragraphs, it would appear that little short of a fundamental change of approach and custodial practice will improve matters dramatically. What has to change essentially is what might be termed the 'culture of containment' that tends to pervade custodial facilities deprived of a prospective purpose, whether this endeavour is described as 'rehabilitative', 'restorative', 'reparative', or even 'reformative'. For as long as prisons remain primarily agencies of retribution, the likelihood of them assuming other than a retrospective (or backward-looking) operational culture is minimal.

This is not, however, a change of direction that prisons alone can undertake. In order for it to come about, the emphasis within criminal justice generally has to be altered away from preoccupation with crime primarily as a violation of the law and the state and towards an understanding of crime as a violation of persons and communities (Zehr, 2002a). Viewed in the latter manner, the central purpose of custodial corrections becomes that of making amends for the harm done by crime and of those imprisoned not merely being made to 'serve time' in satisfaction of some form of tariff that equates guilt and culpability solely with periodic measures.

'Doing time' as the almost universal description within the *argot* of prisons implies, conceptualises custodial sentences as the *quid pro quo* for offences. In present circumstances and particularly in Britain, it amounts to a negative sanction because it makes no further and necessary demands on offenders other than to survive the period spent in detention. In this sense it also makes the punishment preponderantly retributive, simply by depriving it of any other identifiable purpose. What is perhaps even worse, however, is the fact that during at least the past two decades, the underlying political agenda driving the custodial punishment of offenders has been primarily that of social incapacitation and exclusion. That relatively scant pretence has been made in relation to facilitated change or the inculcation of victim awareness is little short of reprehensible, driven as it is by the perceived need of successive governments to be seen to be 'tough on crime'[11] (see, for example, Cavadino and Dignan, 1997a: 12; Roberts and Smith, 2003: 206-7).

If, therefore, one were to describe the social purpose achieved by the existing use of imprisonment as a sanction, it would be difficult not to conclude that the process is primarily exclusive and intended to incapacitate rather than change offenders. This places both prisons and prisoners at a disadvantage insofar as the former lack a guiding social ethos and the latter find re-integration into the community significantly more problematic. The community also suffers from this form of isolationism, because it eventually receives back into its midst numbers of unimproved ex-offenders prone to return to crime because their employability has been diminished rather than enhanced. To make matters even more unsatisfactory, it becomes likely that a further cohort of victims of crime will arise from the recidivist activities of those released from prison.

It is not particularly surprising that in the current penological climate recidivism rates should be so high. A significant proportion of offenders sentenced to imprisonment are unemployed at the time of conviction, many have additional problems of homelessness, drug- or other substance abuse, basic literacy and social skills deficits. Since these dysfunctional attributes remain largely un-addressed during the process of imprisonment and particularly during shorter (two years or less) sentences, the stage is set for further offending.[12]

The question that arises from all of this is that of how adoption of restorative justice principles and practices within prisons might change this situation effectively and particularly in relation to shorter sentences in custody. In this regard it is necessary to sound a note of extreme caution, since attempts to remedy the deep-seated problems noted above might easily lead to *increased* severity of sentencing on the basis of the length of time that might be deemed necessary to address them effectively.[13] Alternatively, it might lead to a return towards a framework of semi-determinate sentencing within which the timing of

---

[11] In this specific respect there has proved to be very little difference in the approaches towards criminal justice adopted by successive governments of either a 'conservative' or 'new labour' political orientation in Britain during the 1990s and the early years of this millennium (Tonry, 2003, op. cit., p. 2).

[12] Estimates differ in relation to recidivism following release from prison sentences, depending on the manner in which data is collated and interpreted. The majority of recent studies indicate reconviction rates of approximately 60 per cent within two years of release in England and Wales (Home Office (2001), *Making Punishments Work: Report of a Review of the Sentencing Framework for England and Wales*, London: Home Office Communications Directorate, p. 126; Home Office (2002), *Justice For All*, CM 5563, London: HMSO, p. 92; and J. Roberts and M. E. Smith, 'Custody Plus, Custody Minus' in M. Tonry (ed) (2003) op. cit., pp. 182-3).

[13] Under present circumstances in England and Wales, a sentence of two years imprisonment results in the offender serving 12 months in custody (less any time spent in custody prior to conviction). The remainder of the sentence is served under supervision within the community.

release would be decided by some process of assessment of the progress made by individual inmates towards addressing the deficits. Since the purpose within this work is to arrive at a situation in which *decreasing* resort is made to custodial sentencing, either of these outcomes would be entirely counter-productive and unsatisfactory.

THE CONCEPT OF REPARATIVE PRISONS

Perhaps the most useful way of addressing the notion of giving prisons a reparative ethos lies in describing how such facilities would differ from those designed and used essentially for containment, or what Fleisher (1989) has described as 'warehousing prisons'.[14] Before doing so, however, it is necessary to indicate a number of basic assumptions that would have to be accepted before restorative practices could be incorporated into the operation of prisons as most presently function.

The first of these assumptions concerns the extent to which sentences involving a custodial element should be viewed in their entirety: that is to say, the relative lengths of the periods spent initially in prison and subsequently under supervision in the community. The case will be made here for the total sentence period to be *strictly* confined to that necessary to mark the seriousness of the offence and the time spent in custody to be similarly limited to the time necessary to satisfy a minimum requirement for retribution. Such an approach serves to reinforce the contention that restorative justice is not the antithesis of retribution, but rather limits notions of retribution to a minimum acceptable level in each individual instance.[15] It does, however, allow the total sentence period to reflect the gravity of the offence, with any additional element over and above the requirement of retribution to be served on a non-custodial basis.

The second assumption is that the financial benefits deriving from reduced use of custody would be re-deployed to both the expansion and the logistical support of supervised community-based programmes and the provision of work-related and better remunerated skills centres and workshops within prisons. Further, that these amenities would operate on a vocational training basis and produce marketable products, the sale value of which would accrue to the development budget of the prisons concerned to enable future growth and also provide restitution for victims of crime.[16]

The third and final assumption concerns the operation of prisons themselves and in particular the regime requirements of those parts of each prison that would

---

[14] See M. S. Fleisher (1989), *Warehousing Violence*, London and Newbury Park, California: Sage Publications.

[15] Here see my original prescription set out in D.J. Cornwell (2006) op. cit. pp. 101-3.

[16] Here it will be noted that financial support for victims of crime would be derived from a fixed proportion of the weekly wage earned by participating inmates, and be paid directly into an auditable charity administered independently of the Prison (or Correctional) Service.

be established and operated on restorative and reparative principles. In particular, offenders opting to participate in reparative custody and adhere to an agreed reparative sentence compact should have an active incentive to do so, but with strict safeguards to ensure compliance. As will become clear later, this implies and proposes regimes and disciplinary arrangements based upon the 'direct supervision' model of correctional practice that is not, at present, followed substantively in any of the existing penal establishments of the United Kingdom, or, indeed, in many other countries.[17]

In the foregoing paragraph, reference was made to those parts of a prison that might be operated within a reparative regime model and the reason for this requires brief elaboration. On the basis of pragmatism alone, it must be recognised that while some offenders might perceive the potential advantages of opting for reparative regimes, others will not do so and should not be permitted to disrupt the operation of such regimes. As will again be made clear later in this chapter, it would become necessary to design (or, in the case of existing facilities, adapt) the estate within each establishment to accommodate separate regimes for both types of inmate. Ultimately, it might be envisaged that entire prisons could be operated on a reparative correctional model, but until the concept gained universal acceptance, an interim arrangement would clearly be necessary. In the concluding part of this chapter, attention is focussed on what are termed 'issues of bifurcation' which are implicit in operating reparative regimes alongside the more traditional models of custodial practice.

In the light of the assumptions indicated above, it will be evident that reparative regimes propose a range of operational features that make the administration of correctional facilities very different from the 'traditional' model almost universally in use in developed contemporary Western-style democracies.

The first and the most fundamental of these features is that in accordance with the principles of restorative justice, reparative regimes absolutely require inmates to take personal responsibility for their own conduct, analyse (with the necessary counselling assistance) and confront their offending behaviour and undertake reparative work (which may include vocational training) of a productive nature.

The second major feature of reparative regimes is the element of self-imposed personal discipline required of participating inmates, and the system of incentives and sanctions that underpins adherence to the regime concept. This particular aspect of reparative regimes is non-negotiable and uncompromising in its expectations of personal and inter-personal conduct, particularly because, as will be seen later, it offers considerable scope for reduction in supervisory staffing and the re-deployment of resources.

---

[17] Direct supervision regime models have proved extremely effective in certain parts of the USA and elsewhere, and are incorporated in the design and operation of GSL's 3,000-bed maximum security facility at Mangaung Correctional Centre near Bloemfontein in the Free State Province of the Republic of South Africa. The author was the consultant operations adviser during the building, commissioning and initial operation of this facility within which the behavioural control of inmates is implemented entirely on direct supervision methodology.

The third important aspect is that, when fully implemented, reparative regimes form a natural and substantive 'bridge' between custodial and community-based sanctions. In no sense should such regimes be perceived in a 'custody-plus' or 'custody-minus' manner (see Roberts and Smith, 2003 *supra*: p. 119, fn.12), but rather as a more substantial means of restricting the use of custody as an imperative in its own right. Indeed, reparative prisons of the future would necessarily incorporate within the design template provision for 'work-out' or 'working-out' hostel accommodation to house inmates in the period immediately preceding release from custody to community supervision.

In summary of the foregoing considerations, the entire concept of reparative prisons is grounded in restorative justice principles that involve offenders in accepting responsibility for their offences and behaviour, acknowledging the harm done to victims and the community and in making a substantial effort to 'put things right'. This concept replaces the present model of 'negative' sanctions with an altogether different one that is inherently 'positive' in nature. Moreover, as will be seen subsequently, the costs of such a transformation are both realistic and affordable.

DESIGNING PRISON FACILITIES FOR REPARATIVE OUTCOMES

Transforming prison estates to deliver reparative regimes is, quite evidently, as much a matter of political choice as is the continuation of existing penal policies and the perpetuation of overcrowded conditions. As will become clear later in this chapter, the potential advantages of opting for change are considerable for individual offenders, victims, communities and society as a whole. The attendant disadvantages are not as extensive as might be imagined, but much depends upon changing both public and political attitudes towards the nature and effectiveness of criminal sanctions. Lesser, but better use of custodial corrections can only be achieved by a deliberate commitment to restrict the use of imprisonment to instances in which it is strictly unavoidable and by greater use of community sanctions that have a clear social and penal purpose.

Realistically, it is altogether unlikely that extensive building programmes designed to provide new facilities specifically to promote reparative regimes would accompany a move towards reparative prisons. At a more pragmatic level, however, existing prisons might be transformed relatively easily to accommodate 'side by side' regimes of a reparative and a traditional nature and without undue cost. Since the geography of existing prisons is of an individualistic nature, few, if any, being identical in design and layout, this discussion is focussed upon general principles of operation rather than detailed prescriptions.

Over 15 years ago now and in the aftermath of a notorious riot at Strangeways Prison, Manchester, England, the concept of community prisons was proposed as a means of enabling offenders to serve sentences closer to their communities of origin and maintain their family ties more easily[18] (Woolf and Tumim, 1991; see also Cavadino and Dignan, 1997a: 126-7). Though the concept received widely based support, it was overcome by a speedy return to more punitive sentencing and a steadily escalating prison population for which a deliberate expansion of the prisons estate was set in place. To make matters worse, the increase in numbers was to occur in tandem with a reduction in opportunities for prisoners approaching the end of custodial sentences to take home leave.[19]

Though at the time there was no suggestion that the concept of community prisons should be based on a restorative or reparative ethos, the idea did imply acceptance of the need for prisoners to serve their sentences while at the same time retaining close links with the communities in which they lived (and, in the main, offended). The initiative proposed that the existing prison estate should be grouped in 'clusters' of establishments able to accommodate inmates of either sex, age, nature of offence(s) and length of sentence in appropriate levels of security. Its achievement absolutely relied upon an overall *reduction* in the prison population in order to use available places more flexibly. It is a matter of penal history that the initiative was frustrated by the 'populist punitivism' of the Conservative government of the day and the bullish statements of the incumbent Home Secretary Michael Howard.[20]

The concept of providing both reparative and traditional regimes implies that living unit accommodation within prisons has to be allocated to either use, but the two should, if possible, be physically separated, each in a zone or compound of its own. Units dedicated to the reparative regime should also, ideally, have minimal visual contact with and be out of voice range of those housing other inmates. This may not always be possible to achieve, but it is desirable in order to prevent disruption or intimidation of the reparative regime by those prisoners who opt not to participate within it.

There is no reason why the majority of the support services within the prison (kitchen, healthcare, visitation, admissions, gymnasia, faith centre, administration, etc.) cannot support both regimes, though it may be desirable, again in the interests of separation, to programme availability of these services to either regime at different times. The reparative regime should, however, have its own allocated

---

[18] The concept of 'community' prisons advanced by Woolf and Tumim initially received some enthusiastic support from a wide range of penal commentators, government officials, and the Penal Affairs Consortium. See H. Woolf (LJ), and S. Tumim (J) (1991), *Prison Disturbances April 1990*, Cm 1456, London: HMSO. Unfortunately, the mid-1990s return to increasing use of custodial sentences made the concept largely inoperable, particularly due to the rising penal population and Home Secretary Michael Howard's insistence on significantly reducing the availability of home leave for prisoners approaching the end of their sentences.

[19] In 1993-4 and subsequently, home leave availability was reduced by some 40 per cent—see the account of Cavadino and Dignan, (1997a. *op. cit.*) pp. 127-8.

[20] As was evidenced in his statement to the Conservative Party conference in October 1993 that 'prison works', and that he would not flinch from implementing measures that would increase the size of the prison population.

workshops and these should have integral classroom areas available for vocational instruction. In addition, it would be desirable for each regime to have its own library, shop and medical treatment facilities provided on a compound basis.

In the event that new generation prisons were to be built on the basis of accommodating both forms of regime, there are many variations on the 'campus style' design template that would allow complete physical regime separation, each regime having its own access to centralised support services. Alternatively, consideration might be given to the construction of two quite separate facilities within the same perimeter, though with a common administration building, kitchen and healthcare complex, but separate admissions, visitation, gymnasium and faith centre provision. [21]

Earlier, mention was made of the desirability of reparative prisons being designed to provide 'hostel type' accommodation for those inmates permitted to work outside the facility within the wider community. Such provision would be difficult to make available in the context of many existing prisons without recourse to additional building and capital cost. For security reasons, however, it is highly desirable that inmates with daily access to the wider community are housed separately from those confined within the prison perimeter. This largely prevents the former from being intimidated by the latter to act illicitly on their behalf while outside the prison, or from attempting to smuggle unauthorised articles into the prison for their use. [22]

In the event that future prisons were to be built to provide reparative regimes alone, or even existing prisons role-changed to meet this purpose, it is possible to envisage a number of physical design economies that might accrue due to the nature and operation of such regimes. These become available because inmates in reparative regimes are subject to stringent requirements in terms of personal conduct, rule compliance and communal behaviour and risk summary removal from the regime in the event that infractions are committed. For these reasons, perimeter security and defence systems need not be as sophisticated and costly as traditional prisons require, cellular accommodation need not be as robustly designed and provided, locking and zoning protocols can be simplified and predominantly of a manual rather than electronic nature and CCTV coverage can be reduced to a realistic minimum. Such facilities would also require less intricate central control room equipment due to the reduced levels of perimeter security, camera deployment, alarm systems and the like.

On the other hand, however, prisons operating restorative regimes require provision of workshop and other production facilities that ensure full and

---

[21] Excellent examples of such design are provided in a number of source texts with detailed illustrations. One such is P. Krasnow (1998), *Correctional Facility Design and Detailing*, New York: McGraw-Hill.

[22] Although as will become evident later in this discussion, serious infractions of prison regulations would invariably result in the removal of inmates from reparative regimes, acknowledged best practice indicates strongly that it is only prudent to remove the temptation and opportunity for such offences to be committed under duress.

purposeful employment is available to all inmates on a daily basis. This should operate on the basis of a 'mixed economy', including as wide a range of productive vocational activities as possible and provide a full working day of eight hours in duration. The forms of training and employment offered should be of the type for which there is a directly related need and opportunity within the wider community and which actively promote the prospects or potential for eventual regular employment of the participating inmates.

At the present time in the United Kingdom and some European countries, prisons do not have a good track record for providing purposeful and productive work. Much of that which is available tends to be of a menial and largely unskilled nature and does not generate a potential for future employability. Reparative regimes should and indeed must be cost-effective to the extent of generating income and may, therefore, incur investment and 'start-up' costs in order to make them viable. This stated, however, there is a range of vocational skills for which there is a constant demand within local communities and which can be operated on an individual or 'small firm' basis.[23]

These reservations notwithstanding, it is also the case that some prisons have attracted high quality industrial work for which there is a consistent demand and market. Due to controllable labour costs, prison-based industries can compete very favourably in the markets for furniture production, upholstery, traffic sign making, printing and a range of other products. In addition, there are products for which government agencies require regular and consistent supply sources, but for which bids for production contracts are not presently made available to prison industries. There might, therefore, be a reasonable case for an element of positive discrimination in favour of these industries if the concept of reparative prison regimes were to be actively pursued.

Reparation forms one of the central pillars upon which the entire concept of restorative justice is constructed. It is part of the process of *putting things right* and of acknowledging the harm caused to victims of crime. There are, of course, limits to the extent to which offenders can make reparation to the victims of crime, but the most obvious way of doing so comes in the form of doing practical work that generates the revenue which can be used to compensate victims to some effective extent.

OPERATING REGIMES FOR REPARATIVE OUTCOMES

It will have become apparent in the foregoing part of this chapter that the emphasis has so far been placed on ways in which prisons can be changed to serve a predominantly reparative purpose. It is, however, the case that reparation forms only a part (albeit a significant part) of the wider concept of restorative justice.

---

[23] These include: horticultural work; electrical and plumbing installation; painting and decorating; bricklaying; carpentry; landscape gardening; and a range of IT-based skills, all of which attract accredited vocational qualifications.

Moreover, the actions involved in making reparation are part of the process of acknowledging responsibility for the harm caused by offences, demonstrating remorse for this harm and doing something practical to make amends for it.

Prisons designed to provide opportunities for reparation also have to have a restorative purpose, which involves many aspects of what used to be described as a 'rehabilitative' ethos. The difficulty that this presents is one of being realistic and pragmatic about the extent to which it is possible to 'rehabilitate' offenders while holding them in custody (Packer, 1973: 183-9; van den Haag, 1975: 190-1; Allen, 1981: 1-12; Hayley, 1984: 393-408; Hudson, 1987: 34-5). Most of the concepts of rehabilitation that have occupied the minds of penologists over past decades have implied, at the least, some sort of process that enhances the prospect of future law-abiding behaviour, even though this can in no sense be guaranteed. Put another way, perhaps, there may be considerable truth in the maxim that 'the proof of the pudding lies in the eating'.

John DiIulio, one of the most influential writers on the operation of prisons in the post-rehabilitative era of the late 1980s in the USA, urged a re-thinking of the purposes of rehabilitation in the following terms:

> There is no good *a priori* reason and to my knowledge no body of empirical evidence, to discredit the possibility that prison inmates, even ones who have a long history of serious offences, may become more law-abiding if they are made to live, work, go to school and recreate in productive, law-abiding ways. Enforced adherence to the norms of a civilised, non-criminal way of life, coupled with a rich menu of treatment and work opportunities, would seem bound to have some good effect on inmates' institutional and post-release behaviour ... Prisons cannot make saints out of demons, or do for the average inmate what families, schools, churches and other institutions may have failed to do. But they may be able to modify offenders' lifestyles while in custody and this experience may help keep some who would otherwise return to crime upon release from doing so. Enlightened self-interest and plain moral duty dictate that any chance that prison may afford to make serious offenders more civil and law-abiding ought not to be discarded without further investigation and debate.
>
> (DiIulio, 1987: 257)[24]

Though DiIulio used the term 'treatment' in his account, this refers more to programmes of counselling and corrective therapy than the modes of treatment formerly envisaged within the rehabilitative model of the 1960s and 1970s.[25] In a more modern sense, corrective therapies comprise programmes to analyse and

---

[24] J. J. DiIulio Jnr. (1987), *Governing Prisons: A Comparative Study of Correctional Management*, New York: Free Press.

[25] Treatment as formerly proposed was largely conceived on a medical model of intervention and behaviour modification through the use of drugs, aversion techniques, and even electro-therapy. It became discredited because it was both morally questionable and uncertain in outcome terms. Belief in the efficacy of treatment programmes also led to sentencing indeterminacy or semi-determinacy, both of which extended sentences and placed excessive power over release in the hands of criminal justice professionals.

address forms of offending behaviour in addition to protocols to reduce drug-dependence, alcoholism and other addictions.

There is a direct link between the ideas set out by DiIulio and the operation of prisons on reparative and restorative principles. This link is most visibly evident in the effectiveness of prisons that employ the philosophy and practice of Direct Supervision in the daily control and governance of the inmate population. Since direct supervision and its mode of operation are not widely known about or practised in many European countries (and particularly the United Kingdom), it may be helpful to sketch its under-pinning philosophy and methods of implementation, since both have a direct relevance for restorative and reparative prison regimes.

Direct supervision is a prescription for regime management that has profound implications for the design, staffing and operational control of inmate populations within prisons. First and foremost, it requires inmates to take responsibility for their own behaviour, conform with basic rules and requirements, respect the rights of others at all times and take a full part in the day-to-day life of the establishment. These are absolute and basic requirements, set out in codes of behaviour and 'house rules' and form a 'compact' between the inmate and the prison that places obligations on both parties.

Direct supervision regimes require inmates to conduct themselves in the same civil manner as would be expected of them within their families and communities and display appropriate behaviours both personally and inter-personally with other inmates and correctional staff. These behaviours and daily regime requirements are explained and demonstrated during the period of induction that immediately follows arrival into the prison and thereafter become an expectation of each individual. In return for this compliance, the prison undertakes to provide a good quality of living facilities, food, medical care, access to purposeful work, educational and recreational opportunities and, in addition, support and guidance in addressing the causes of their imprisonment.

Once the inmate has agreed to this 'compact', it is demonstrably assumed that he or she will abide by its requirements unless or until there is any evidence of non-compliance. The inmate then enters the wider regime of the prison following induction and having agreed a personal programme of work and activities (including the requirement to engage with correctional officials in examination of offending behaviour).[26] Within the main prison regime, penalties for non-compliance are both immediate and invariable. The regime operates strictly on a 'three strikes and you're out' basis: on the first occasion of non-compliance the inmate is advised again of the requirement; on the second, a written warning for

---

[26] The period of induction into the prison is normally of at least seven days in duration, but can be extended in the event that the inmate demonstrates unwillingness or inability to adopt patterns of reasonable behaviour or compliance with house rules. If, after two weeks, no further progress has been made, the inmate is moved to an Intermediate Treatment Unit with a regime that is subject to more extensive control and discipline than the main prison regime, and permits of a much reduced range of privileges.

amended behaviour is issued; and on any subsequent occasion the inmate is removed to the Intermediate Treatment regime for a specified period (see fn.27 below).

The Intermediate Treatment Unit is not a punishment regime, but rather one in which individual supervision is more extensive and access to privileges is reduced automatically. Practical experience in maximum-security conditions in South Africa indicates very strongly that once direct supervision regimes are established and operating well, very few inmates wish to regress to intermediate treatment, or, if they do, few wish to remain there for longer than the imposed period.[27] It is, however, necessary to operate a segregation unit or punishment regime alongside that of intermediate treatment, solely in order to deal with serious infractions of prison disciplinary rules.

The main advantages of direct supervision regimes are that these become considerably less staff intensive than their 'traditional' counterparts and operate in a more relaxed manner on a daily basis.[28] Compliance with 'house rules' is, in reality, not particularly onerous and most inmates respond relatively willingly—if only on the basis of 'enlightened self-interest'. It is also arguably the case that the reduced presence of correctional staff makes the atmosphere within living units less oppressive and encourages compliance with basic regime requirements. More importantly, it makes possible the employment of staff in a wider capacity than that of routine 'turn-key' duties, and this contributes to job satisfaction and enhanced professional development.

Basic 'house rules' require inmates to rise each morning when unlocked, wash and make their beds and clean their cells before breakfast. Meals are taken communally at which reasonable behaviour and consideration for others is mandatory. Inmates are then responsible for presenting themselves on time and suitably dressed to attend for work or other activities and for their conduct wherever they are during the day. The average day envisages up to 13 hours spent unlocked, of which at least eight are work or programme related and others permit exercise and recreation. Smoking is only permitted *outside* living units during exercise or recreational periods and never within any other part of the prison. There is no allocation of inmates to units (or administrative segregation) on the basis of the nature of their offending, thus enabling sexual offenders in particular to have unlimited access to the full prison regime.

---

[27] The entire purpose of the Intermediate Treatment Unit is to reinforce the importance of the basic rules of the regime, and, where necessary, to provide a period of re-assessment for inmates who persistently disrupt the main regime by committing petty breaches of routines, failing to meet behavioural expectations or other forms of anti-social behaviour. The unit affords its inmates reduced privileges and closer personal supervision than the main prison regime.

[28] Employment of direct supervision practice within living units enables a single staff member to supervise effectively the behaviour of up to 75 inmates in full association within a house-block 'spur'. The direct supervision officer (DSO) is immediately supported by the unit supervisor on duty within the unit on a continuous basis during the hours in which prisoners are unlocked.

Family ties and relationships with close friends are important and to encourage the maintenance of these bonds, visitation capacity should be sufficient to permit a weekly visit for each inmate and include the availability of evening visiting. There is considerable merit in making additional visits available on the basis of positive performance within the mainstream regime, particularly at weekends and on public holidays. On the same reasoning, visitation allowances should be to some extent reduced in the Intermediate Treatment regime as an incentive towards mainstream compliance. The visitation facility should, however, be comprehensively CCTV-monitored to detect the importation of contraband items and searching procedures for visitors must be sufficiently robust to intercept attempts to bring classified drugs or other prohibited items into the prison.[29]

From the foregoing and somewhat summary account of the way in which reparative regimes might be operated, it will be apparent that these regimes have three primary purposes and that these operate in a sequential order. In the first place, behavioural expectations are clearly expressed and reinforced with an easily understood system of incentives and sanctions. Standards of personal and inter-personal conduct are entirely non-negotiable and the response to non-compliance is immediate and invariable. Secondly, clear emphasis is placed on the requirement for offenders to address their offending behaviour and acknowledge the harm caused to victims. This process starts in the induction unit and is continued consistently through casework and counselling on an individual basis within the main regime. The third strand of the sentence management process requires every participating inmate to undertake purposeful work on a daily basis, a proportion of the pay for which is allocated to a central fund for victims of crime.

One of the most important aspects of reparative regimes lies in the potential for 'testing' the reliability and responsibility of prisoners approaching the end of their sentences through participation in work projects outside the facility which would be of direct benefit to the local community. It might also be envisaged that the help of members of the community might be enlisted to identify such projects and assist prison management in assessing the potential risks and benefits that would inhere in these being undertaken by inmates under the joint supervision of prison staff and local residents or employers. While it has to be admitted that there are always risks that attend such initiatives, within the type of regime proposed here, there are also counter-balancing risks to be faced by prisoners in the event of failure. The most significant of these risks is undoubtedly that of being summarily removed from the reparative regime and possibly re-located to the 'traditional' regime of a more distant facility.

---

[29] Searching technology is now available to indicate with relative certainty the fact that a person has recently been in immediate contact with controlled drugs, whether these are carried externally or internally. In the event of positive indications, it becomes a matter of operational choice whether the visitor should be refused entry, or, alternatively, whether the visit should be permitted to take place in 'closed conditions'. The latter requires that there is no physical contact between an inmate and his or her visitors by providing a visit booth in which the two parties are separated by a glass partition that prevents any form of intimate contact.

Viewed in its entirety, the regime within a prison operated on restorative and reparative principles is purposeful, active and demanding of the individual inmate. From the induction stage onwards it requires and promotes self-examination, self-discipline, victim awareness and, in addition, a willingness to make a positive attempt through purposeful work to provide reparation for the victims of crime. Such regimes are no 'soft option' for offenders, requiring them to take responsibility for their past wrongdoing, analyse their behaviour and empower themselves to adopt law-abiding lives in the future. DiIulio sums up his own research into prison governance in the following terms:

> From everything I was able to learn in the course of this research, it seems that the quality of prison life depends far more on management practices than on any other single variable. Indeed, the evidence leads me to conclude that, given certain administrative conditions, prisons can be improved, even in the face of crowded cells, tight budgets, faulty architecture and inmate populations polarized along racial and ethnic lines. Prison officials can form a government behind the walls that produces safe, civilised conditions. These officials are neither pawns of inmate society nor captives of broader socio-political developments. Prisons are no more likely to fail than are schools, armies, state hospitals, regulatory agencies, or other important public organizations. If most prisons have failed, it is because they have been ill-managed, under-managed, or not managed at all.
>
> By the same token, it may be that where prison managers effect a strong administrative regime that enforces adherence to the norms and values of a civilised, non-criminal, 'straight' way of life—dressing neatly, washing regularly, being punctual, working hard, speaking respectfully to peers and authorities, delaying gratifications for the sake of future rewards—serious disorders are less frequent, meaningful programmes more frequent and recidivism rates less startling.
>
> (DiIulio, 1987: 6-7)

Reparative and restorative regimes, based on the same precepts, take DiIulio's analysis an important step further down the road towards constructive justice. The broader vision of offenders, correctional officials, communities and penal administrators combining to deliver 'better justice' is realisable if the political landscape can be changed away from traditional dogma and entrenched beliefs towards a more enlightened concept of corrections that fulfils a better social purpose than at present.

MAKING PRISONS COMMUNITY-FRIENDLY: ENCOURAGING COMMUNITY INVOLVEMENT

Prisons operated within restorative and reparative principles must necessarily be integrated within the communities that surround them and cannot operate effectively in isolation from the immediate social environment.(CIO, 1978: 50-55; Rutherford, 1986: 91). For this to happen realistically, traditional public attitudes towards prisons have to be changed and the 'isolationist' tendencies within the conduct of correctional services have also to be modified.

Public (and notably also political) attitudes towards prisons have historically been shaped by the treatment of penal affairs by the media in many countries and prison inmates become a 'soft target' for 'demonisation', particularly when serious crimes become sensational national headlines. The difficulty that has to be faced is that sensationalism sells newspapers and the more salacious or notorious the reportage can be made, the greater the volume of sales becomes. Prisons seldom attract positive or supportive media coverage, partly because of the traditional secretiveness that shrouds what happens within them from public view and also because there exists in the public psyche an 'out of sight: out of mind' perception of prisons that consigns prisoners to social obscurity.

If a restorative justice agenda is to be pursued by correctional agencies, there is a need for greater 'permeability' in both directions: the public has to perceive prisons as serving a useful social purpose beyond that of incarceration; and prisons have to encourage a greater extent of public participation within their regimes. Both, it might be contended by many observers, are rather more easily said than done. Restorative practices can, however, be seen to work for the general welfare of society, though in relation to the penal system it is essential that these are not perceived as a 'soft option' for offenders. Indeed, in the contemporary situation of criminal justice almost worldwide, it is the *demonstrable* credibility of restorative justice that is probably the greatest obstacle to its more universal adoption.

Packer's assertion quoted in *Chapter 1* (at p. 46 *supra*) that the law has to take some chances has a particular relevance for this situation. It is simply impossible to *prove* the efficacy of a new philosophy of justice without allowing it to be tested in all its potential applications in a realistic environment. If the case for using restorative and reparative practices in prisons is to be made substantively, then trials have to be conducted in real prisons with real prisoners and real staff. In default of willingness to make a genuine attempt to evaluate the potential of restorative prescriptions, the entire concept becomes marooned at the margins of the justice system and cannot hope to enter the mainstream.

One way of approaching the task of making prisons more community-friendly and at the same time promoting restorative and reparative practices is to undertake a risk: benefit analysis of the potential advantages and difficulties that such a course of action might entail. Such an analysis would necessarily include the potential gains to be made by both communities and the criminal justice system, and would balance these carefully against any dysfunctional outcomes that might be anticipated to arise. This assessment is attempted in summary form as follows:

Potential benefits within communities

- Prisons seen to be actively concerned with reduction of crime;
- prison regimes demonstrably addressing needs of victims of crime;
- prisoners required to address their offending behaviour and take responsibility;
- prisoners undertake work of direct benefit to local communities;

- community members involved in identifying projects of community value;
- prisoners remain geographically closer to families and friends;
- prisoners' reliability and responsibility 'tested' before release; and
- reparative regimes eventually seen as no 'soft option'.

Potential benefits for criminal justice systems
- Concept of 'negative sanctions' eventually dismantled;
- criminal justice process perceived to have a more positive purpose;
- restorative practices can result in crime reduction;
- lower rates of recidivism due to enhanced prisoner employability;
- restorative prisons reduce construction and capital costs;
- reparative regimes have lower staffing requirements;
- local communities benefit directly from reparative prisons;[30]
- needs of victims of crime more evidently addressed;
- logical 'bridge' between custodial and non-custodial sanctions; and
- potential to revise sentencing practices and reduce use of custody.

Potential risks for local communities
- Inevitable risk involved in external work projects undertaken by prisoners;
- earlier return of ex-offenders into communities; and
- some victims may feel insufficiently vindicated.

Potential risks for criminal justice systems
- Need to take political risk to introduce restorative prisons or regimes;
- restorative justice changes the traditional view of offences, law and state;
- requirement to review sentencing practices;
- reparative regimes require production resources;
- public may be reluctant to place confidence in restorative justice;
- media may foster hysteria about external community work by prisoners; and
- restorative justice may seem opposed to 'tough on crime' approaches.

This brief summary excludes entirely the range of activities and initiatives that can be and frequently are set in place between prisons and local communities to promote relationships and mutual trust. Many prisons presently become involved in such activities through the auspices of faith groups, prison visitors, educational and cultural programmes, addiction counselling and the like, all of which are potentially valuable, helpful and deserving of encouragement. In addition, access by inmates to caring agencies such as the Samaritans can be a vital factor in dealing with despair and personal trauma. Each of these, in different ways, involves

---

[30] Where it can be seen that productive work is completed by inmates that has 'amenity value' for the community, while at the same time providing reparation for victims of crime. Such work, when completed within the community, may also contribute towards a reduced 'public fear of crime'.

positive aspects of community involvement in prisons, the benefits of which are frequently under-estimated or overlooked.

The reader will ultimately decide, in the light of the foregoing analysis, whether the potential advantages of introducing restorative and reparative practices within penal systems outweigh the attendant disadvantages. He or she will also have to consider alongside this the implications of leaving matters within contemporary penal systems as they presently stand, of accepting the existing cost to taxpayers and economies, and of contemplating increases in the future if nothing of substance is changed. In the concluding part of this discussion it is clearly necessary to consider how, within existing custodial arrangements, those prisoners should be dealt with who decline to involve themselves in reparative and restorative processes (or who are considered to be entirely unsuitable to do so).

ACCOMMODATING THE UNREPENTANT AND INCORRIGIBLE: ISSUES OF 'BIFURCATION'[31]

Every prison has its 'difficult' inmates, some of whom can be violent, disruptive and abusive towards correctional staff. There is also always an element of those who show no remorse whatsoever for their offences and are entirely indifferent towards the victims of their crimes. A number also receive long sentences (including life) for heinous acts and cannot therefore be trusted—at least during the earlier years of their sentences. As a consequence, it would be unrealistic in such circumstances to expect that these prisoners would participate willingly or effectively in reparative regimes unless or until they are able to modify their attitudes and behaviour.

In the cases of such inmates, a regime more similar to that of the 'traditional' model with more intensive control and supervision arrangements is both necessary and entirely appropriate. It is also important that such people are not permitted to disrupt more progressive regimes that can accommodate those with better intentions within a reparative and restorative ethos. This creates a situation in which two regimes might have to co-exist within a single correctional facility, the 'reparative' one becoming considerably more desirable and rewarding than the 'traditional' one. Alternatively, it might eventually become the case that two geographically adjacent prisons operate entirely different regimes that would also be likely to lead to different outcomes for those inmates concerned.[32]

It has been an accepted precept in the past that, at least in principle, like offences should be dealt with similarly, and that those in custody should not be discriminated against on the basis of the nature of their offences. Neither of these

---

[31] See *Chapter 1*, p. 52 and fn. 29 *supra.*, and A.E. Bottoms (1977), 'Reflections on the Renaissance of Dangerousness', *Howard Journal of Criminal Justice*, Vol. XVI, No.2, pp. 70-97.

[32] This is particularly likely in terms of consideration for parole release, and in relation to other processes such as release to home detention curfew arrangements or on life licence in the United Kingdom.

propositions is objectionable in any theoretical sense; both are morally logical; and yet there are reasons why neither works entirely in practice. By way of example, the demonstration of remorse and contrition has long been accepted as a mitigating factor within sentencing considerations and frequently leads to different outcomes in relation to markedly similar offences. It is also evident that from time to time in many jurisdictions, particularly prevalent offences are singled out for exemplary penalties in an attempt to reduce the incidence of the crimes in question.

Within the Prison Service of England and Wales it has become the established practice for prisoners at risk of violence or intimidation from others to be housed in Vulnerable Prisoner Units (VPUs) for their own protection. The majority of those thus accommodated have been convicted of sexual offences which, within the inverted morality of the prisoner culture, are regarded as particularly despicable and deserving of violent or abusive treatment by inmates themselves.[33] Though there is no deliberate intention on the part of the prison authorities to discriminate against vulnerable prisoners specifically, the almost invariable outcome of their segregation is evident in diminished regime conditions subject to inevitable restrictions resulting from their protective isolation.

Each of these briefly described examples to some or another extent indicates different elements of bifurcation, albeit not strictly in the terms in which Bottoms originally perceived it.[34] In practice, however, the outcomes might be remarkably similar. The question then is whether in certain circumstances bifurcation is necessarily improper or immoral. Here we are dealing with what might be termed a 'positively discriminatory bifurcation' that is specifically conceived to promote reparative and restorative objectives by dealing more favourably with offenders who opt to show remorse, take responsibility for their offences and make reparation to victims. In so doing we do not propose to impose increased penalties upon those who do not do so (for whatever reason): rather it is proposed that such offenders remain to be dealt with within the 'traditional' correctional model.

It will be recalled from earlier discussion that one of the more important potential outcomes of restorative and reparative custodial practice was to reduce reliance on 'negative' sanctions. The form of bifurcation proposed here would seem to satisfy this purpose and do so in a morally defensible manner. A further objective was to reduce, where possible, the use (and extent) of imprisonment and, ultimately, the size of the prison population. Once again, the selected mode of bifurcation might enable this to happen. From a utilitarian perspective, therefore, bifurcation may be seen to offer potential advantages that are not forthcoming from within the 'traditional' model.

---

[33] Segregation of individuals for their own safety and protection is especially prevalent where prisoners have been convicted of offences against children, rape and kindred offences.

[34] In his original comments, Bottoms was more concerned with the (then) increasing tendency to select groups that he described as 'the mad' and 'the bad' against whom serious action should be taken, while being prepared to reduce penalties for the remainder (Bottoms, 1977: 89).

The final consideration is, somewhat inevitably, the extent to which engagement with reparative regimes should be allowed to affect the balance between the time to be spent in custody and that to be spent subsequently in the community under conditional release arrangements. This implies that in relation to each offence it is possible (and, indeed desirable) to specify the period considered necessary to meet the requirement for retribution and separate this from other sentencing considerations.[35] In instances of serious offending, it seems altogether reasonable for the retributive element of a sentence to be spent in custody (whether within a reparative or 'traditional' regime), but thereafter it becomes possibly counter-productive to extend the custodial phase unnecessarily, merely to mark the overall gravity of offences.

The important point to be made here is that an integrated or inclusive concept of criminal punishment allows the legal system to adopt a more flexible approach towards sentencing, particularly in relation to those offenders who are prepared to engage in reparative processes, having accepted responsibility for their offences. This principle has already been accepted within the legislative provisions in both New Zealand[36] and Canada[37] and a similar approach has been evident in Australia also (Strang, 2001).[38] This form of sentencing framework does, however, suggest the necessity for statutory maximum and minimum provisions: if only to ensure that proper safeguards are set in place to prevent excessive (exemplary) or inconsistent use of sanctions.

The concept of bifurcation has, in the past, presented some criminologists, moral philosophers and lawyers with an ethical difficulty. In the circumstances of its proposal here it may, however, be positively helpful. There seems to be some merit in the contention that like offences should be treated similarly, but this need not extend beyond the strict requirement for a retributive element in sentencing. In determining the residual element of a sanction marking gravity or culpability, it seems entirely reasonable to behave more leniently towards those who are prepared to accept guilt and make reparation than towards those who are unwilling to do so. In a utilitarian sense also, a disposition towards leniency in such cases can be seen

---

[35] In earlier work (see Cornwell, 2006 *op. cit.*, pp. 101-3) suggestions have been advanced as to how a model of sentencing might be created that enabled the separate custodial and non-custodial elements of an overall 'individualised' sentence to be viewed as logically consecutive, while still retaining the notion of retribution as a necessary ingredient of the former. The concept is not repeated here, but the reader will note that the broad conception enabled a judicial view to be expressed at the time of sentencing as to the appropriate portion of the total sentence that should be spent in custody to satisfy the requirement for retribution and desert, while allowing that the remainder of the sentence period might reflect the overall seriousness of offences. The latter period need not be spent in custody, and, indeed, should preferably be spent under conditional release within the community.

[36] Here see McElrea's account of the New Zealand Sentencing Act 2002 (in Cornwell, 2006: *op. cit.*, pp. 120-121).

[37] Also see Cormier's description of developments in Canada following the landmark judgement in *R. v. Gladue* (1999) 1 SCR. 688, and subsequently (in Cornwell, 2006: *op. cit.*, pp. 153-5).

[38] H. Strang (2001), *Restorative Justice Programs in Australia: A Report to the Criminology Research Council*, Australian Government: Criminology Research Council.

to have a generally beneficial effect in reducing the use of custody in favour of community-based alternatives.

SUMMARY: A DIFFERENT APPROACH TO CUSTODIAL CORRECTIONS

Within this chapter, an argument has been advanced in favour of adopting a reparative and restorative approach within custodial corrections and the reasons for doing so have been set out in some detail. The suggestion has been made that continued use of the 'traditional' model of custodial punishment imposes unacceptable human, social and fiscal penalties that are largely unaffordable, unsustainable and unnecessary within modern democratic societies. More than this, however, there are better ways of doing justice for offenders, victims and society in general.

Adoption of a reparative ethos within the custodial penal systems of most countries today would require a significant shift in policy-making terms, but is in no sense unthinkable. Penal policies are instrumental aspects and reflections of contemporary politics and the exercise of state power over the citizenry. Moreover, viewed dispassionately, a dominant motivation of politics is the assumption and retention of the power to govern with the consent of the electoral majority.

Public attitudes towards crime and criminal offenders are significantly affected by media influences and these same influences tend also to inform the judgement of politicians and policy-makers in terms of risk-taking. Thus, where public attitudes are inherently punitive towards crime (or can be induced into being so), the politics of criminal justice normally follow suit. Even in circumstances in which the need for change is evident, a preference for the *status quo* is a politically safer option than that of risk-taking.

Prisons certainly can be given a reparative ethos, but not all prisoners will wish to be concerned with making some effort to make good the harm caused by their offending. This means that two processes of imprisonment have to be accommodated: one for those prepared to make reparation and another for those unwilling to do so. Prison design and operation can meet both requirements, but legal systems also have to be convinced of the morality of this form of 'bifurcation'.

Designing (or converting) entire prisons to deliver reparative regimes is much simpler than adapting existing prisons to serve both the reparative and 'traditional' models of custody. Decisions also have to be made about the extent to which participation in reparative regimes should permit those who choose to do so to return to their communities earlier than those who do not. Of equal importance, reparative regimes have to be resourced and operated in a manner that provides a combination of vocational training and marketable employment that enhances the 'survivability' of ex-prisoners on their release back into their communities.

Reparative prisons, whether strictly localised or otherwise, require a greater commitment on behalf of correctional authorities and their immediate communities to work together in the interests of crime reduction rather than of social incapacitation. Both reparation and the restoration of individual offenders rely upon opportunities being made available for visibly purposeful work to be undertaken for the direct benefit of victims of crime and communities themselves. Without these opportunities, local communities will, with reason, remain sceptical in relation to the risks involved in any expansion of conditional release from prison custody.

If restorative and reparative initiatives are to gain credibility, both sides within the community and correctional services equation have to adopt less entrenched attitudes towards each other and offenders. Each has to accept some extent of reliance upon the other and acknowledge that the potential advantages may actually be considerably greater than the risks to be faced. Restorative and reparative justice seeks to reconcile offenders, victims and communities and can only do so effectively if opportunities are made available to make this a possibility. This, ultimately, may be seen to be of greater moral importance than that of the imperatives of retributive justice being seen to be satisfied.

Implementation of restorative and reparative justice concepts and practices leads almost inexorably towards a measure of bifurcation in penal policy deliberation. Even within the uncertain territory of penal politics, it must be both logical and morally defensible to deal somewhat differently with the repentant and the unrepentant. Without such a compromise, justice itself becomes diminished. Restorative justice has a message of hope for the former, but is still able to accommodate the latter. This is both its strength and its challenge to modern societies.

Above all else, perhaps, reparative regimes in prisons hold out a prospect of greater hope for victims of crime, offenders and communities. Though these regimes offer no 'soft options' for offenders in custody, they provide a more logical 'bridge' between custodial and non-custodial corrections than is widely available at present. In the chapter that follows, this particular theme is developed further in discussion of community-based sanctions. Prisons cannot operate effectively in isolation from the realities of the world around them and neither can those housed within them, most of who must, inevitably, return to their place in society in due course. This transition should, ideally, be of a graduated and supervised nature rather than a sudden event, particularly if prisons are to play an active part in reducing recidivism. Coyle provides a very apt postscript to this discussion:

> Prisons as we know them today are based on the notion of exclusion from society. Such a notion sits very uneasily with the concept of a society which is integrated and in which everyone is meant to contribute to the good of others, It is naïve of us to assume that by excluding large numbers of people from our society behind the high walls of a prison for a specified period of time [we] will somehow turn them into better citizens. The successful experiments which are now emerging from other countries about restorative justice and community penalties give us real reason to

hope that there may indeed be, in Vaclav Havel's words, 'a better way of coming to terms with certain things'. This alternative is not an easy way. It is a very difficult way. But eventually it will be a much more successful way. (Coyle, 2001b: 4)

In the chapter that follows, the focus of the discussion changes to examine the ways in which the use of community-based corrections might be expanded by making lesser use of imprisonment in the future. It is, however, important to maintain an explicit link between the custodial and non-custodial sectors of correctional practice, rather than to perceive them within a 'stand alone' context. In this current chapter we have seen how reparative prison regimes would rely upon a community service element to provide a natural progression from custody to restoration of full social status. The corollary of using prisons less is that, given the political will to do so, many less serious offenders so sentenced presently might be adequately sanctioned within the community. In spite of the evident fiscal and social advantages of such a change of direction, the political will can only materialise if public perceptions of the effectiveness and appropriateness community corrections can be reassured.

Within this chapter it has been proposed that the processes of reparation and restoration are essentially part of a natural continuum and that, indeed, restoration is contingent upon reparation having been made in a substantial manner. This is, I believe, a central tenet of restorative justice in action and an indispensable ingredient of the new penology proposed in *Chapter 2*. The issue is, however, one that extends far beyond a more positive use of custody. Public confidence in the role of prisons has been eroded because custodial sanctions have been negatively perceived and have evidently failed to have any measurable impact on recidivism. Political confidence in the effectiveness of imprisonment has become confined to its incapacitative effects alone and remains sceptical of any change-facilitative benefit that may derive from custodial sanctions. These two influences, viewed together, have resulted in the isolation of prisons within a neo-penitentiary time warp, particularly in Britain, but also widely elsewhere.

Both public and political confidence will only be restored when prisons are seen to have a prospective purpose, when victims of crime are afforded more evident consideration and corrections become more community focussed. This means greater community involvement in prisons, greater prison involvement in communities, and a coherent linkage between custodial and non-custodial sanctions. Inevitable risk attaches to making the concluding part of custodial sentences semi-custodial in nature, but the risk is, to a marked extent, a manageable one. Restoration implies social re-acceptance that has to be earned: social re-acceptance implies law-abiding behaviour that also has to be tested.

CHAPTER 6

Community Justice: The Potential for Expanding Non-custodial Corrections

Throughout this book, an attempt has been made to provide the reader with a commentary upon the ways in which the principles of restorative justice might be applied within the criminal justice systems of developed and developing democracies. To this end, this work is not specific in relation to any particular country, though examples have been drawn from the United Kingdom and elsewhere, entirely for illustrative reasons where this seems appropriate.

THE POLITICS OF COMMUNITY PENOLOGY — PRELIMINARY OBSERVATIONS

Insofar as the penal systems of every nation are, to a greater or lesser extent, unique, developed differently over time and shaped to meet national priorities, the common thread that unifies them is the overall pursuit of crime reduction. In a more specific sense, however, the penal systems of many of what are often referred to as the 'Western-style' democracies display adherence to a range of criminological principles that are identifiable and form the basis of the international discourse of penology.

If the majority of these democracies presently share a dominant characteristic, it is probably that of incarcerating a higher proportion of the population than they would wish to do, for longer than might be strictly necessary and at unacceptably high cost to the tax-paying public. The outcome of such behaviour is that other social priorities (such as education, healthcare, welfare provision and the like) suffer diminished access to finite national resources.

The non-custodial sector of corrections in every country reflects two important and sometimes conflicting aspects of the national agenda for crime prevention. The first of these is the extent of public acceptance of identified (and sanctioned) offenders at liberty within communities; the second is the threshold of national tolerance of criminal acts before resort is made to the use of custodial punishment. These two determinants of criminal justice policy remain in a perpetual state of potential conflict because where public attitudes are antipathetic towards offenders, or can be encouraged to be so, community-based sanctions will be perceived as lacking 'penal bite' and politicians anxious to be seen as 'tough on crime' will favour policies of social incapacitation when this is strictly avoidable. The outcome of both situations is, illogically, an increase in the use of imprisonment[1] (Tonry, 2003: 5-6; Tonry and Green, 2003: 488-9).

This is unfortunate because it suggests that intransigent public attitudes towards certain forms of offending, frequently fuelled by sensationalist media coverage of particular incidents, create a reactionary climate that can be used by politicians to bolster the case for ever more stringent measures against offenders.[2] Levels of public tolerance are closely linked to what is termed a 'fear of crime' that is a complex dynamic within modern societies (Garland, 2001: 152-4; Tonry, 2003: 5). Certainly it is based in part on public perceptions about the prevalence of crime that may be exaggerated by media reporting and also, in part, on other influences such as selective communication of statistical data relating to particular forms of offending.[3]

It remains the case, notwithstanding, that widespread feelings of public insecurity—however misconceived or exaggerated—create a social and political climate in which it becomes difficult to envisage an expansion of community-based sanctions and a corresponding decrease in the use of imprisonment. The evidence does, however, point conclusively in a somewhat different direction. Between 1995 and 1999 there was an average fall in police-recorded domestic burglary of 14 *per cent* across the member states of the entire European Union, the greatest decreases being in England and Wales (31 *per cent*), Germany (29 *per cent*) and Austria (26 *per cent*). In the USA also, over the same period, the corresponding decrease was 19 *per cent*.[4]

Viewing crime historically since the new millennium, the *British Crime Survey* published in October 2001 reported a reduction of 19 *per cent* in violent crimes between 1999 and 2000 and, in particular, a 34 *per cent* decrease in the offence of

---

[1] Illogical, simply because there is clear evidence to show that in England and Wales since the mid-1990s, crime rates—excluding those for violent crime in 2005/6 which increased by two per cent—have shown an overall decrease, while the prison population has continued to rise (Home Office, 2006a, 2006b and 2006e). The same falling crime rate situation is reflected in almost every Western country during the same period, irrespective of whether imprisonment rates have risen (England, The Netherlands, the USA), fallen (Finland, Canada, Denmark) or remained much the same (Germany, Scotland, Sweden) (Tonry and Frase, 2001; Tonry, 2001 and 2003: 3).

[2] The evidence for this assertion derives from the government White Paper (Home Office, 2002), *Justice for All*, CM 5563, London: TSO, which proposed, *inter alia*, the confinement of certain violent and sexual offenders on an indeterminate basis, until the Parole Board was 'completely satisfied' that the public risk they presented had become significantly diminished (Home Office, 2002: 95). This provision was augmented within the form of extended (or incremental) sentences for violent and sexual offenders whose offences were regarded as 'not serious', but whom the courts considered to pose a serious public risk. These increments were to be additional to the punishment based on desert, amounting to up to an additional five years imprisonment for violent offences and up to nine years for sexual offences (sections 227 and 228, Criminal Justice Act 2003).

[3] Here see the account presented by Lord Windlesham (2003), 'Ministers and Modernisation: Criminal Justice Policy', in L. Zedner and A. Ashworth (eds), *The Criminological Foundations of Penal Policy*, Oxford: Oxford University Press, pp. 271-4.

[4] Home Office (2001), *The 2001 British Crime Survey: First Results, England and Wales*, Statistical Bulletin 18/01 (October), pp. i-viii.

wounding.[5] The result of this downward trend in violent crime indicates that in the particular year 2000, only 3.7 *per cent* of people in England and Wales were subject to one or more incidents of violence (Windlesham, 2003: 272-5). More recently, the same survey published in October 2004 confirmed the downward trends for the crimes of domestic burglary and violence and, indeed, of all crime in England and Wales during 2003/4. Burglary stood at the lowest level since 1985 and had reduced by 47 *per cent* since 1995. Crimes of violence had similarly reduced by 36 *per cent* over the same period and the total figure for all crime showed a 39 *per cent* reduction on 1995 levels.[6]

The most recently available statistics relating to crime (Home Office, 2006d; 2006e; and the Office for National Statistics, 2006) are to some extent confusing, since the data record information from both the British Crime Survey (BCS) and offences recorded by the police. The BCS data relate to offences convicted in the courts, while the latter is based upon offences alleged to and subject to police enquiries. However, all three sources indicate falling rates for domestic burglary and theft, relatively stable rates for violent and sexual offences excluding robbery, and increases in drug related crime, robbery and criminal damage.

Over the same decade (1995-2006) the average daily prison population of England and Wales increased by some 50 *per cent* from just over 52,000 to more than 78,250 and the number of sentenced prisoners increased similarly from 38,000 to a figure in excess of 61,500.[7] It is, therefore, demonstrably the case that in a decade in which a significant (over 30 *per cent*) decrease in crime affecting individual safety and security occurred, the number of offenders sentenced to imprisonment *increased* by a much greater proportion.

This situation represents the backdrop against which community-based corrections have to be considered in contemporary England and Wales and also in a number of other European and North American countries that display similar trends in the use of sanctions. In such circumstances it would evidently be fanciful to suggest that the prevailing mood of political and public punitivism is likely to change dramatically, since present projections of custodial penal populations reveal an expectation of further increases (Home Office, 2006b, op. cit.).

These increases, and even current rates of imprisonment, are by no means inevitable: rather, they represent deliberate political choices made by national governments and pursued through criminal justice policies and practices. Lest there be doubt, the history of the Finnish penal system provides a clear example of how matters can be different. In the 1950s, Finland incarcerated 187 offenders *per* 100,000 of its population—a rate subsequently deemed by the Finnish government to be unsustainable. By 1960 this figure had decreased to 154, by 1970 to 113, by 1980 to 106, by 1990 to 69 and by 2000 to 55. In 2006 it stands at 66,

---

[5] Ibid., page viii.

[6] Home Office (2004), *The 2004 British Crime Survey*, www.crimestatistics.org.uk/output pp. 55-63.

[7] Source: Home Office (2006b), *Prison Population*, www.statistics.gov.uk/cci as at 3 January 2006.

the same as Denmark and slightly below Norway at 68 and Sweden at 78 *per* 100,000 of the national population. By contrast, the corresponding rate in England and Wales is 143 and rising[8] and in Scotland 135.[9]

Community-based corrections can only be viewed in the context of being sanctions of a lower order than imprisonment, but this does not preclude lesser use of custody and increased use of community sanctions where the use of imprisonment is *not strictly necessary*. The main question then is: Why is imprisonment so consistently overused and what makes the public risk posed by offending in some jurisdictions apparently so much more acute than in others that use imprisonment much more sparingly?

CHANGING PUBLIC ATTITUDES AND PUNISHMENT RHETORIC

With the benefit of hindsight, it is clear that in Britain, the USA and a cluster of other countries worldwide, the climate of public and political opinion in relation to crime and criminals changed dramatically as the mid-1990s approached. Though the reasons for this are far from straightforward, a number of factors conspired to influence events—particularly in Britain—and advance the adoption of more punitive penal strategies. Declining confidence in the 'just deserts' concept of proportionate punishment proposed within the 'justice model' of the late 1970s and 1980s resulted in what might be described as a 'punishment stalemate' in which retribution and deterrence became the dominant purposes of criminal sanctions—largely for want of any other plausible justifications.

Intractably high rates of recorded recidivism fuelled the belief that the 'nothing works' thesis of Martinson (1974) was, in fact, a reality. This, in turn, led to a more belligerent approach towards repeat offenders and to a hardening of attitudes in relation to violent and sexual offending in particular (Cavadino and Dignan, 1997: 51; Matravers and Hughes, 2003: 55-59[10]). The result was to be seen in the 'prison works' declaration of Michael Howard, the Home Secretary in the government of John Major, to the British Conservative Party Conference in October 1993.[11] From that time onwards, the emphasis of subsequent criminal

---

[8] See: Scottish Consortium on Crime and Criminal Justice (2005), *Reducing the Prison Population: Penal Policy and Social Choices*, Edinburgh: SCCJ, p. 18.

[9] Source: International Centre for Prison Studies (ICPS) (2006), *World Prison Populations (UK and Western Europe)*, London: ICPS, available at http: //news.bbc.co.uk/2/shared/sp1/hi/uk/06/prisons/html/nn1page1.stm

[10] See: A. Matravers and G. V. Hughes, 'Unprincipled Sentencing? The Policy Approach to Dangerous Sex Offenders' in M. Tonry (ed.) (2003), *Confronting Crime: Crime Control Policy Under New Labour*, Devon, UK: Willan Publishing, pp. 51-79.

[11] Michael Howard declared to the conference that 'prison works' and that he would not flinch from measures that would increase the prison population. This, the measures certainly did and in the

justice legislation became heavily slanted towards 'public protection', delivered under the guise of a 'law and order' agenda of incapacitation and deterrence.[12] It was particularly directed against serious violent and sexual offenders, extending the sentencing powers of the courts to impose longer prison sentences (including discretionary life sentences) and also the arrangements for post-release supervision of released offenders.

Public protection continued to be the dominant theme of legislation introduced post-1997 by the 'New Labour' government of Prime Minister Tony Blair and successive Home Secretaries (Jack Straw, David Blunkett, Charles Clarke and latterly John Reid) within that administration. Both the Criminal Justice and Court Services Act 2000 and the Powers of Criminal Courts (Sentencing) Act 2000 contain measures for public protection against serious sexual offenders in relation to disclosure of their identities and arrangements for extension of post-sentence supervision (for up to ten years) respectively. In addition, a raft of reports and White Papers during the years 2000-2 all further addressed issues directly related to sentencing, serious offenders and public protection.[13] All in all, David Garland appears to have been entirely correct in his assessment made in the following words:

> Protecting the public is a perennial concern of crime policy and the correctionalist system was by no means casual about this. It was, after all, the penal-welfare reformers who invented preventive detention and the indeterminate sentence and the system that operated for most of the twentieth century reserved to itself special powers to incarcerate 'incorrigible' and dangerous offenders for indeterminate periods. But in an age when crime rates were low and fear of crime was not yet a political motif, protecting the public was rarely the motivating theme of policy-

---

following five years the prison population of England and Wales rose from just over 50,000 to almost 65,000.

[12] This process started with the Criminal Justice Act 1991 which contained specific measures for the extension of sentences for sexual, violent and drug offenders and extended parole provisions (in section 44) in the name of 'public protection'. It continued with the Crime (Sentences) Act 1997 and the Sex Offenders Act 1997 which were both specifically targeted against sexual offenders (see Matravers and Hughes (2003), op. cit., pp. 56-7) and the Crime and Disorder Act 1998 ,which gave courts the power to impose discretionary life sentences for a second serious violent or sexual offence and to add an extended period of post-release supervision in cases in which the offender was deemed to pose a risk to the public on release. The latter Act introduced the Sex Offender Order (SOO) which augmented the provision made in the Sex Offender Act 1997 requiring all offenders cautioned for, or convicted of, offences identified in Schedule 1 of the Act to notify the police of their place of abode and any change to that place of residence. The SOO was a civil measure, available to the police, to compel offenders convicted of sexual offences to register with the police within a specified period. Breach of these conditions constituted a criminal offence, carrying a maximum penalty of five years imprisonment.

[13] In particular: Home Office (2000), *Setting the Boundaries*, London: Home Office—the Review of Sex Offences; Home Office (2001), *Making Punishments Work*, the report of a Review of the Sentencing Framework for England and Wales, [The Halliday Report], London: Home Office (July); Home Office (2002a), *Justice for All*, CM 5563, London: TSO—a White Paper; Home Office (2002b), *Protecting the Public*, CM 5668, London: Home Office; Home Office (2002c), *Justice for All: Responses to the Auld and Halliday Reports*, London: Home Office.

making. Today, there is a new and urgent emphasis upon the need for security, the containment of danger, the identification and management of any kind of risk. Protecting the public has become the dominant theme of penal policy.

(Garland, 2001: 12)

All of this leaves the world of community corrections in a very difficult position. For although countries like Britain have a wide range of non-custodial sanctions available to courts, there has occurred a rather unsubtle change in the political rhetoric of the 1990s and early 2000s that speaks not of 'alternatives to imprisonment' as heretofore, but of 'punishment in the community' and 'community penalties'—presumably to guard against such measures being perceived as a 'soft option' both by sentencing officials and the public.

It is of some interest to note that although the Criminal Justice Act 1991 established for the first time (for England and Wales) a three-tier hierarchy of sentences that was intended to 'grade' severity in a clear and unambiguous manner, the ambitions of the legislators largely failed to materialise in effect. The levels identified ranged from fines and compensation orders at the lowest level[14], through a range of orders (probation, community service, curfew, combination, attendance centre and supervision) at the second level, to imprisonment (immediate or suspended for adults and detention for young offenders) at the third and highest level.[15] The problem was, however, that what might be described as the 'thresholds' or 'filters' between the levels were, in fact, described in a manner that was *not* entirely unambiguous and allowed a measure of subjectivity to permeate sentencing decisions.

For instance, the 'threshold' between the lowest and second levels was described in the Act in terms of the offence being 'serious enough' to warrant the more punitive level of sanction (section 6(1)) and 'suitable' for the offender 'in the opinion of the court' (section 6(2)a). Similarly, the 'threshold' for custodial consideration was described in terms of the offence being 'so serious that only such a [custodial] sentence can be justified' (section 1(2)a), or the 'need for public protection in the case of violent or sexual offences' (section 1(2)b). As a result, many non-serious offenders who were unwilling or unable to pay a fine inevitably attracted an enhanced (level 2) sanction and subjective assessments relating to the 'seriousness' of offences or the 'need for public protection' propelled many (level 2) offenders into custody. The latter effect was particularly marked in cases in which offenders (and particularly young offenders) had previously breached the conditions of level 2 sanctions.

In any event, the governmental *volte-face* in penal policy announced by Michael Howard in October 1993 opened the floodgates to an increasing use of custody that effectively negated the very well-intentioned prescriptions of the Criminal Justice Act 1991, and the prison population in England and Wales quickly began its

---

14 Including provisions for absolute and conditional discharges.
15 For a clear and concise explanation of these measures, see M. Cavadino and J. Dignan (1997a), op. cit., pp. 205-47.

inexorable rise to the levels presently experienced. It is also the case that similar escalations have been evident in the USA, The Netherlands, Australia, South Africa and a number of other countries across the world today. As Garland further indicates:

> The politicisation of crime control has transformed the structure of relationships that connects the political process and the institutions of criminal justice … 'Politicisation' sometimes suggests a polarisation of positions, but the populist form that penal politics has taken has had exactly the opposite effect. Far from there being a differentiation of policy positions, what has actually emerged, in the 1980s and 1990s, is a narrowing of debate and a striking convergence of the policy proposals of all the major political parties. It is not just one party that has moved away from the old correctionalist orthodoxy: they all have. The centre of political gravity has moved and a rigid new consensus has formed around penal measures that are perceived as tough, smart and popular with the public …
>
> In vivid contrast to the conventional wisdom of the previous period, the ruling assumption now is that 'prison works'—not as a mechanism of reform or rehabilitation, but as a means of incapacitation and punishment that satisfies popular demands for public safety and harsh retribution. Recent years have witnessed a remarkable turnaround of the fortunes of the prison. An institution with a long history of utopian expectations and periodic attempts to reinvent itself—first as a penitentiary, then a reformatory and most recently as a correctional facility—has finally seen its ambition reduced to the ground-zero of incapacitation and retributive punishment. But in the course of this fall from grace, the prison has once again transformed itself. In the course of a few decades it has gone from being a discredited and declining correctional institution into a massive and seemingly indispensable pillar of contemporary social order.
>
> (Garland, 2001: 13-14)

If, then, the world of community justice has to be reinvented, something far-reaching has to be done to reverse the contemporary rhetoric of penology, or, perhaps more realistically, to put the concept of *correction* back into the linguistics of criminal punishment. In the final analysis, community justice will only be seen to be just if it is perceived by politicians, legislators, policy-makers and the public as having an achievable purpose of changing offenders for the better. In the concluding sections of this chapter, it is appropriate to suggest how such a massive task might be approached and identify the extent to which the principles and practice of restorative justice might assist in this endeavour.

MAKING COMMUNITY CORRECTIONS CREDIBLE

Any attempt to re-shape the concept of sanctions operated in the community must necessarily retain a relationship with that higher level of penalties that involves custodial punishment. We have seen (in *Chapter 5*) how prison regimes can be designed to achieve reparative and restorative outcomes and the extent to which community involvement in the life of prisons is not only desirable, but also manifestly necessary. This is particularly important if the transition of offenders from custody to the community is to be a natural progression to social re-integration.

Although the concept of making reparation for offences to victims of crime lies at the heart of restorative justice principles, this is, as has been discussed in *Chapter 5*, only part of the process leading to restoration. As important is the insistence that offenders accept responsibility for their actions and the harm caused by criminal acts, and do something substantial to 'put things right'. This means, in effect, being prepared to analyse and address offending behaviour and, with appropriate professional assistance, to make plans to ensure that it does not recur. These same principles are immediately transferable to sanctions that operate within the community setting[16] (Zehr and Mika, 1998: 47-55; Zehr, 2002a: 40-41).

The credibility of sanctions and particularly of those measures operated within the community is, undoubtedly, a crucial issue for victims, the public and those involved in the formulation of penal policies. One of the main strengths of action taken within communities by offenders to make reparation to victims of crime is that it provides a visible manifestation that some benefits can derive from the processes of justice. Work done by offenders for the immediate benefit of communities also has a number of tangential effects in addition to creating revenue for victim compensation: it engages the community with offenders and the penal process; it can lead to a reduction in the 'fear of crime'; and it creates confidence in the criminal justice system itself. Such is only the case, however, if the work undertaken is evidently purposeful, demanding, adequately supervised and creates outcomes of real social benefit.

As we have also seen in *Chapter 3*, the issue of victim satisfaction and vindication has important implications for the credibility of the criminal justice system. Insofar as community-based sanctions are concerned, it must be assumed that there is a considerably greater scope for victim–offender mediation in relation to offences—particularly those against the person and property—than might be the case in the custodial sector of corrections. This is largely because community sanctions are normally imposed for less serious offences committed within communities and offenders tend to remain within the geographic areas in which their offences were committed and their victims also reside.

Restorative justice in action promotes not only reparation of victims and communities, but also victim–offender mediation (where this is possible and acceptable to the parties concerned) through both direct and indirect inter-personal contact, and also through the wider medium of restorative conferencing (in which victims, offenders, relatives, prosecuting authorities and counsellors all participate) (Galway *et al.*, 1995; Mika, 1995; Sharpe, 2003; Umbreit, 1994; Wright and Galway,

---

[16] Here see, for instance, H. Zehr and H. Mika (1998), 'Fundamental Principles of Restorative Justice', *The Contemporary Justice Review*, Vol.1, No.1, pp. 47-55. Also what these authors describe as the 'signposts of restorative justice' in H. Zehr (2002a), op. cit., pp. 40-1.

1989; Wright, 1996; McElrea, 2006).[17] Mediation can take place at a number of different stages following the commission of offences. At the pre-trial point it can be powerful in reducing victim trauma[18] and also in making the offender aware of the harm done and the reasons for this. At the trial stage, victim–offender mediation can enable offenders to demonstrate genuine remorse and make apology to those harmed, thus possibly affecting the selection of sanctions, or the extent of these. Post-trial, it can assist in the essential process of offending behaviour analysis by perpetrators of crime; and even post-sentence, it can assist in victim vindication.

The essential point here is that victim–offender mediation is not just a palliative process designed to make victims feel acknowledged and considered: it is much more a powerful means of enabling all the parties affected by crime to come to terms with the reality of it and recover from its effects. This has as much to do with victim vindication as it has to do with the effective re-integration and restoration of offenders within communities. It therefore has a central role to play in the concept of community justice and the effectiveness (and therefore the credibility) of community sanctions.

There is an ever-increasing body of research evidence from across the world[19] which suggests very strongly that the various forms of mediation approach offered by restorative justice have potential and actual beneficial effects for all the participant parties in criminal justice.[20] Governments that have funded restorative justice programmes and implemented the European Union and United Nations initiatives 'to incorporate restorative practices within their laws, regulations and administrative provisions', have agreed that from all the available evidence, these assist in reducing the fear of crime and increasing confidence in criminal justice (Umbreit, *et al.,* (2005 and 2006); Hayes and Daly (2004); Morris and Maxwell (2001)).

Public perceptions of crime and, in particular, those shaped by sensationalist media sources in relation to community justice and the effectiveness of sanctions, may well prove more difficult to alter. From the public viewpoint, evident reduction in criminal activity provides the 'acid test' of whether or not the 'war on crime' is being won. Much can, however, be done to make the processes of criminal justice more easily understood, to make sanctions more direct and relevant and to involve communities in the entire apparatus of law enforcement and crime

---

[17] Here see also the abstract of the proceedings of the European Forum for Victim-Offender Mediation (2000), *Victim-Offender Mediation in Europe*, Leuven: Leuven University Press.

[18] Frequently evident in the form of post-traumatic shock disorder (PTSD) which can require long-term medical treatment and therapy in addition to physical injury, absence from employment and material loss.

[19] And in particular from New Zealand, Australia, Canada, the USA and the UK (Umbreit (2004); Morris and Maxwell (2003); Sherman and Strang (2004); Bonta, *et al.* (1998)).

[20] These include victims, offenders, relatives, police, prosecuting authorities, legal professionals and, ultimately politicians and their advisers who determine criminal justice policies and sanctions. Much of this research derives from pilot projects in which initial indications are positive in relation to both victim satisfaction and the subsequent recidivism of offenders—in particular juvenile offenders.

reduction. Once again, restorative justice principles can be of considerable assistance in enabling all this to happen, as the following example indicates.

THE 'COULSFIELD' REPORT 2004

In 2001, in Britain, the Esmeé Fairbairn Foundation (EFF) established a programme named Rethinking Crime and Punishment (RCP) that funded an independent Commission of Inquiry into the criminal justice system under the chairmanship of Lord Coulsfield.[21] Significantly, the remit of the commission covered many of the issues discussed in the foregoing parts of this chapter, but in particular, sentencing, the courts, public attitudes, delivery of community penalties and reparation. The commission's report, entitled *Crime, Courts and Confidence* (EFF, 2004a) highlighted, within its wide-ranging and well-balanced recommendations, a number of important prescriptions for improving the quality of criminal justice delivery and reducing the present over-use of imprisonment.

In defining the present problems of the criminal justice system—specifically the system in England and Wales—the commission identified a lack of public confidence in criminal justice, despite the fact that crime rates have generally fallen significantly in recent years and a widespread popular belief that crime has actually increased. This belief, the inquiry noted, had led to pressure for increased severity in sentencing from, amongst others, the government. It also commented upon the extent of prison over-crowding, the recent steep increases in women and black offenders in custody and the situation of over-stretch and low morale in the probation service sector of the National Offender Management Service (NOMS).

Significantly, for our purposes here, however, the commission made the following observations that are relevant to the issues discussed in this chapter.

- Many of those subject to community penalties and some of those in prison, present a low risk of re-offending and an even lower risk of causing significant harm (p.4);
- short custodial sentences do very little to reduce crime and it is unlikely that these have a significant deterrent effect: they certainly have no rehabilitative value (p.5);
- the evidence on what has driven the increasing severity of sentences shows that it is not due to an increase in the level or seriousness of crime coming before the courts (p.5);
- the government sends out mixed messages to the public and the courts about sentencing. It wants to reduce the prison population but, at the same time, introduces policies and legislation which have the opposite effect.

---

[21] Lord Coulsfield is a distinguished former Scottish judge who, in 2001, had recently retired. The Commission reported in November 2004 in a comprehensive document entitled: *Crime, Courts and Confidence: Report of an Independent Inquiry into Alternatives to Prison*, EFF (2004a), London: The Stationery Office.

These often fail to take account of the research evidence, which the government itself has sponsored (p.5);
- public opinion, or rather public opinion as perceived by the mass media and politicians, is presented as being considerably more punitive than research shows it to be—this should be recognised when developing policy (p.5); and
- parts of the media portray crime as rising and serious. Alarmist reporting of high profile cases gives a distorted picture. However, it is not solely the media's responsibility to ensure the public knows the real facts—that rests with the government and individual parts of the criminal justice system (pp.6-7).

The report also included a comprehensive assessment of the potential for expanding the use of community penalties,[22] and suggestions for increasing public confidence in these measures. In particular, it proposed that community sanctions should be locally delivered and local communities should be much more closely involved in this delivery. The proposal was directly made that:

members of the community should play a key part in deciding on the work which offenders will undertake as part of community punishment orders. The projects identified should be delivered by local people including local businesses to maximise the possibility of longer term employment for offenders.[23]

The significance of the Coulsfield Commission's findings and recommendations for the analysis presented in this work lies in the extent to which these outcomes independently underscore the central argument that the contemporary penal crises in so many developed democracies are not only avoidable, but are also, to a considerable extent, the result of political mismanagement. It is, ultimately, an indisputable fact that national prison populations will be of the size that governments consider to be tolerable. Moreover, when reluctance to reduce these populations can be 'justified' on the grounds of social protection and by deliberately ignoring the potential effectiveness of community sanctions through failure to challenge populist perceptions of the 'fear of crime', the crises become more acute.

Critics of existing penal systems frequently make the claim that the systems, of themselves, create their own crises (Cavadino, 1992; 1994). This seems often to be the case because the structures of criminal justice are complex, bureaucratic, secretive and pursue different professional agendas depending upon their primary orientations. Police services are judged on the extent to which they pre-empt and prevent crime and also on the 'clear-up' rate of bringing offenders to justice when crimes are committed. Prosecution services and courts exist to deal with alleged offenders according to the evidence presented and to sentence those found guilty in

---

[22] At Chapter 8, entitled 'Courts and Community Penalties' pp. 56-66.
[23] See p. 7 and, in particular, the discussion in Chapter 9, 'Offender Management', pp. 67-73.

accordance with prevailing provisions for punishing crime. Prisons are expected to accommodate securely those offenders committed to custody by the courts, for as long as necessary and without undue concern for the number or nature of offenders assigned to their charge. Correctional services within the community are expected to 'sweep up' the balance of lesser offenders not sentenced to custody under a range of different 'orders' and provide effective programmes of supervision and improvement to combat recidivism.

The Coulsfield Inquiry report robustly challenged this state of affairs by identifying very clearly within its executive summary[24] and subsequent analysis, the reasons for the present lack of confidence in the criminal justice system. It cited, in particular, the following reasons for the contemporary crisis:

- public misinformation about crime levels;
- increased severity in sentencing;
- prison overcrowding and in particular the rise in the numbers of women and black offenders in custody;
- over-stretch and low morale in the recently (twice) re-organized probation service;
- the increased volume and range of community penalties; and
- overstatement of the public risk presented by many less serious offenders.

The report was reinforced shortly after its publication by a further analysis produced by the EFF's RCP Project under the title *Rethinking Crime and Punishment* (2004b).[25] This document specifically addressed the potential for extended use of restorative justice principles and practices in the adult sector of the criminal justice system and 'with proper arrangements for judicial oversight and a presumption that *all* sentences include an element of reparation'[26] [emphasis added]. Further recommendations urged that restorative justice should be organized in ways that maximise victim participation within the criminal justice process and that a national agency should be created to oversee arrangements for the implementation of restorative justice, which, in the longer term, should not involve police as facilitators.[27]

Now while these recent initiatives provide clear and evident signs that prestigious groups and professional bodies are considering very seriously the nature and implications of the existing penal crises that affect Britain and a number of other nations remarkably similarly, the impetus has to be reinforced if it is to

---

[24] At p. 4.
[25] The Executive Summary and full text of this document produced by the EFF's RCP Project are available at www.rethinking.org.uk . The full title is: Esmeé Fairbairn Foundation (2004b), *Rethinking Crime and Punishment* (Chair: Baroness Linklater), London: Beacon Press.
[26] Recommendation 6 of the Executive Summary, p. 7.
[27] Ibid., at recommendations 7 and 8. But see also the divergence of view over the appropriateness of using the police in this role as a result of experiences in Australia and New Zealand described by McElrea in Cornwell (2006), op. cit., at Chapter 9, pp. 119-134.

have any incisive effect. While it is also encouraging to note that these same observers perceive the potential benefits offered by implementation of restorative justice principles and practices, community corrections in particular are still beset with a range of difficulties that have to be overcome.

However, if both politicians and the public are to be convinced that community sanctions can be made to work effectively in reducing recidivism and promoting social cohesiveness, then all the principal issues identified by the Coulsfield Inquiry have to be addressed in a coordinated manner across each of the sectors of criminal justice. This involves the creation of a clear and simple ethos for the operation of community corrections, telling the truth about crime rates and offender risk, and providing the courts with measures that have sufficiently evident penal 'bite' to satisfy sentencing officials and the public that these are viable alternatives to custody. In addition, once these measures have been identified, the means of implementing them with demonstrable effectiveness and reliability has to be set in place and properly resourced.

There is no doubt that the concept of offenders making reparation to victims of crime has widespread appeal and is entirely appropriate. Reparation (or 'putting wrongs right') is a guiding principle of restorative justice, arising out of the assertion that violations create obligations on offenders to repair the harm done as far as possible. In addition, making reparation is the primary means by which offenders can be restored to full status within communities when crimes are committed. This is a clear and uncompromising message that is easily understood and has almost universal acceptance. It also provides a useful platform upon which to construct effective sanctions.

The actions required of offenders in the process of discharging a community penalty and making reparation are similarly capable of simple and unequivocal expression. The offender will consent to undertake an agreed programme of allocated and supervised work within the community, for a stipulated period of time and this work will have an evident social value to the community. The offender will be remunerated for this work, from which remuneration a fixed proportion will be deducted for the support of victims of crime. In the event that the offender defaults in discharging the penalty, he or she may be returned to the sentencing court for reconsideration of the sanction imposed.[28]

The entire concept of community penalties advanced here is that, as the Coulsfield Inquiry suggested, these should be locally administered with the direct involvement of community members and business organizations. It would also seem entirely sensible to follow the logic of the RCP recommendation that a nationwide agency should oversee the implementation of community penalties,

---

[28] Within such a definition it would be necessary to stipulate what behaviours might constitute a 'breach' of the community penalty and the arrangements for reporting default to the sentencing court. It would also be essential to identify the powers of the court in re-sentencing the offender, in order to pre-empt unnecessary resort to the imposition of custodial sentences in breach proceedings.

setting common standards and monitoring performance of locally delivered community programmes. It might also be considered appropriate for such an agency to administer, as a registered charity, the fund subsequently generated for the support of victims of crime. However, before any hopes of such progress can be entertained, the existing approach towards community corrections has to be significantly altered.

'HALLIDAY' AND PUNISHMENT IN THE COMMUNITY: CONFUSION AND COMPROMISE

The question inevitably arises concerning the extent of and necessity for the residual powers of courts to impose other restrictions, subsidiary sanctions or prohibitions upon offenders sentenced to community penalties. Here it will be noted that in England and Wales at present there exists a raft of different legislative provisions or 'orders',[29] all now subsumed under the generic community order arrangements set out in the Criminal Justice Act 2003.[30] This legislation is not only extremely complex, but it is also subject to a number of conditional provisions indicating when such orders may or may not be used, or restrictions on the use of them.[31] The Act has much of its origins in the 'Halliday Report' of 2001[32] that specifically addressed sentencing issues in England and Wales. The report, entitled *Making Punishments Work: Report of a Review of the Sentencing Framework for England and Wales* (Home Office, 2001), contained a number of contentious recommendations that were not subsequently adopted by government, or subsumed within the Act. Others were incorporated in a somewhat piecemeal manner, significantly at odds with the original intentions envisaged by those who contributed to its authorship.

The difficulty presented by the arrangements for community orders is that many of the measures subsumed within the 2003 Act are designed to promote measures of social control and prohibition, rather than provide a simplified framework for the operation of community sanctions.[33] To make matters even worse, the Act introduced the concepts of 'custody plus' and 'custody minus'

---

[29] Here it will be recalled that in Britain up to 2003, the courts had access to no fewer than eight different forms of non-custodial order (probation, community service, curfew, combination, attendance centre, supervision, drug treatment and testing, anti-social behaviour), each of which contained its own set of regulatory conditions.

[30] Within the Criminal Justice Act 2003, these were drawn together in a single generic community order with 12 separate subsidiary provisions, conditions and prohibitions.

[31] See sections 147-151 in particular.

[32] The report is widely referred to as the Halliday Report after its director, John Halliday, who submitted it to the government in 2001 (London: Home Office Communications Directorate).

[33] These measures include participation in specified activities, prohibition from certain activities, curfew provisions, exclusion from specified areas, residential restrictions and provisions for the treatment (with consent) of offenders with mental health, drug and alcohol related conditions. Only four of the 12 provisions focus directly on the requirements of community penalties (compulsory work, participation in offending behaviour programmes, community supervision and the use of Attendance Centres for people aged 25 years or less).

sanctions that have served to confuse rather than to clarify an already complicated sentencing situation. These hybrid sentencing options emerged from within the Halliday Report and are similar in many respects to the 'split sentence' provisions that are available in the USA (Tonry, 2003: 9-10). The measures therefore require brief mention here because of their extraordinary incongruence with evidence-based research, their illogical conception and their ill-disguised political motivation at a time when the custodial penal system was approaching its highest level of use in living memory. It has since reached record proportions.

'Custody plus' was used to describe a composite sentence that would combine an initial period in custody,[34] followed by a period on licence supervision in the community. The licence period might, in effect, impose any of the conditions within the concept of the community order described above. The measure was thus effectively designed to replace existing sentences of immediate imprisonment for periods between three and six months in duration, but also provided for a 'short, sharp, shock' component that would appeal to punitively minded sentencing officials who might, otherwise, have considered a non-custodial disposal.

The illogical nature of the 'custody plus' proposal lay in the fact that, by its own admission in the White Paper *Justice for All* published in 2002,[35] the Home Office recognised that available research evidence indicated that short custodial sentences of less than 12 months in duration are not only 'usually ineffective' (p.92), but also 'increase the chances of re-offending' (p.102) (Roberts and Smith, 2003: 182; Home Office, 2002). The main reason why short custodial sentences are relatively ineffective is that these are, in effect, almost entirely incapacitative and do not permit sufficient time for prisoners to attend programmes to address their offending behaviour or prepare constructively for release.

'Custody minus' was, to some extent, a 'mirror image' of 'custody plus', proposing a non-custodial initial disposal (including a selection of licence conditions from the menu available within the community order), but backed by a suspended sentence of (i.e. non-immediate) imprisonment for a specified period in the event that the conditions were breached. Within the Criminal Justice Act 2003, the 'custody minus' provision is termed a suspended sentence order, but the total or maximum sentence period that it embraces is more than slightly deceptive. For in the cases of offenders for whom the courts might consider a custodial sentence of 12 months or less to be appropriate, but deserving greater punishment than a community order, 'custody minus' can impose a suspended sentence of between 28 and 51 weeks duration within a community order of between six months and two years in length.

---

[34] In effect of between two and 13 weeks in duration, but without any provision for remission. The maximum custodial period was thus the equivalent of a former six months sentence of imprisonment, from which the offender would previously have been released without a requirement for mandatory supervision in the community.

[35] Home Office (2002), *Justice for All*, CM 5563, London: HMSO.

In the parallel situation of 'custody plus', the court might impose a prison sentence of between 28 and 51 weeks duration, of which between two and 13 weeks must be served immediately. This would be followed by a period of at least 26 weeks on licence under community order conditions, but with the remaining element of the custodial sentence held in abeyance. Given what is known of the reconviction rate within two years of release from short term custody and the similar rates following non-custodial penalties—both in the order of 60 per cent (Home Office, 2001: 126)—it seems altogether likely that the prison population would soon feel the full impact of these measures. This is the ultimate irony of the situation, since the declared objective of the government within the legislation was to contribute to an overall reduction in the prison population.

The same criticism also attaches to the arrangements for 'intermittent custody' that formed the third element of the sentencing provisions 'below 12 months' within the 2003 Act. This measure envisaged a period of between 14 and 90 days served in custody, but of a duration specified by the court, and followed by the remaining sentence period served on licence within the community. Within this latter period the court could impose conditions available within the community order relating to unpaid work, activities, programmes or prohibited activities, the penalty in default of which is an immediate return to custody. The sentence is, in effect, a variant of the concept of 'weekend imprisonment', allowing for a total period of between 28 and 51 weeks and the number of custodial days between 14 and 90.

The final point to be made about these measures is that they are, on the face of it, based upon the non-custodial concept of the community order and were conceived to enhance public confidence in the penal 'bite' of 'punishment in the community'. Each of the sanctions defies, in different ways, the widely available evidence of criminological research, but all have been promoted by an administration that had committed itself publicly to legislation (in all sectors of public life) compiled on an 'evidence-led' basis of policy-making. Michael Tonry sums up the situation very accurately as follows:

> Part of the backdrop is the government's expressed but schizophrenic commitment to 'evidence-based policy-making'. The schizophrenia can be seen in sometimes startling contrasts between the government's rationalistic claims to engage in evidence-based policy-making and its determination always and on all issues to be seen as tough on crime. Many millions of pounds have been devoted to piloting and evaluating new criminal justice programmes in the name of evidence-based policy. Preoccupation with media imagery, however, has led to support for policies for which there is no significant evidence base—including mandatory minimum sentences, Neighbourhood Watch, ubiquitous CCTV, preventive detention and weakening procedural protection against wrongful convictions—to knee-jerk responses to shocking incidents like the New Year's Eve gun killings in Manchester and to rhetoric like this from the 2002 White Paper: 'The people are sick and tired of a sentencing system that does not make sense' (Home Office, 2002: 86).
>
> (Tonry, 2003: 1-2)

To which 'list' might now reasonably be added the provisions for 'custody plus and minus', 'intermittent custody' and the deceptively opaque motivations for the community order which is more a device for social control than for community justice.

Viewed together, the provisions of the Criminal Justice Act 2003 have the potential for significant impact on the already stretched NOMS and, most particularly, upon the daily workload of the prison and probation services. The short periods of custody envisaged by the 'custody plus' and intermittent custody sentences would inevitably increase the rate of 'throughput' in many prisons and also the workload involved in licence preparation, admission, discharge procedures and the like. Caseloads within the probation service will be similarly affected by the increased requirement for community supervision of offenders, delivery of offending behaviour programmes and monitoring of compliance with conditions imposed by the courts within community orders. It has to be questioned whether the resource and logistical implications of these measures were rigorously researched before decisions were made to bring them into effect.[36]

It is of some interest to note that the 2003 Act makes only incidental reference to the issues of offender reparation and victim–offender mediation which form a central element of the restorative justice approach to the implementation of sanctions both in custody and within the community. Both of these issues are addressed, albeit briefly, in the Coulsfield Inquiry report,[37] but they seem to have evaded the attentions of Halliday and his co-authors to the same extent as they evaded the drafters of the legislation.

The importance of the Coulsfield and Halliday reports lies not so much in the coterminous nature of the period within which both were prepared, but rather in the significant difference of approach that each reveals. The Coulsfield Report, commissioned independently of government, made explicit references to incorporating restorative justice principles within penal policies, greater use of community sanctions, lesser resort to the use of custodial sentences and, in particular, to the use of prison terms of short duration. The Halliday Report, commissioned by government, made no such references and focused upon measures that would inevitably lead to increased use of short custodial sentences. Most bizarre of all, perhaps, remains the fact that the 2003 Act reflected the main recommendations of the latter report: recommendations that flew in the face of the clear evidence that short prison sentences achieve little if anything in the reduction of recidivism and may be instrumental in enhancing it.

The further irony lies in the fact that both the 'custody plus' and 'custody minus' provisions of the 2003 Act were bound, if fully implemented, to lead to large numbers of offenders serving terms of imprisonment in breach of the wide-ranging

---

[36] The relevant provisions have been piloted in some areas but have not yet been brought into force and are possibly now permanently on hold. This may be at least in part due to their somewhat chaotic and ill-thought out nature.

[37] In Chapter 5 pp. 42-4.

conditions that could be imposed within the generic community order. With a prison population approaching all time record levels, evidence-based statistics on recidivism and recorded levels of breach proceedings indicating high rates of failure, the provisions resemble more a recipe for political suicide than a serious attempt to enhance the cause of justice.

All things considered, the prospects for designing community sanctions based upon restorative justice principles appear to be extremely bleak in the present circumstances and particularly so, given the general tenor of the Criminal Justice Act 2003. For although this Act will undoubtedly have a community impact, possibly in enabling even more offenders to experience custody, it is doubtful if it will contribute much of social value beyond increasing levels of social control. Though this might be considered by some to constitute a virtue, it is certainly a far cry from what restorative justice seeks to propose. The question that remains to be answered is whether all of this could, realistically, have been done differently and altogether more constructively from the viewpoints of offenders, victims and society. In the penultimate section of this chapter, we shall examine briefly an entirely different approach to contemporary justice administration based on the Finnish model of justice and its underpinning values.

THE FINNISH PERSPECTIVE AND ITS IMPLICATIONS

It will be recalled from the earlier part of this chapter that in the 1950s Finland made a deliberate decision to reduce its high prison population, which was reflected in a rate of 187 per 100,000 of the population, and that progressively this rate was reduced to its present level of 59 per 100,000—the same as that of Denmark and slightly lower than that of Sweden at 63 per 100,000.[38] The Finnish approach to sentencing offenders is based upon uniformity and predictability of outcome using specific statutory sentencing principles based on proportionality, harm and culpability within each offence. The sentencing principles set out specific aggravating and mitigating factors, the latter being expressed in a more flexible and open manner than the former, to allow the courts greater discretion in *reducing* the severity of punishment[39] (Joutsen, Rahti and Pölönen, 2001: 30).

Courts in Finland may waive punishment entirely in specific circumstances,[40] but notably if punishment is deemed to be unreasonable or pointless, considering the (extent of) victim–offender reconciliation, or the action taken by the offender to prevent or eliminate (mitigate) the effects of the offence, or to further its being cleared up. In addition, offenders involved in narcotics offences may have

---

[38] The rate of imprisonment in England and Wales was 143 per 100,000 of the population in 2006, (International Centre for Prison Studies (2006), *World Prison Populations*, London: King's College, pp. 1-2).
[39] Chapter 6 of the Criminal Code adopted in 1976 (466).
[40] Set out in Chapter 3, Section 5 of the Criminal Code, as amended by the Acts of 23 March 1990 (1990/302) and 12 December 1996 (1996/1060).

punishment waived if they agree to treatment approved by the Ministry of Social Affairs and Health.[41]

Only four general forms of punishment are available in Finland: these comprise the 'summary penal fee',[42] a fine,[43] community service and imprisonment. Community service is defined as 'a punishment in place of unconditional imprisonment' and consists in at least 20 and a maximum of 200 hours of unpaid work under supervision. It can also be imposed in the place of sentences of up to eight months imprisonment. It requires the consent of the offender and the assumption that he or she will successfully complete the sentence. Community service is supervised by the Probation and After-Care Administration which can take action in serious cases of breach to inform the Public Prosecutor, who in turn may request the court to convert the sentence to one of imprisonment.

Imprisonment is generally imposed for periods of between 14 days and a maximum of 12 years, or, in the case of multiple offences, 15 years. Murder is punishable by life imprisonment. Sentences of up to two years can be imposed 'conditionally' (suspended) and a subsidiary fine can be attached to conditional imprisonment. Any new imprisonable offence committed during the period of a conditional sentence may result in the court ordering the suspended sentence to be enforced in full or in part. In practice, more than half of all sentences of imprisonment are suspended.

Victims of crime occupy a prominent place within the Finnish criminal justice system and the Finnish Victim Compensation Act (1973/935) provides a right to compensation on a comprehensive basis that includes personal injury, medical expenses, disability, loss of earnings, damage to property or articles and the like. In addition, the employer of an injured person has the right to compensation for any wages paid to the victim while disabled.

Victim–offender reconciliation programmes exist throughout Finland, managed mainly by municipal social welfare offices. These programmes have a recognised legal status through an amendment to the District Prosecutor Act 1196/1059 because reconciliation between the parties may influence the decision of the prosecutor to waive further measures, or the decision of the court to waive punishment. While victims of crime may bring private prosecutions where a prosecutor decides against

---

[41] Chapter 50, Section 7 of the Criminal Code.

[42] Imposed for minor traffic offences, littering, etc. and which cannot be converted to imprisonment in default.

[43] Finland adopted the 'day fine' in 1921 as the first Nordic country to do so. Day fines can extend from one to 120 days, the size being calculated on the monthly income and assets of the offender, but normally one sixtieth of monthly income less taxes and fees defined by decree and a fixed deduction for personal expenditure. In cases of persistent default, the fine can be converted to imprisonment at the rate of one day in custody for each two day fine. The minimum period of imprisonment in default is four and the maximum 90 days. A 'unit fine' system was introduced in Britain similarly in England and Wales under the Criminal Justice Act 1991 but abandoned in 1993 following a public outcry.

prosecution, they do not have the right to address the court in matters relating to sentencing.[44]

This brief cameo of the Finnish approach to penal administration reveals very evidently the extent to which the processes and delivery of justice can be simplified and made understandable if the fundamental philosophy of corrections is clearly thought through. This same philosophy in Finland is morally underpinned by a humanistic desire to punish only when this is strictly necessary and to the *minimum* extent consistent with the seriousness of offences. Above all else, perhaps, it exemplifies the Nordic preference for parsimony rather than punitivism and a sensitivity towards all concerned in the commission of offences. This, in particular, distinguishes it from the traditional Anglo-Saxon preoccupation with the inevitability of punishment.

For the purposes of this book, there is much to be learned from Finland and from a number of other countries that follow broadly similar penal philosophies. Penal codes do *not* have to be complicated to be effective; high rates of imprisonment *are* avoidable; the extent of punishment *can* be moderated to a minimum necessary extent; victims *can* have a central place in justice processes; and justice *can* be designed to provide restorative outcomes without the appearance of being 'soft on crime'. Of equal importance, Finnish justice demonstrates a largely apolitical quality which is about social regulation and cohesion rather than social control and its penal system, unlike some others, is evidently not used as a political shuttlecock for the expression of partisan agendas designed to placate misconceived perceptions about crime and its extent in a modern society. There is no particular reason to suppose that Finnish society is any more or less law-abiding than its European neighbours, but it manages its justice system in a simpler, more economical and more understandable manner than most countries around it.

COMMUNITY CORRECTIONS IN A *CUL-DE-SAC*

The criminal justice systems of all the nations that over-use imprisonment are in or approaching a situation from which, ultimately, retreat is the only practical remedy. Even the most crude of economic analyses indicates that excessive use of custody represents a high cost–low reward strategy for crime control. Reliable research evidence also indicates that resort to short prison sentences does little to reduce crime and probably increases recidivism. In short, it represents a strategy of despair.

While it is evidently true that every society needs to be protected from criminals who are truly dangerous, violent and predatory, rigorous research indicates that the extent of dangerousness in most penal populations is routinely over-estimated

---

[44] The source of the information used to provide this outline description of the Finnish legal system is a government sponsored digest, prepared for the European Institute for Crime Prevention and Control, entitled *Criminal Justice Systems in Europe and North America—Finland*, compiled by M. Joutsen, R. Rahti and P. Pölönen in 2001. It can be viewed at http://www.vn.fi/om/heuni and is also available from the Academic Bookstore, Helsinki.

(Bottoms, 1977; Brody and Tarling, 1980; Monahan, 1981; Bottoms and Brownsword, 1983; Cornwell, 1989). Also, it is well known that many inmates who display grossly violent behaviour within prisons do not necessarily behave in the same way within the wider community (Shah, 1981; Cornwell, 1989: 158-9). The majority of non-dangerous offenders do not merit the high cost of long-term incarceration to mark the gravity of their anti-social behaviour and the longer they are kept in prisons, the less likely they are to become responsible citizens.

Increasing numbers of academics and practitioners within criminal justice consider the principles upon which restorative justice practices are based to offer a better, more humane and more inclusive quality of justice than is widely available at present. Correctional strategies informed by the concepts of reconciliation, reparation and restoration create genuine opportunities for offenders, victims and communities; those insistent primarily on retribution, incapacitation and exclusion create only bitterness, disillusionment and despair.

Restorative justice recognises the requirement for just retribution, but does not contemplate excessive punishment for its own sake, or vicariously for the satisfaction of other purposes.[45] Because it perceives custodial punishment as a strategy of last resort, restorative justice works best *within* the communities where offences are committed and where offenders, victims and other citizens ultimately have to co-exist. Above all else, however, restorative penology makes no concession to 'soft options' for offenders: rather, it makes them face reality, take responsibility for their behaviour and do something that is evident to make good the harm done.

Community-based corrections are a visible manifestation of justice in action and in this important sense, justice can be creative rather than destructive. Well-planned and carefully supervised community service projects, of immediate social and amenity value to local areas and their inhabitants, provide the ideal launch pad for community justice. It is, however, essential to return to a situation in which community service is identified as an *alternative* sanction to imprisonment, rather than as a conditional release from custody. This does not imply that community service should not be capable of being converted to imprisonment in serious cases of default or non-compliance: rather, that there is an expectation of compliance since the offender has consented[46] at trial to abide by the conditions of the sanction.

As we have seen in previous chapters, the concept of making reparation is the pivotal requirement of restorative corrections. If it becomes possible for victims, offenders and other legitimately interested parties to become reconciled at any stage in the sanction process, then this is not only desirable, but it also deserves consideration in the sentencing and supervisory processes of justice. It cannot, however, be relied upon and its absence should not, therefore, be seen as an aggravating factor in sentencing. To this end, the fact that offenders make reparation to victims of crime in a wider or more general sense becomes the dominant consideration.

---

[45] Such, for example, as general deterrence (Cornwell, 2006 op. cit., pp. 58-60).
[46] Under English law, consent is not now a pre-requisite except in a limited number of situations.

There seems to be no good reason why a community service sanction should not be accompanied by a specific form of licence to carry out reparative work for a specified period and include a requirement to attend approved courses to address particular forms of offending behaviour delivered locally. Alternatively, some offenders might benefit more from a requirement to attend classes of instruction in basic literacy and numeracy, social survival and communication skills, substance abuse or parenting, in order to repair deficits that have contributed to offending.

As to other forms of licence condition that impose measures of social control and surveillance, it seems altogether more constructive to reduce these to the absolute minimum *consistent with encouraging sanction compliance*. The plethora of prohibitions involving residential conditions, curfews, exclusion from specific areas and the like, are broadly inconsistent with expectations of law-abiding conduct and also create a wider potential for failure and licence revocation. It seems wiser to proceed from the premise that offenders sentenced to community sanctions remain responsible citizens which, in any event, they will be required to be at the expiry of the sanction period. Setting them up to fail by imposing unnecessary or inappropriate prohibitions creates an atmosphere of mistrust and discrimination that can, ultimately, be counter-productive.

Lastly, it is clear that the correctional *cul-de-sac* into which many governments have manoeuvred themselves at the present time could have been avoided and a way now has to be found to navigate out of it. Overuse of custodial punishment and the creation of other sanctions that heavily rely on incarceration as a component to satisfy misconceptions about crime and punitive agendas, have become the confining aspects of the situation. These have proved to be politically dominated prescriptions with a 'bound to fail' label attached to them. There are other, better, less expensive, more humane and much simpler ways of approaching the problem of crime control. Substitution of a restorative for an essentially retributive ethos within penology might go a long way towards putting *correction* back into criminal justice. The Finnish model noted earlier is a good starting point for such an endeavour: it economically restricts itself to few but entirely purposeful sanctions, is victim-conscious, reparative and ultimately restorative.

CAN RESTORATIVE JUSTICE RESOLVE THIS *IMPASSE*?

If the answer to the question were an unequivocal affirmative, this book would have been much simpler to write. There is no doubt that the emergence of restorative justice over the past decade has opened the door to a new and more progressive form of justice, particularly where the law allows for disputes between offenders and victims to be resolved to mutual satisfaction without recourse to the full weight of legal processes. In relation to juvenile and youth offending in particular, there has developed a consistent body of restorative justice practices in many countries that increasingly permits mediated settlement of inter-personal conflicts and victim reparation without the absolute necessity for full, formal court intervention prior to adjournment or sentencing (McElrea, 2005: 2-3).[47]

Victim–offender mediation, of either a direct (face to face) or indirect (third party facilitated) nature,[48] is gaining increasing credibility as a means of resolving many less serious inter-personal incidents to the satisfaction of all the parties directly affected, though in most instances in which a criminal offence has been committed, the courts require to be satisfied as to the nature of the outcome. A number of broadly similar studies undertaken in the USA, Canada, Australia and New Zealand have revealed high rates of victim, offender and other participant satisfaction with such conflict resolution strategies and the outcomes (Umbreit *et al.*, 2006: 4).

Family or community group conferencing, which includes a wider range of participants including community members in resolving conflict situations, reveals similarly high levels of satisfaction with both the process and its outcomes (Latimer, *et al.*, 2001; Hayes and Daly, 2004; cited in Umbreit *et al.*, 2006: 4-5). These are encouraging beginnings, pointing to a widespread willingness on the part of offenders, victims, families and communities to engage in restorative processes to resolve the harm occasioned by offending behaviour. A more extensive resort to restorative practices, where these are accepted by all concerned, has considerable potential to reduce reliance upon costly court procedures, increase victim vindication and reduce sentencing severity in the future.

All of this stated, however, it remains necessary to be realistic and practical in the prevailing climate of penology worldwide. Restorative justice has proposed a realistic agenda for change within many aspects of contemporary criminal justice and much of this change is undoubtedly for the better, rather than merely for the sake of change. There is no doubt whatsoever that far fewer offenders need to be imprisoned and that many more would be adequately punished within the community. Much more could and should be done for victims of crime and much of this could and should be done by offenders in the form of reparation. In a more forgiving, less media-driven world, attitudes towards other than the most serious of offenders would be more tolerant and greater political emphasis would be placed on being as tough on the causes of crime as on crime itself.

Entrenched attitudes, both social and political, are difficult to change, especially where it might appear that change, however necessary, involves taking risks with people who have given evidence of their unreliability or their indifference towards law-abiding behaviour. Restorative justice extends the potential for tolerance and restoration towards those who are genuinely willing to 'put things right' and accept responsibility for the wrong they have done. It does not extend the same tolerance

---

[47] In some instances in, for example, New Zealand, a court may take account of the nature of a mediated settlement and the reparation offered by a defendant and adjourn (or defer) sentencing for sufficient time to allow the plan to be put into effect (McElrea, 2005: 3).

[48] Frequently referred to as 'shuttle' mediation—see Umbreit *et al.* (2006: 1).

towards the unrepentant, or those who show no concern for those harmed by their actions or the effect of these actions upon their communities.

Many offenders fall within the former category, yet have no genuine opportunity to make reparation because our over-crowded and over-stretched criminal justice systems make no space for them to do so either in custody or in the community. A significant number of those in prisons present low levels of social risk and the cost of imprisonment is wasted on them. Few, very few indeed, are improved by the experience of imprisonment and the life chances of the majority are diminished significantly by it. The social cost of unnecessary imprisonment extends far beyond that incurred by maintaining people in custody.

Community corrections can be expanded given the political will to do so, and expanded to the direct benefit of communities, offenders and victims. The Finnish experience suggests that, given a similar political will, reliance on custodial corrections can be reduced dramatically, and arguably with greater social benefit and less risk than might be imagined. These are evidence-based facts, but ones that politicians, anxious to retain power and electoral credibility, choose to ignore. Restorative justice provides at least a means of engaging with these problems and its momentum and credibility increases with every genuine opportunity it gets to demonstrate its effectiveness.

There are, at the present time, encouraging signs that the need for significant change has been acknowledged by enlightened members of the judiciary in Britain and elsewhere in the world. The Lord Chief Justice of England and Wales (Lord Phillips of Worth Matravers) in a lecture delivered in Oxford,[49] criticised certain sections of the British media for inciting the public to

> exact vengeance from offenders not dissimilar to the emotions of those who thronged to public executions in the 18th century ... Media pressure such as this cannot fail to have an effect on the public, on politicians and on judges.

Importantly, for the purpose of this analysis, Lord Phillips further remarked:

> Some of the media, and some sentencers, are sceptical as to whether community sentences provide adequate punishment and whether they are any more effective in preventing re-offending than imprisonment. They are not a panacea, but I believe they offer a better chance of preventing re-offending than short spells of imprisonment and can leave room in the prisons for effective intervention for those whose crimes require detention. (*The Times*, 11 October 2006: 11)

Such public statements by influential members of the criminal justice community are genuinely helpful to, and encouraging for, the development of restorative practices and increased use of community sanctions. Wider use of non-custodial penalties, providing that these are of a demanding, socially useful and constructive nature, benefit victims of crime and communities, while decreasing

---

[49] On 10 October 2006, reported in *The Times*, 11 October 2006, p. 11 under the headline: 'Law Chief Attacks Longer Sentences', by Frances Gibb and Richard Ford.

pressure on over-stretched and largely ineffective prison systems. Viewed in such a manner, there are potentially more winners than losers in such circumstances, even though some offenders will inevitably re-offend when in the community while they might otherwise have been in custody.

The potential for expanding community justice has never been greater or more urgently needed than it is at the present time. To achieve this potential does, however, require a shift in attitudes predominantly within the media and politics and a greater public tolerance towards offenders who are willing to take responsibility for their criminal acts and make reparation to both victims of crime and the communities within which these acts are committed.

CHAPTER 7

Doing Justice Better: Making Restorative Justice Work

Any book that seeks to promote the adoption of restorative justice principles within the contemporary setting of most democracies of the world will, almost inevitably, attract a measure of criticism from politicians, policy-makers and some academics and criminal justice system practitioners. The main source of this criticism is usually that restorative justice may sound all right in theory, but it is largely untried in practice—particularly in relation to custodial corrections and serious adult offending. Even worse, perhaps, restorative justice requires an entirely new and different approach to the administration of criminal justice and this approach does not fit comfortably alongside existing popular demands for punitive sanctions. Those who exercise power and influence in the formulation of penal policies, set these into legislation and give them operational effect have a political constituency to satisfy if they are to retain this authority: it is, therefore, hardly surprising if they are risk-averse when confronted by the need to do justice rather differently.

SHIFTING THE CRIMINAL JUSTICE PARADIGM

The present vogue in political circles in many democracies is to demand 'evidence-based' strategies from policy advisers, the 'evidence' being extracted, in the main, from research commissioned to produce outcomes that are at least consistent with prevailing ideologies (Tonry, 2003: 1, 20; Garland, 2002: 133). Put somewhat more bluntly, most governments will not normally fund research that will eventually tell them what they do not wish to hear. Insofar as new approaches to criminal justice administration are concerned, this 'chicken and egg' situation becomes a comfortable option since what cannot, or will not, be tried and evaluated can 'reasonably' be disregarded as having no evidence to sustain its claims.

In the modern world, the intrusiveness of the mass media within the consciousness of the general public—and of politicians—is undeniably immense. Crime creates victims who can be used both to 'demonise' criminals and, at the same time, express the popular moral outrage at the prevalence of crime. As Garland points out:

> The crime victim is no longer represented as an unfortunate citizen who has been on the receiving end of a criminal harm. His or her concerns are no longer subsumed within the 'public interest' that guides prosecution and penal decisions. Instead, the crime victim is now, in a certain sense, a *representative character* whose experience is

assumed to be common and collective, rather than individual and atypical. His (or more often her) suffering is represented in the immediate and personalised idiom of the mass media and speaks directly to the fears and angers of the viewing public, producing effects of identification and reinforcement that are then turned to political and commercial use. (Garland, 2002: 144) [Emphasis in original]

Politicians who disregard, or fail to respond to expressions of popular anger and concern in relation to crime do not enjoy longevity in powerful positions. As the experience of the last decade has shown very clearly in Britain, the USA and in many other countries, it has suited the purposes of politicians admirably to pursue 'tough on crime' agendas, since our contemporary social cultures propel the discourse of crime in that particular direction. It would, however, be an entirely different world if moral outrage were to be expressed in relation to the extent to which many governments resort to punitive segregation in pursuit of crime control.

Certainly in the majority of European countries during recent years, a rational and unemotional debate in relation to crime should have provoked just such a reaction. As we have seen in the previous chapter, crime rates in most categories have fallen significantly while rates of imprisonment have followed an upward path. There is also clear evidence, at least in Britain, that increased severity of sentencing, accompanied by restrictions on the use of premature release, have contributed in no small measure to the dramatic escalation in the penal population. What, then, is the logic that sustains such practices? If anything, evidence-led research should have prompted an entirely different response from governments anxious to reduce the costs of maintaining needlessly excessive numbers in custody.

Neither are excessive prison populations incapable of reduction given the political will to do so. The Finnish example discussed in *Chapter 6* is but one example (Lappi-Seppälä, 2001). Similar initiatives have been pursued in Germany in the 1960s and 1970s[1] (Wiegend, 2001) and in North Carolina in the USA during the closing two decades of the previous century (Wright 2002; Tonry, 2003: 212-3). In addition, other countries such as the Netherlands, Denmark and Norway have all imposed limitations on the admission of offenders to prisons operating at (or above) full capacity (Tak, 2001; Kyvsgaard, 2001; Larsson, 2001). The Netherlands, in particular, specified an upper limit of 95 per cent of operational capacity as the 'cap' figure, on the basis that a predictable element of the total capacity was always unavailable or under repair.

The virtual abandonment of any substantive penal policies promoting the rehabilitation of offenders in custody almost worldwide has resulted in a widespread return to fundamentally retributive punishment. In addition,

---

[1] During the 1960s and 1970s, the (then West) German government decided that short prison sentences (of six months or less) did more harm than good and deliberately reduced the number of offenders so sentenced from 130,000 per annum to a figure below 30,000 within a year. This level has remained more or less constant ever since. The reduction was achieved by increased use of fines and diversion from prosecution.

increased use of short-term custodial sentencing where non-custodial measures might otherwise have been considered sufficiently robust and effective—particularly in England and Wales—has exacerbated the difficulties. The problem is that national governments will sustain (and maintain) penal populations of the size that secure the support of electorates as affordable and appropriate. This is the perverse logic of contemporary corrections, particularly since it is clear that media influences have induced voters into believing that crime is more prevalent than it actually is on the basis of recorded statistics. Some governments, the British being the most notable, have done little to correct this misconception, since it fits neatly with the need to be seen to be 'tough on crime and tough the causes of crime'.[2]

It is against this somewhat unpromising backdrop that proponents of restorative justice are obliged to make its claim to deliver better justice for modern societies. The most appropriate starting point for such a task is to identify the ways in which restorative justice perceives the processes of justice differently from the traditional approach to criminal justice—particularly as it is presently implemented within many contemporary democracies. This discourse has been presented in some depth in *Chapter 1* and only the more salient aspects of that discussion need detain us here. It is also important to emphasise that the entire purpose of effective criminal justice is to reduce crime within societies, rather than merely to contain it and punish it when it occurs. Moreover, when we speak of crime reduction, perhaps we should not consider only the phenomenon of crime itself, but also and of equal importance, reduction of the *effects* of crime within societies.

There is, after all, an important difference between strategies designed to *control* crime and those conceived to *reduce* it and its dysfunctional outcomes. As Garland argues, most of the advanced democracies live in a new era in which populations have become accustomed to high crime rates which are a focus for media attention and in which concerns about victims, public risk and public safety dominate public policy deliberations (Garland, 2002: 163-4). The now typical state response is to attempt to 'manage' the risk more than to remove its causes and change the behaviour of offenders. Risk management strategies are not only heavily dependent upon measures of social incapacitation, but also upon the development of technological 'solutions' to contain risk by reducing the opportunities to offend.[3] Public expressions of fear and vulnerability, accentuated and amplified by media attention, drive the political discourse of sanctions in an ever more punitive direction.

---

[2] A political slogan that first appeared prominently when the present British Prime Minister Tony Blair was Shadow Home Secretary and addressed the Labour Party Conference in October 1993. Originally published in an article: T. Blair (1993), 'Why Crime is a Socialist Issue', *New Statesman and Society*, 29 January, pp. 27-8.

[3] Most notably by widespread use of CCTV, domestic security systems, electronic monitoring ('tagging'), computerised recognition and access control systems, DNA applications and the like.

Strategies to reduce crime are of an altogether different nature. Their primary focus is on offenders and the victims of crime who bear the immediate brunt of criminal behaviour. Crime reduction results more from the changed patterns of offender behaviour than from reduction of opportunity through technological and incapacitative risk management, though the latter may play an important part in reinforcing law-abiding conduct by increasing the risks of detection.[4] A restorative approach to justice is devoted more towards crime reduction than crime control, primarily because it is humanistic rather than mechanistic in its underlying motivations.

RESTORATIVE JUSTICE POSES DIFFERENT QUESTIONS

It will have become evident within each of the chapters of this book that the concept of restorative justice re-draws the map of criminal justice to a considerable extent by asking a range of different questions about the nature of justice and its desired outcomes. Its central focus is placed on the needs of victims and on offender responsibility for repairing harm, rather than offenders 'getting what they deserve'. Crime itself is perceived as a violation of people and relationships much more than of the law and the state as traditional criminal justice supposes. These violations, restorative justice insists, create obligations rather than guilt and justice involves offenders, victims and their communities in an effort to put things right (Zehr, 2002a: 21).

Where offenders are prepared to engage with the obligation to 'put wrongs right', restorative justice is able to exercise parsimony in the extent of necessary retributive punishment, in the interests of restoring the offender to full community status. The act of making reparation is thus a powerful mitigating factor in limiting punishment in an economical manner, but it does not, in any sense, negate the need for sanctions. In other words, where offenders are prepared to acknowledge the harm caused to victims, accept responsibility for this and make reparation for it, restorative justice is able and willing to ask how *little* punishment is strictly necessary, rather than how much is desirable in requital of retribution and desert.

Traditional criminal justice clings to the dubious belief that substantial punishment deters both offenders and would-be offenders in an exemplary manner. Restorative justice does not engage in this substantialism because it is incapable of proof in any exact sense and represents more an appeal to moral sentiment than to reason.[5] In any event, to endorse such notions implies a

---

4 While it would be disingenuous to suggest that technological innovations do not contribute to crime reduction, the central issue here is that recidivism is reduced much more by reducing the causes and motivations for offending, than from increasing measures of social control or the widespread use of custodial punishment.

5 For an expanded version of this debate see Cornwell (2006) op. cit., pp. 53-65.

necessary move away from parsimony for reasons that are not amenable to adequate justification.

Contemporary criminal justice is, in its approach to the punishment of offenders, largely unconcerned about sustaining any fundamental belief in a rehabilitative ethic, mainly because it displays an ambivalent attitude towards the 'nothing works' and 'some things work sometimes' debates that have plagued criminology since the mid-1970s.[6] This is, perhaps, in some respects fortunate, since a full-blown return to belief in rehabilitation (whatever that means in a custodial setting) would most probably herald a renewed enthusiasm for sentencing indeterminacy.

Perhaps the most important of all its claims to deliver better justice lies in the fact that restorative justice potentially frees the apparatus of state from the *inevitability* of inflicting punishment on offenders. This is because it does not insist primarily upon retribution and deterrence and is thus not constrained to punish in satisfaction of these justifications merely to retain its own credibility. Restorative justice would prefer to see a measure of reconciliation between offenders and victims (where this is possible) and reparation made, rather than the inevitable imposition of punishment for its own sake.

In the final analysis, restorative justice asks not what laws have been broken, but who has suffered from crime and to what extent? State-centred justice demands to know who committed crime and the extent to which punishment must be imposed because it is deserved: restorative justice seeks to know what the needs of victims are and to whom the obligation to meet these needs falls. Offenders within restorative justice are not allowed the luxury of avoiding responsibility for their actions and ignoring the plight of those whom they harm: the traditional concept of criminal justice makes no such demands, neither does it apparently feel that to do so is necessary or appropriate. Restorative justice perceives reparation as infinitely more important than retribution, since reparation can heal all parties to offences and retribution heals none of them.

THINKING DIFFERENTLY ABOUT CRIME AND PUNISHMENT

One of the principal difficulties posed by the ever more widespread interest in restorative justice is that it does not merely invite consideration of an entirely different penology: it actually compels it. It is perhaps this particular aspect of the initiative that is intellectually and practically threatening to politicians, policy-makers and some criminal justice professionals whose natural instincts

---

[6] This situation emerged with Robert Martinson's (1974) assertion that was widely misinterpreted to imply that no rehabilitative programmes had a measurable effect on recidivism (see: Martinson, 1974; Lipton *et al.* 1975; Brody, 1976; and for a concise commentary Cavadino and Dignan, 1997a: 36-7). Subsequent studies have reversed this assertion to some extent (Gendreau and Ross, 1987; McGuire, 1995; Underdown, 1995).

favour preservation of the *status quo*—with all its manifest shortcomings—over the evident necessity for reform. The discussion in *Chapter 2* has identified the implications of the need for an entirely different penology and, in particular, for a new formulation of what was traditionally described as the concept of rehabilitation.

The main obstacle to such a re-formulation lies not just in the tarnished image of rehabilitation and its virtual demise from contemporary criminological discourse, but rather in the practical difficulties that attend the very real need for offenders to be reintegrated into society and their communities having fulfilled the obligations that crime and sanctions impose upon them. The prevailing practice, in Britain in particular, of selecting certain forms of offending for exemplary and extended punishment exacerbates this situation to a significant extent. For while all offenders have the notional right to full social restoration having 'paid the price' of their offending, it is clearly evident that this right is deliberately curtailed in the cases of sexual and some violent offenders.[7]

The simple fact is that specific measures taken against certain groups of offenders have nothing whatsoever to do with punishment philosophy, culpability, desert or even commensurability, but are unashamedly designed for public protection and risk-management purposes as political responses to media sensationalism of a 'public fear of crime' (Garland, 2002: 12; Matravers and Hughes, 2003: 51). Such is, at the least, a perverse penology and one that ultimately subverts justice in a manner almost as barbaric as the biblical '*jus talionis*'.[8] Importantly, for our purposes here, however, these are practices that restorative justice would be unable to contemplate and this makes its prescriptions all the more difficult for politicians and policy-makers to accept.

There are, as we have seen in *Chapter 2*, other and compelling reasons why a new penology would be necessary to accommodate the operation of restorative justice. Two of these reasons have a direct bearing on the administration of criminal justice within modern democracies in a general sense, but also upon the operation of prisons and community penalties in particular. The first concerns the concept of 'negative sanctions' and the second relates to the issue of 'bifurcation'. Since both of these concepts recur in the discussion within other chapters of this work, it is appropriate to deal with their implications at this juncture.

The concept of 'negative sanctions' has particular resonance for the aims of restorative justice because it implies that once an offender is sentenced—and in particular to imprisonment—there is no particular requirement for that person to do anything constructive to repair the harm done by his or her offences. In other

---

[7] See also the discussion in *Chapter 7* in relation to the adoption by the New Labour government of Prime Minister Tony Blair of measures extending the 'prison works' agenda pursued by the previous Tory administration of Sir John Major and his Home Secretary Michael Howard.

[8] The punitive doctrine of 'an eye for an eye and a tooth for a tooth', *The Bible*, Exodus, Chapter 21, verse xxiv.

words, the prevailing mode of custody allows, and to some extent also encourages offenders to merely 'survive' the sentence period with reasonable behaviour and without, necessarily, either addressing offending behaviour or making any form of reparation. Though there are offending behaviour programmes available in British prisons,[9] and of a mandatory nature for sexual offenders, these are of a generic format and do not, necessarily, explore the individual pathology of offenders to any significant extent.[10] As has been made clear in *Chapter 6*, prisons designed and operated to deliver reparative and restorative outcomes would approach this situation entirely differently.

'Bifurcation' is a term within contemporary criminology that has come to have different meanings in different contexts. As originally proposed by Bottoms, the concept relates to the deliberate strategy of dealing more severely (than desert alone would allow) with what might be termed 'really serious offenders' and more leniently with 'ordinary' offenders (Bottoms, 1977: 88). This 'twin track' approach to sentencing was widely questioned in the 1970s and 1980s, particularly because it also extended into the parole system to the detriment of those offenders adjudged to have committed 'grave crimes'. On the other hand, relatively lesser offenders, many with extensive records of minor property crime, attracted parole because of the increasing pressure on prison places.[11]

Similar instances of 'bifurcation' arose again in the mid-1980s, though with a somewhat different implication for those serving sentences of five years or more for violence or drug trafficking in England and Wales (Cavadino and Dignan, 1997a: 186-7).[12] The main point of contention in relation to issues of 'bifurcation' is, however, that for whatever reason and justification, these provisions result in some extent of discriminatory practice in relation to certain groups or classes of offender as opposed to others. This sort of behaviour restorative justice would, in principle, naturally abjure.

The discussion within *Chapter 6* that deals with making prisons reparative and restorative therefore presents us with a considerable dilemma. For however

---

[9] The main ones comprising Anger Management and the Sex Offender Treatment Programme (SOTP), though these are not universal and many short- term prisoners do not have the opportunity to participate in them.

[10] See the more detailed discussion in *Chapter 6* and, in relation to reparation, in *Chapters 4* and *5*.

[11] Bottoms (1977: 88-9). This policy was devised by the (then) Home Secretary Roy Jenkins in conjunction with the Parole Board and promulgated in a set of guidelines for release on parole licence. See: Home Office (1976), *Review of Criminal Justice Policy*, London: HMSO, Appendix 4, paras.19-24 and 29-30). In fact, these lesser offenders were to be granted parole unless there were substantial reasons for withholding it.

[12] In July 1984, Home Secretary Leon Brittan lowered the eligibility threshold for parole from 12 to six months and introduced a fast track review process which obliged Local Review Committees to operate on a presumption in favour of parole for short-term prisoners. At the same time, however, he introduced the policy of 20-year minimum sentences for certain forms of murder, and offenders serving sentences of five years or more for violence or drug-trafficking were told that they would be unlikely to obtain parole until a short time before their normal date of release.

much we may disapprove, both morally and intellectually, of bifurcation in practice, we are inevitably confronted with the operational issue of managing prison regimes to secure reparative and restorative outcomes. This means that a way has to be found around the problem of dealing with those offenders who are willing to make reparation and those who are reluctant or who decline to do so, within the same prison estate and at the same time.[13] This is far from an insurmountable problem, though it does raise the issue of differential conditions, external work opportunities and release arrangements for prisoners who opt to participate in reparative work. The issue is discussed somewhat further later in this chapter.

The need for a new penology suggested in *Chapter 2* has manifestly far-reaching implications for the delivery of justice in many countries of the world today. Restorative justice proposes an altogether different approach to what has hitherto been understood to represent the rehabilitation of offenders. To a significant extent within a restorative justice concept, offenders effectively 'rehabilitate' themselves through their commitment to examine their conduct, take responsibility for it and make reparation to victims of crime. This is, however, only one element of the new penology that becomes necessary in a restorative concept of corrections. The same penology has to accommodate demands legitimately placed on offenders, the victims of crime and communities—however these are defined.

PROCEDURAL CONSIDERATIONS

In *Chapter 2* and in former work,[14] it has been suggested that extensive change would be necessary to the way in which legal—and particularly court—systems operate if restorative justice principles were to be followed. Indeed, what is proposed represents a more 'democratic' form of justice process that allows for a measure of conferencing, victim–offender mediation and pre-trial diversion such as that found in New Zealand (McElrea, 2006; Morris and Maxwell, 2003), Australia (Sherman *et al.* 2000; Nugent *et al.* 2001), Canada (Bonta *et al.* 1998; Cormier, 2006) and parts of the USA (Umbreit, 2001; Umbreit *et al.* 1994).

Restorative justice identifies victims, offenders and communities as the principal stakeholders in criminal justice, and in this sense is at odds with the traditional model that perceives the state and the law as primarily violated by crime (Zehr, 2002a: 23; Zehr and Mika, 1998: 47-55). Such a view, it has been suggested in *Chapter 3*, may require some modification, since the state clearly has a responsibility within the restorative justice process to make available the means

---

[13] Here see, in particular, the discussion in *Chapter 5*, pp. 122-5. From this particular point of view, it would be infinitely preferable for entire prison establishments to be devoted to reparative and restorative regimes, rather than attempt to operate two forms of regime within a single prison.

[14] This reference is to the accounts of McElrea, Blad and Cormier in Cornwell (2006), op. cit., at *Chapters 9, 10* and *11* respectively.

by which reparation can be made by offenders. In a secondary sense also, the state has a role to play in enacting a legislative framework within which all the sectors of the criminal justice system should operate in a restorative setting.

Such a legislative framework implies provisions to allow, before and at the trial stage, offenders who accept guilt and opt to make reparation to be dealt with differently from those who decline to do so. This, effectively, suggests a further measure of 'bifurcation' alluded to earlier, but which would, operationally, enable courts greater discretion to deal more leniently with those offenders who demonstrate remorse and a willingness to compensate victims. In dealing with these offenders 'differently', it is, of course, implicit within the framework of restorative justice that this means punishing economically, or to the minimum extent strictly necessary to mark the seriousness of offences.

Economical punishment is not exactly the prevailing fashion in relation to certain classes of offenders—particularly in Britain—as has been indicated in *Chapter 6*.[15] This stated, however, one of the primary purposes of restorative justice is to create a judicial and penal environment in which the inevitability of punishment is significantly reduced and the extent of punishment is strictly limited to the necessary minimum from a retributive viewpoint. If this can be achieved, then it becomes possible to envisage an era in which retrospective punishment becomes of lesser importance than the imposition of sanctions with a positive prospective purpose.

Dealing with intransigent and unrepentant offenders is a commonplace aspect of the life of criminal courts and of prisons and, human nature being what it is, this is unlikely to change in any dramatic sense within the foreseeable future. There is, however, an extensive literature that suggests that these attitudes derive, at least in part, from the deeply held perceptions of many young, socially unskilled, sub-culturally subverted and ultimately delinquent people that due to their areas of origin, ethnicity, peer relationships, group identities and the like, they are permanently consigned to a social under-class (see, for instance, Box, 1971 and 1987; Wiles, 1976; Lea and Young, 1984). This under-class, as a result of the perceived (and often real) circumstances of injustice and lesser eligibility in which it exists, develops antipathetic and antagonistic attitudes towards all forms of authority—attitudes reinforced by additional perceptions, justifiable or imagined, of being subject to excessive surveillance, suspicion, police activity and measures of social control.[16]

Offenders within such a profile are altogether unlikely to comply readily with reparative sanctions, some even seeing non-compliance as a 'badge of honour' that preserves a sense of identity and defies the agenda of authority. However, to punish them *excessively* in relation to other more compliant offenders, serves only to reinforce their sense of prejudice and discrimination. It

---

[15] Particularly violent and sexual offenders—see *Chapter 6* and particularly footnotes 9-12 thereto.

[16] David Garland deals with these issues at some length in his account of the 'contradictions of official criminology' in Garland (2002), op. cit., Chapter 5 and particularly at pp. 135-8.

is for all these reasons that policies of bifurcation, however well-intentioned, must at all costs avoid the accusation of punishing the unrepentant and intransigent gratuitously merely for being what they are. This does not, of course, negate the idea of punishing *less* where this is appropriate and compliance is forthcoming.

VICTIM INCLUSIVENESS: THE HALLMARK OF RESTORATIVE JUSTICE

The status and situation of victims of crime is one of the central threads of the discussion within the entire content of this work, although *Chapter 3*, in particular, deals with the place of victims within the procedural processes of restorative criminal justice. The ever-expanding literature and the extensive bibliographies that catalogue its development are replete with immediately evident references to the centrality of victims within all aspects of the subject material.[17]

It is in no sense illogical or accidental that restorative justice places victims of crime centre stage in its principal purpose of delivering 'better justice'. Even though undeniably it is the state's law that is broken by crime, the state is not the primary sufferer from the wrongful action: the victim is ,and in this sense has the first claim to consideration. Victim–offender mediation, where this is possible, has an immensely important part to play in determining not only if and how, victims receive reparation, but also the residual extent to which retributive punishment is necessary or appropriate *when* reparation is made. At this point it is necessary to point out that restorative justice perceives an important distinction between reparation and compensation. Reparation made by offenders to victims of crime forms part of the process of expiation, part of the process of victim vindication and an equally essential part of the process of offender restoration. State funded compensation, on the other hand, may well not derive from the actions of offenders to 'put things right' and frequently takes the form of social welfare 'tokenism' that does little to make victims feel vindicated or adequately considered.

As we have further seen within the discussion in *Chapter 3*, the issue of whether and to what extent, victims should have 'procedural rights' within the criminal justice process is a matter of considerable debate and contention (Watson *et al.*, 1989; Cooper, 1991; Ashworth, 1992 and 1993a and b.; Cavadino and Dignan, 1997(b)). Recent developments in Britain have, ostensibly, appeared to acknowledge the concept of victim's rights,[18] though a more recent *Code of*

---

[17] Two of the most extensive bibliographies on restorative justice are provided by Catherine Morris (1999 and with updated entries to 2004) and the Victim Offender Mediation Association (VOMA) (2005), both available on the Internet.

[18] See *Chapter 3*, particularly pp. 81-3 and fn. 17 and 18 thereto.

Practice for Victims of Crime (Home Office, 2005c) does not appear to afford other than tangential 'rights' to victims beyond the expectations that they might reasonably have of the prosecution and justice processes. There is no suggestion of the participation of victims within trial processes (other than as witnesses), although research has been undertaken on a continuous basis since the late 1990s (Hoyle *et al.*, 1999) to evaluate the impact and usefulness of Victim Personal Statements (VPSs) and Victim Impact Statements (VISs), particularly in relation to cases of domestic violence (Graham *et al.*, 2004).[19]

Admission of such statements is not, however, without its difficulties. While it may provide victims with a significantly increased hearing within the court process, it also has some important implications for both accused people and for victims themselves. By way of instance, two individuals could be convicted of almost identical offences, though in one case the victim might opt to make a VPS and in the other the victim might decline to do so. Thus, the outcomes, where a court must consider any VPS submitted to it prior to sentencing, might be significantly different as between the cases. This situation might be said to infringe the principles of fairness and proportionality.

The same inequality might also affect victims themselves, insofar as those victims who are less articulate or willing to adopt the procedure for making a VPS to the police might be at a disadvantage in comparison with others more articulate and willing to do so. As one firm of legal practitioners in Britain has already noted, the decision of the Lord Chief Justice seems to have followed broadly that made in the United States Supreme Court judgement in 1996 in the case of *Payne v. Tennessee* to restore the constitutional status of VISs.[20] Moreover, as these practitioners point out, it will remain to be seen whether the admission of VPSs will be a matter of challenge under Article 6 of the European Convention On Human Rights (right to a fair trial). Certainly, the duty of criminal courts to give reasons for their decisions would seem to impose a requirement for the court to indicate the extent that consideration of a VPS had an influence upon the sentence passed.

As we have also seen in the concluding part of *Chapter 3*, the debate continues in relation to the extent to which victim participation in court processes can reasonably be permitted.[21] The larger question, for the purposes of

---

[19] In fact, in England and Wales since 2001, there has been provision for victims of crime to make VPSs to the police when a police officer takes a witness statement from them. Courts presented with VPSs must take them into consideration prior to passing sentence. This procedure was initiated under a *Practice Direction* issued by the Lord Chief Justice, 16 October 2001under *The Consolidated Criminal Practice Direction*, III, 28, 1 and 2—Personal Statements of Victims.

[20] Shulmans Solicitors, *Legal Update—Crime Victim Personal Statement*, http: //www.shulmans.co.uk/update/ 20 January 2006.

[21] At the time of writing, a pilot scheme is being introduced in five Crown Courts in England and Wales (Birmingham, Cardiff, Manchester, Winchester and the Old Bailey in London) to permit evidential statements in murder and manslaughter trials from Victims' Advocates on behalf of bereaved relatives or close other persons. The scheme has been introduced in the face of considerable criticism from the judiciary and legal professionals in relation to the lack of clarity in

this work, is whether, if courts were to adopt the principles and practices of restorative justice, the situation would alter significantly. The obvious response has to be that much would depend upon the willingness of governments to contemplate seriously the necessary shifts in criminal justice policy development that would allow the entire sanctions process to become less punitive merely for the sake of being seen to be punitive. Within a number of contemporary jurisdictions, notably in Britain, the United States and a cluster of the European countries, this would mean deliberately distancing criminal justice policy considerations from political stances designed more to placate media sensationalism and perceived popular punitiveness, than to deliver better justice.

Restorative justice creates the opportunity to punish *less*, to punish *differently* and to punish *for different reasons*, while at the same time showing greater consideration for victims of crime. If the agenda to punish in order to deliver retribution and social incapacitation were to be discarded and if misplaced belief in the effectiveness of deterrence could be abandoned, then the inevitability of punishment could be reduced—particularly the inevitability of custodial punishment. For as long as punishment remains necessary to sustain its own credibility, imprisonment will continue to be used when its use can be avoided and prison populations will continue to exceed reasonable levels of provision. Excessive use of custody prevents prisons from carrying out a useful social role (other, perhaps, than of incapacitation) and also from delivering a potentially change-facilitative purpose. Such a situation adversely affects society, offenders and victims of crime and ultimately benefits no one.

Demonstrable inclusion of victims of crime within criminal justice processes is a rational response to a social imperative to consider the needs and obligations of all the parties to criminal acts. Victims and those close to them need their suffering to be acknowledged and vindicated; offenders have an obligation to 'put wrongs right' and a need to be able to do so in order to resume full citizenship; society needs less crime and the knowledge that criminal acts are constructively dealt with. The contemporary reliance upon punitive incapacitation and measures of social control to 'manage risk' deliver none of these objectives in a constructive sense. Moreover, if current rates of recidivism are any index of the social usefulness of existing measures, these serve only to highlight monumental ineffectiveness.

---

its conceptual and operational effect and the evidently political nature of its inception without wide consultation. See A. Miles (2006), 'Misery, Anger, Hurt, Confusion. Yep, a Politician Just Had Another Bright Idea', *The Times*, 19 April, p. 19.

REPARATION AND PRAGMATISM: MEANS TOWARDS ENDS

The forgoing chapters of this book to some considerable extent take for granted the unsatisfactory situation that the present climate of 'politicised' criminal justice has created, and they seek to provide a platform for doing justice differently. In doing so, however, it has been necessary to try to understand why the present situation is so fundamentally change-resistant, why attitudes have become so deeply entrenched and thus why making a case for doing justice differently is so profoundly difficult. It is relatively much easier to describe what restorative justice proposes, why it does so and the apparent advantages that might derive from accepting the 'restorative logic', but this does not bridge the gulf that presently stands between the existing and prospective positions.

In *Chapter 4* an attempt has been made to present a discussion that proceeds from the present unsatisfactory position towards an ultimately more promising situation and explain the reasoning for doing so. As will have become evident, this explanation goes only part of the total distance that would have to be travelled on the journey from contemporary to restorative justice, but acceptance of the potential value of reparative justice in place of predominantly retributive justice would prove a useful and substantial point of departure.[22] Such is not an attempt to make a virtue out of compromise, but rather to adopt a pragmatic approach to the inevitability of political rather than philosophical objection and obfuscation.

For all its objectionable qualities, the demise of the rehabilitative ethic of the 1960s and 1970s created a vacuum in penology of much greater extent and durability than ever the justice model that replaced it was capable of filling.[23] The difficulty that remains lies more in the legacy of the political persuasiveness of the notions of desert and retribution that dominate the contemporary discourse of criminal punishment. Whether or not it will ultimately prove possible to re-shape the more informed sectors of public consciousness to accept a prospective motivation for criminal punishment is, of course, the quintessential question.

Within the same chapter, we are confronted with yet another of the operational problems that inevitably arises when significant shifts in criminal justice administration have to be accommodated. This involves the potential difficulty of dealing rather differently with those offenders prepared to make

---

[22] If only because it makes possible a revised view of sanctions that might operate in a prospective manner for both offenders and victims. This change of emphasis is essential if a retreat from a predominantly retributive view of the purposes of punishment is ultimately to be entertained.

[23] Primarily because however flawed in terms of its operation and outcomes, the rehabilitative model was of a prospective nature and conditioned criminological thinking in terms of the social re-integration of offenders. The justice model, based on the 'just deserts' concept of punishment enabled retribution to dominate the punishment 'debate' in an almost exclusively retrospective manner (Hudson, 1987; Box, 1987; Bean, 1981).

reparation for their offences from those who decline to do so. The issue of 'bifurcation' is, without doubt an emotive one at both the ethical and practical levels of consideration and it recurs at intervals both implicitly and explicitly within this work.[24] There seems little doubt that from an essentially practical and utilitarian perspective, an extent of bifurcation can be justified on the grounds that it enables a more desirable mode of sanctions to be implemented than would otherwise be the case. Viewed another way, perhaps, without an element of bifurcation, it becomes altogether unlikely that victims of crime and offenders themselves would be enabled to benefit from the reparative regimes that have been discussed in *Chapters 5* and *6*.

However this situation is viewed, it has become evident (in *Chapter 6*) that— at least in England and Wales—the government has opted for a deliberate measure of bifurcation in its 'custody plus' and 'custody minus' prescriptions within the Criminal Justice Act 2003. This being so, the general argument in favour of reparative justice becomes less open to objection on the grounds that it deals differentially with those prepared to make reparation as opposed to those unwilling to do so.

REPARATION, RESTORATION AND REINTEGRATION: A SEQUENTIAL PROCESS

The discussion within *Chapter 4* derives directly from the suggested need for a new penology proposed in *Chapter 2* and the desirability of increased victim awareness and participation within criminal justice that was recommended in *Chapter 3*. However, in order to envisage a new penology, it is clearly necessary to dismantle the constraining rhetoric that underpins and sustains the contemporary approach to the punishment of criminal offenders. This makes it essential to indicate why preoccupation with penal policies grounded in retribution and deterrence inevitably lead towards incarceration and incapacitation and directly away from outcomes that are in any way reparative and restorative.

Such is not to deny the necessity for a retributive element within criminal punishment, but it is to insist that retribution need not be the *primary* purpose of that process. The necessity for a measure of retribution has, after all is said and done, a sound moral philosophical basis and particularly so when offences violate people rather than merely laws. In this respect it remains morally right to impose sanctions upon offenders for the harm caused by offences, but this is altogether different from making excessive retribution a predominantly political imperative and an instrument of social control. In addition, to visit retributive punishment upon offenders in pursuit of general deterrence becomes both

---

[24] But see the explanations offered in *Chapter 1*, p. 52; *Chapter 3*, p. 76, fn. 6; and, in particular, in *Chapter 5*, p. 100 and fn. 34 thereto.

vindictive and excessive—manifestly so where it may be shown to be largely unnecessary.

The obligation of offenders to make reparation to victims for offences that cause them harm is, arguably, as much an imperative within criminal punishment as is the need for retribution. The significance of reparation is, however, that it has a prospective purpose that can be beneficial to all the parties involved in criminal acts—victims, offenders and communities. This cannot be claimed for the retrospective nature of retribution other than in its denunciatory and retaliatory effects. It is for this central reason that restorative justice offers the vision of a new and inclusive, rather than an outdated and exclusive penology for the future.

The concept of reparative justice advanced here is designed to convey the contention that the actions involved in making reparation are the first stage in an expiative process[25] which, when completed, leads logically to restoration. Indeed, restoration becomes contingent upon reparation having been made because reparation is the means by which offenders discharge their 'debt' to society and also through which victims are vindicated. Although the idea of crime invoking the notion of a 'social debt' may appear somewhat anachronistic, it has an essential usefulness in relation to reparative justice simply because of an implicit insistence that something substantive by way of 'making matters right' has to be part of the process leading to personal restoration of offenders within society.

The act of making reparation also implies that offenders have, in a prior sense, accepted responsibility for the offence and its harmfulness and this, in itself, becomes an active element in addressing the nature of offending behaviour. Since our ultimate purpose is to achieve a reduction in crime rather than the inevitable infliction of punishment, it becomes more likely that this will occur through a prospective rather than a retrospective approach to sanctioning offenders.

The reintegration of offenders within society and their immediate communities is a much more difficult matter, particularly when offences are of a serious nature or involve punishment of a protracted duration.[26] Public attitudes towards offenders, often inflamed by media presentation of crime and its supposed prevalence and influenced by the 'tough on crime' rhetoric of politicians, are at the least ambivalent and frequently ill-disposed. Sexual offenders, in particular, bear the brunt of this widespread attitudinal intolerance that has, in recent years, been amplified by specific measures of restrictive social surveillance against them.[27] Pressure for the provision of public protection

---

[25] The term 'expiation' is used here to convey the moral imperative to make atonement for harm done in a socially constructive manner (Ewing, 1929: 30-31; Radzinowicz, 1972: 238).

[26] The reader will note here the discussion in *Chapter 6* concerning the approach of the British government towards legislation of measures of public protection against violent and sexual offenders in 1997 and subsequently. (Here see, in particular, fn. 11 and 12 to that chapter, p. 142-3.)

[27] In particular the mandatory provisions for residence and reporting once someone is placed on the Sex Offenders Register created under the Sex Offenders Act 1997 and re-enacted within the Sexual

measures such as a 'Megan's Law' and a 'Sarah's Law' within the United States and Britain have undoubtedly added to the problems of successful offender reintegration.[28]

These pressures notwithstanding, the overwhelming majority of offenders sentenced to imprisonment simply have to be released from custody on the expiry of their sentences and resume a life in the community. Of course it is reasonable for the public to want to be protected—and, particularly, to have their children protected—from serial sexual or violent predators, but far from all sexual offenders in particular repeat their offences, or do so with significant regularity. Serious sexual offenders do present a different picture once a definitive offence pattern has been established. Compared with violent offenders, sexual offenders accumulate their offence patterns more slowly and over a longer period of time. In addition, the proportion of serious offending within their total offence patterns is significantly higher than that of offenders who commit violent offences only.[29] There is, however, no particular evidence to indicate that sexual offenders commit serious offences with greater frequency than do violent offenders, or offenders who commit both violent and sexual offences (Cornwell, 1989: 190-2).

These factors inevitably confront criminologists and penal policy-makers with the problems of prediction of serious offences and this is an area in which significant difficulties arise. Rigorous research in the field of criminal dangerousness very clearly indicates that predictive methods, however refined, are highly unreliable and that the extent of dangerousness is widely over-predicted. False-positive rates[30] within specific periods of time for dangerous offending seem to vary between 55 and 70 per cent, thus making it entirely unreasonable to impose measures of predictive restraint on a universal basis (Steadman, 1973; Steadman and Cocozza, 1974: 152; Monahan, 1976: 20, 1981a and b; 1984; Bottoms, 1977: 79-80; Cornwell, 1989: 201-2).

Offences Act 2003. There are also a number of other restrictive lists such as the Department for Education and Skills (DfES) List 99 which excludes from educational employment in England and Wales all people barred or restricted on the grounds of misconduct or on medical grounds *vide* DfES Circular 11/95. Similar provisions are made in Scotland and Northern Ireland under delegated legislation arrangements. At the time of writing, a new Violent and Sexual Offenders Register (VISOR) is in the early stages of implementation within the United Kingdom.

[28] Here see the discussion in *Chapter 3* and fn. 14 and 15 thereto.

[29] There is research evidence that indicates that serious sexual (only) offenders accumulate offence patterns at a different (slower) rate than serious violent (only) offenders, but do so over a longer period of time. In addition, the proportion of serious offences within their total offence patterns is higher than that for violent only offenders. Those who commit violent and sexual offences display remarkably similar offence pattern accumulation rates to violence only offenders. However, mean time between failure rates (at large) for each of these groups are remarkably similar, averaging some 12 months between significant events (Cornwell, 1989: 190-5).

[30] False-positive predictions concern those offenders whom predictive techniques indicate are more than likely to offend or re-offend in a particular form of dangerous behaviour and who subsequently do not do so within the time frame identified within the predictive process.

This situation produces a profoundly serious moral dilemma that encompasses the competing rights of society for protection and of offenders not to be subjected to discriminatory practices without reasonable cause. Where it can be shown that the likelihood of predictive accuracy is considerably less than 50 per cent, measures of predictive restraint become both morally unsupportable and a gross violation of individual rights. Moreover, penal policies that permit such practices, on whatever basis of supposed justification, are equally reprehensible. This, as we have seen in *Chapter 6*, has demonstrably been the case in Britain and elsewhere within the present decade.

Penal politics frequently have to confront dilemmas of this nature and accept evidence-based outcomes that do not support measures that might seem, on the face of matters, socially desirable. Intolerant governments, goaded by and responsive to media pressures to act in a morally irresponsible manner, frequently place themselves in positions in which ideologically flawed policies have to be modified or rescinded under challenge in the courts. This is unfortunate, but it is also entirely avoidable if the voices of reason and prudence are permitted a suitable hearing.

Ironically, reason and re-integration in relation to criminal offenders seem to be incompatible partners within contemporary penal politics. This accounts, in many respects, for what James Dignan (2002) has so perceptively described as the 'fault lines' in restorative justice.[31] These 'fault lines' critically affect the acceptance of restorative prescriptions because they clearly identify the ways in which proponents of restorative justice tend to become preoccupied with the extent to which it becomes at odds with the conventional model and fail to emphasise the many similarities that exist within either. This much stated, however, where clear divergences of approach are inevitable, it is necessary for these to be made evident.

Re-integration of offenders is one such area. For however ill-disposed public opinion and media attitudes may be towards certain ex-offenders, once the offenders have been punished they have a moral right to social restoration, unhindered by unwarranted and gratuitous preconceptions about their future conduct. Unless the sequential process of accepting responsibility for harm, making reparation to victims and thereby earning restoration can take place, the entire concept of social re-integration becomes impossible to achieve. Worse still,

---

[31] James Dignan has clearly indicated the danger that advocates of restorative justice principles and practices tend to adopt polarised positions in relation to 'traditional' criminal justice that can hinder what might otherwise be more widespread acceptance of the restorative concept of justice. In agreeing with this analysis, my view is that this may occur partly out of frustration at the more obvious inequities of the traditional approach and partly also from despair at the 'un-reasoned' responses of politicians and penal policy-makers who promote policies and measures that, far from being evidence-based, are primarily responsive to media pressures and ill-informed public opinion. See J. Dignan (2002), 'Restorative Justice and the Law: The Case for an Integrated Systemic Approach', in L. Walgrave (ed), *Restorative Justice and the Law*, Devon, UK: Willan Publishing, pp. 168-90.

ex-offenders become social outcasts: marginalized, less eligible and all the more likely to re-offend. This is the cycle of discrimination and disadvantage that restorative justice seeks to consign to the past.

In many respects one might argue that such an approach is not so much a 'fault line', but rather more a return to moral values in penology that were aspired to before the agendas of criminal justice became so heavily politicised by the 'justice model' and 'law and order' debates of the late 1980s and 1990s. At the very least, restorative justice, through its insistence on responsibility, reparation, reconciliation and self-examination, demonstrably and actively seeks the reformed behaviour of offenders and the vindication of victims. These are no shallow ambitions in a contemporary world in which penal policies are so often pursued for the purposes of short-term electoral advantage.

REPARATIVE CUSTODY: SOCIALLY RESPONSIBLE EXCLUSION

The practice of locking human beings away from public view within institutions, removing their liberty, reducing their autonomy and limiting their communication with those close to them is one of the most extreme and unnatural measures practised by mankind on one another. Ironically, of the two traditional bastions of institutional social exclusion—prisons and hospitals for the mentally-ill—it is the latter which in recent years have, in Britain, seen a deliberate measure of 'decarceration', while the former have almost universally been expanded in their use.[32]

The irony of the situation is that the primary motivation to 'outsource' mental patients into the community was that of cost-reduction in the maintenance of long-stay beds in psychiatric hospitals in Britain in the 1970s and 1980s. Though the doctrine of 'care in the community' was evidently considered by the government to be appropriate for the mentally ill, the same principle was clearly considered inappropriate for criminal offenders for whom the demand for 'long-stay beds' considerably increased then and subsequently.[33] In other words, perhaps, it might be concluded that public attitudes in tolerance of

---

[32] The term 'decarceration' was first used by Rothman in the early 1970s to describe the state-sponsored policy of decanting the inhabitants of asylums and reformatories back into the community to be cared for there. It was taken up, most notably, by Scull some few years later to propose a similar process of limiting the use of imprisonment and decreasing the size of the prison population. See D. Rothman (1973), 'Decarcerating Prisoners and Patients', *Civil Liberties Review*, 1, 8 and A. T. Scull (1977), *Decarceration, Community Treatment and the Deviant: A Radical Review* (First edition), Englewood Cliffs, New Jersey: Prentice-Hall.

[33] Indeed, there might be said to be a 'double irony' in the situation, since the removal of many mentally-ill patients into the community has passed largely without major public reaction, whereas proposals to make extended use of temporary release from prisons have met with widespread public and media opposition.

mental illness are considerably more charitable than those extended to offenders in the community context.

The discussion in *Chapter 5* has focussed on the need to provide prisons with a more constructive social ethos, to make these places less exclusive of the communities in which they operate and to make the process of custody part of a broader sentencing philosophy that perceives a natural relationship and linkage between custodial and non-custodial sanctions. Some observers of contemporary criminal justice in Britain might propose that this was what was intended within the 'custody plus and minus' provisions brought forward in the Criminal Justice Act 2003 that were considered in *Chapter 6*. There are, however, sound reasons for believing otherwise and that, as Roberts and Smith (2003: 185-7) have suggested, these measures were actually devised for the altogether different purpose of 'toughening up' community sanctions with a dose of imprisonment— immediate or suspended.

The Coulsfield Report (EFF, 2004a), discussed at some length in the same chapter, provided an independently honest and timely assessment of the existing situation affecting prisons in England and Wales (and many other countries in a similar manner), from which there is much of value to be learned. Perhaps the most incisive of its observations for our purposes here were that, first of all, prisons do not work simply because there are too many prisoners, many of whom do not need to be in prison at all. Secondly, the pressure for increased severity of sentencing as a political response to the apparent (though misconceived) lack of public confidence in criminal justice urgently needs to be reversed. There is certainly nothing new in the over- and unnecessary use of prisons, but their use primarily for the purposes of social incapacitation is politically cynical where it is unjustified. The 'custody plus' and 'custody minus' provisions provide an evident example of just this cynicism.

Against this rather unpromising background, restorative justice proposes an altogether different and more constructive use of prisons—predominantly for reparative purposes. There is nothing that is massively intellectually challenging about such a proposition; indeed, it suggests little more than that prisons could, given the will to do so, be given a constructive rather than a destructive purpose. But, and here once again the same stumbling block is evident, this would depend upon using prisons much more sparingly. The corollary of this is also not difficult to perceive: it is that increasing use would have to be made of community-based sanctions. Once again, it must be supposed that the second stumbling block immediately comes into play and misplaced public perception of 'soft option' penalties, inflamed by media sensationalism, would make increased use of community sanctions appear politically suicidal.

Prisons with positive and demanding regimes dedicated to purposeful use of time and resources for victim reparation serve three quite distinctive purposes: the first to make constructive use of time spent in custody; the second to dismantle the prevailing tradition of imposing 'negative' sanctions[34] and the third to vindicate victims of crime. Making prison regimes much more demanding of inmates represents no 'soft option' for them, while at the same time raising the level of public respect for what prisons represent. Increased public respect for more purposeful prisons might, in turn, be expected to result in increased public confidence in criminal justice—particularly in relation to the treatment of victims of crime. In such circumstances, shorter rather than longer sentences in custody would be perceived as beneficial and appropriate.

The Coulsfield Inquiry quite rightly identified the fact that short custodial sentences, as presently operated, do very little to control crime, have very uncertain effect in terms of deterrence and certainly have no rehabilitative value (EFF, 2004a: 5). The key words here are: *as presently operated*. There is, however, no reason to suppose that significantly more demanding and rigorous regimes, encompassing strictly earned and limited privileges, full engagement and linked to community-based release entirely dependent upon full participation, might not have an altogether different impact on offenders. Such regimes would actively encourage full participation over the entire period identified as necessary to make adequate reparation and permit early release to community work only when offending behaviour had been substantively addressed.

Neither is it impossible to conceive sentences of imprisonment being calculated on a 'day penalty' basis, the overall duration being assessed on the number of working days necessary to earn the proportion of wages appropriate to victim reparation for the harm occasioned by the offence(s) and/or the seriousness of the offence(s).[35] Such a sentence calculation protocol would have the merit of being closely related to desert and, if imposed within minimum and maximum sentencing guidelines, would result in reducing excessive sentencing practices. It would also bear a stronger correlation with decisions made in relation to non-custodial sentencing that might be approached on a similar basis for the fines and community service sanctions discussed later in this chapter.

Perhaps the most important requirement is for reparative custody to be linked very visibly to the local community within which prisons are situated and

---

[34] Here it will be recalled from the discussion in *Chapter 5* that the term 'negative' sanctions refers primarily to use of prison regimes that make no specific demands of prisoners either to address offending behaviour, work to make constructive use of time or otherwise respond to life in custody in a positive and self-improving manner.

[35] In very broad terms this implies providing a standard weekly wage (of, say, £40) for working satisfactorily a specified number of hours each day (a minimum of 8 hours = 40 hour week). Of this sum a set proportion would be allocated to victims of crime (perhaps 60 per cent—or £24) and of the remainder 15 per cent saved towards discharge (£6). The remaining £10 per week might be spent in the prison. Thus if a court decided that the harmfulness of the offence merited a total penalty equivalent to a custodial fine of £1,000, the number of custodial days would be assessed as £1,000 ÷ 8 = 125 days—approximately equivalent to a four month sentence. The actual period spent in prison custody might be reduced by a remission factor as at present, or by specifying a minimum custodial period of (say) 50 per cent, with the remaining period spent working on temporary release within the community.

that those inmates permitted to work outside the prison undertake work of direct social value to that particular community. Once it becomes evident to local people that prisoners are regularly to be seen doing purposeful and properly supervised work that adds amenity value to the area and its environment, then it becomes more likely that public attitudes towards offenders will become more tolerant. In ideal circumstances it might be envisaged that prison management, local community leaders and businesses would routinely combine to plan and prioritise the work to be undertaken, the resources needed and its qualitative supervision. There also seems to be no particularly good reason why responsible community members cannot be involved in the supervisory process.

Chapter 5 has also included some discussion of how the issue of unrepentant and uncooperative inmates might be addressed and, in particular, how problems associated with 'bifurcation' could be dealt with. Viewed realistically, there will always be a proportion of prisoners who will decline to participate in reparative regimes and insist on serving their sentences in an 'old style' manner. These people can, of course, be accommodated, but there should be stringent disincentives to such attitudes[36] and in ideal circumstances they should be housed in different prisons from those delivering restorative custody. There is, however, a positive aspect of this situation, since the necessity for basic regimes for the uncooperative provides also a powerful incentive for those within reparative regimes to participate fully and to ensure that they are not 'relegated' to 'non-reparative' conditions.

PURPOSEFUL COMMUNITY PENOLOGY

Every criminal justice jurisdiction develops its own provisions for community corrections and these broadly indicate the prevailing attitudes of each society towards less serious criminal offending. It might be supposed that because sanctions served within the community are reserved for offences that do not merit the use of imprisonment, there exists a strong case for them to be simple for the public to understand, speedily enforced and capable of delivering visible justice while at the same time correcting (or changing) deviant behaviour. Such is, after all, what the essential nature of 'corrections' is about.

Setting on one side for the moment the evident wastefulness of using imprisonment when to do so is unnecessary, community sanctions may be said to serve two important social purposes: the evident punishment of relatively minor offences and the reinforcement of law-abiding behaviour. Thus far, relatively simple but also, within most advanced democracies, extremely naïve. The reasons for this assertion lie within the fast-changing nature of modern

---

[36] Possibly including minimal remission of sentence, reduced availability of privileges and visits, a minimum wage structure and the like. The regime should, however, include the potential for genuinely changed attitudes to permit probationary transfer to reparative regime conditions.

societies, of policing methods, of political reality, of media influence and of penology itself. As Garland points out:

> A new relationship between politicians, the public and penal experts has emerged in which politicians are more directive, penal experts are less influential and public opinion becomes a key reference point for evaluating options. Criminal justice is now far more vulnerable to shifts of public mood and political reaction. New laws and policies are rapidly instituted without prior consultation with the criminal justice professionals and expert control of the policy agenda has been considerably reduced by a populist style of policy making.
>
> The populist current in contemporary crime policy is, to some extent, a political posture or tactic, adopted for short-term electoral advantage. As such, it can quickly be reversed if 'popular' initiatives cease to coincide with calculations of political gain. … There is, as Nils Christie might put it, a more streamlined system of pain-delivery, with fewer intervening obstacles between the political process and the allocation of individual punishments. Public demands for greater punishments are now more easily and instantly translated into increased sentences and longer jail terms.
>
> (Garland 2002: 172)

Clearly written and carefully considered assessments by accredited professionals such as those who compiled the Coulsfield Report should, normally, prompt reasoned governmental responses and action to remedy shortcomings in policies and practices. That is, unless the message conveyed, however distinctly, is precisely what the government does not wish to receive. Here it will be recalled that both the Coulsfield Report (EFF, 2004a) and that of the Esmeé Fairbairn Foundation entitled *Rethinking Crime and Punishment* (EFF 2004b) were issued after the passage of the Criminal Justice Act 2003, with its provisions for community orders, 'custody plus' and 'custody minus', intermittent custody and associated issues. Both of these documents contained clearly stated prescriptions for lesser use of custody, the extension of the use of restorative justice practices and victim inclusiveness that ran entirely counter to the increasingly punitive intentions of the Act. Neither document, however soundly reasoned, was therefore in the least likely to elicit positive responses from the British New Labour government.

Purposeful and restorative community penology would dictate the need for significant repeal of the 2003 Act and its prescriptions for community punishment, but this is extremely unlikely to occur—at least within the foreseeable future. The result of this is that however persuasive and logical the case made for implementation of restorative justice practices may be, it is altogether likely to fall upon deaf governmental ears—at least in Britain at the present time. The same situation seems to prevail in a number of the other democracies within Europe, North America and elsewhere.

This same restorative penology for community sanctions would also, ideally, be of a much less complex and more easily understood nature than the raft of different 'community order' provisions within the British model set out in the

2003 Act.[37] It would also, desirably, be more honest in its underlying intentions. We have seen (in *Chapter 6*) the simplicity of the Finnish concept of criminal sanctions and the way in which, in that country, it has been possible to reduce dependence upon imprisonment in favour of community measures. If ever a more evidence-based prescription for punishing *less* were needed, the Finnish model provides an excellent datum point.

It is the case that community penology can only become effective if there is a logical relationship between it and custodial corrections. In this particular respect the proposals within the Halliday Report (2001) and the subsequent arrangements within the England and Wales Criminal Justice Act 2003 may aptly be said to have placed the horse firmly behind the cart. 'Custody plus', in attaching a custodial period[38] to a subsequent community order, denies the received wisdom that short prison terms are largely ineffective and may even increase recidivism (Home Office, 2001b: iv; 2002a: 92 and 102; Roberts and Smith, 2003: 182). 'Custody minus', in its introduction of an activated 'suspended sentence' of imprisonment for breaches of community orders, will doubtless result in increased use of imprisonment because, as is a well established fact, a high proportion of those people previously sentenced to probation, community service and combination orders were subject to breach action for repeated non-compliance (Tonry, 2003: 10; Home Office, 2002b: Appendix 6).[39] The problem is particularly acute in cases in which offenders are sentenced for drug-related offences, since this group displays high relapse and reconviction rates (Hough and Mitchell, 2003).

The 'custody plus' and 'custody minus' provisions certainly provide a relationship between community and custodial penalties, but this is a long way removed from the type of linkage suggested as necessary in this work. In fact it operates in a diametrically opposite direction from that in which restorative justice would seek to move. The Criminal Justice Act 2003 makes no mention of reparation, makes no provision for victim inclusiveness, fails to simplify the already comprehensive and complicated provisions for community sanctions[40]

---

[37] In total, the Criminal Justice Act 2003 provides for no fewer than 12 species of order, three of which involve the consent of the offender to undergo treatment (for mental-illness, drug or alcohol dependency). The provisions for 'custody plus' and 'custody minus' and 'intermittent custody' are described in Part 12, Chapter 3 of the 2003 Act as Prison Sentences of Less Than 12 Months (section 181), Suspended Sentences of Imprisonment (section 189) and Intermittent Custody (section 183) respectively.

[38] Effectively of between two and 13 weeks in duration, or 12 months and over, though in the latter case only half of the sentence period would be spent in custody—subject to the full 50 per cent remission available. The Act therefore completely removes the powers of courts to impose custodial sentences of between three and six months in duration.

[39] Home Office (2002c), *Justice for All—Responses to the Auld and Halliday Reports*, London: Home Office. The official 'breach' rates cited related to the year 1999-2000 and were 18 per cent for probation orders, 30 per cent for community service orders and 29 per cent for combination orders.

[40] Other than by subsuming the existing raft of formerly separate community sentences under the blanket title of a community order.

and increases the likelihood of short custodial sanctions being imposed where this is avoidable. A restorative penology would move in precisely the opposite direction in each of these important areas.

MOVING TOWARDS 'JOINED-UP' CORRECTIONS

The situation described in the immediately preceding section of this chapter presents a dismal view of the current situation within the British criminal justice system and particularly of the most recent legislation introduced in the Criminal Justice Act 2003. The title of this chapter implied the possibility of 'doing justice better' through making restorative justice work in practice: all of this seems like an illusion in the present climate of penology, not only in Britain, but in the many other countries worldwide that presently overuse imprisonment.

Two central themes have recurred throughout the chapters of this book: these are that it is possible to 'do justice better' and that criminal justice stands where it presently does in many democracies entirely because political choices are made that ensure this is the case. It is possible to 'do justice better' because this has been achieved by countries like Finland that have made deliberate decisions to use imprisonment less and, at the same time, to simplify the delivery of justice in a manner that makes sense to its population. History reminds us also that the Netherlands pursued a similar path in the second half of the last century, but this progress regressed as political decisions were made to adopt increasingly punitive practices in the face of a 'fear of crime' generated predominantly by media pressures and governmental responses designed to secure short-term electoral gain.

The contemporary 'correctional divide' is a deliberately contrived dichotomy between the sanctions of imprisonment and community justice. Overuse of imprisonment is tolerated because of its apparent incapacitative advantages for social control and the political legacy of the 'prison works' assertion of the mid-1990s, which, in spite of its evident deceitfulness, persists in the political imagination. All the evidence-based research points to a contrary conclusion, but in order to maintain a 'tough on crime' stance, the myth has to be perpetuated by both politicians and policy-makers as though it were a self-evident truth.

What, then, is this evidence? It lies in the Halliday Report's assertion (Home Office, 2001b: 3), repeated in the subsequent White Paper *Justice for All* (Home Office, 2002a: 92 and 102), that short prison sentences are 'usually ineffective' and that they 'increase the risk of re-offending'. The reasons for this are clear: neither prisons nor non-custodial sanctions, as presently practised, require anything of offenders, or change them or their circumstances in ways that might avert new offences. These are both, in effect, doubly-negative sanctions: negative in that they do not change the behaviour of offenders; and negative in that they do not reduce crime. The same contention has been reinforced in the Coulsfield Report (EFF 2004a) discussed earlier. The outcomes, also demonstrated in evidence-based research, can be seen in reconviction rates widely accepted to be as high as 65 per cent within two years for many offences and offenders (Home Office, 2001a: 126).

The prescriptions of restorative justice provide the potential to reverse this situation, but they imply significant change throughout the criminal justice systems of most contemporary jurisdictions. Reparative custody represents a positive sanction because it demands much of offenders, provides for and vindicates victims, and addresses offending behaviour and the personal circumstances of offenders and those close to them. More than this, however, it seeks to combine with community justice by testing out the behaviour and reliability of prison inmates within the community as part of the custodial process. In this way it proposes more sparing use of custody where this becomes unavoidable, but links directly with delivery of sanctions within the community.

The term 'unavoidable custody' within the restorative concept of justice means precisely what it implies: that custodial sentencing becomes a strategy of final resort and is imposed only when *no other penalty* will suffice to meet reasonable requirements for retribution *and* the safety of victims of crime (or potential victims). This is altogether different from public protection, since the general public safety is not necessarily improved or ensured by the use of imprisonment—other than in an imagined manner. Research into criminal dangerousness indicates very forcefully that predictions of dangerous behaviour are widely unreliable and that custody imposed for public protection would be unnecessary in more than 60 per cent of false-positive cases.

This in turn implies the urgent need to dismantle the culture of media-induced 'fear of crime' that presently dominates decision-making in penal policy.[41] It also requires politicians, of all political persuasions and party affiliations, to be considerably more honest about the realities of crime and cease to use criminal justice systems as 'political footballs' as a means of securing electoral popularity. There should, after all, be no perceived merit in expending vastly unnecessary public funds on the maintenance of penal establishments and

---

[41] A typical example is provided by articles carried in two reputable British Sunday newspapers in relation to the extent to which offenders subject to electronic monitoring (or 'tagging') appear to breach regularly the terms of their community orders. *The Observer* (29 January 2006, p. 7) published an article entitled 'Violence Fears Grow as Offenders Go Unchecked', alleging that arrangements for monitoring offenders by private companies are defective or inefficient in England and Wales to a significant extent. *The Sunday Times* of the same date carried the headlines on two separate pages: 'Tagged Criminals Shun Curfews and Run Amok' (p. 1) and: 'Revealed: The Tags Offenders Ignore' (p. 4). The clear implication within both articles is that the government should foreclose on the contracts awarded to private sector firms that operate monitoring services that default (or appear to default) in meeting contractual conditions for follow-up action on abuses of the curfew conditions imposed by the courts. Such default, under the terms of community orders imposed under the Criminal Justice Act 2003 should result in immediate imprisonment under the terms of 'custody plus' and 'custody minus' provisions. Of deeper significance, however, is the inference that 'the offenders released to community supervision and who carry the lowest (Level 1) risk assessment are responsible for 80 per cent of the serious crimes committed by those released from prison and subject to supervision orders' (*The Observer*, 29 January 2006, p. 7).

populations where this is both avoidable and unnecessary. If doing so were to be seen to be a matter more of imprudence than of appropriateness, then contemporary criminal justice might start to make sense within overall social policy.

The more widespread and constructive use of non-custodial sanctions flows directly from more sparing and effective use of imprisonment. Restorative community justice would dispense with the multiplicity of community orders or measures by focussing on reparative community service or fines with a last resort back-up of conversion to custody. The Finnish experience indicates that this comprises adequate provision and has even enabled almost half of all custodial sentences to be suspended in favour of community-based sanctions. In such a manner, communities and victims benefit directly from community penalties and offenders are enabled to retain their close community ties in the process.

It is, however, the flawed logic of contemporary social control measures that most stands in need of correction. Locking up offenders unnecessarily within overcrowded and diminished regimes is a strategy of despair. While it may appear to 'buy time', it changes nothing and returns the same (or worse) 'bad apples' to the barrel.[42] Ultimately, the vast majority of prisoners *have* to be released back into communities, regardless of the extent of the administrative and extended sentencing measures employed to delay their freedom.[43] However, as Tonry insists:

> Nonetheless, the bottom line is that current policies, political rhetoric and punishment patterns are as they are because politicians, however motivated, wished it so.
> Looking on the bright side, that conclusion means that directions can change if politicians wish it so. Looking on the dark side, however, as the proposals in [the Criminal Justice Act 2003] testify, the Labour government shows no signs of wishing to return to policies that are more moderate, substantive, humane and effective than those it has promoted since taking office. (Tonry, 2003: 6)[44]

CONCLUSION

Tonry's analysis of the situation is an apt and timely reminder that things simply do not have to be as they presently are within criminal justice—either in Britain, or elsewhere. This book has been written to propose how acceptance and implementation of restorative justice principles could move criminal justice into

---

[42] Worse, very probably, since the experience of imprisonment within impoverished regime conditions encourages frustration and is widely held to have a criminalising effect (DiIulio, 1987: 15-18; Fleisher, 1989; Cavadino and Dignan, 1997a: 16-18).

[43] Such as restrictive parole consideration, increased sentencing provisions for specific forms of offending and indeterminate sentencing for offences other than murder or deliberate acts causing loss of life.

[44] The words within the square bracket have been changed from the original: 'the White Paper and the Criminal Justice Bill', for the sake of clarity in this account.

a new era: an era that would be more moderate, substantive, humane and effective for offenders, victims of crime, communities, the wider society and ultimately for the law itself.

It is not difficult to perceive why restorative justice is such a challenging concept and neither is it difficult to see how its essential reasonableness poses such a threat to existing attitudes, policies and practices. Perhaps the deeper questions are those of whether it is right and appropriate for criminal justice policies to be forged on the anvil of political expediency as the response to misinformed and sensationalist media pressures, and of why politicians find it acceptable to fail to correct this misrepresentation when evidence-based information and advice indicate its deliberately misleading nature.

Those who work within criminal justice and corrections, or who care about the quality of justice within contemporary democracies, are right to be deeply concerned about this very evident political ambivalence. Their concerns are not so much about how politicians behave, but are more about the socially dysfunctional outcomes of this behaviour. Worse still, perhaps, because many practitioners are government employees, their demanded professional loyalties prohibit or inhibit them from criticism of the unjust policies and practices that are set in place by their political masters. This much I know, from half a lifetime spent as a practitioner in corrections within Britain and other countries of the world, and recognise as having caused considerable moral and ethical distress.

Restorative justice deserves more than casual attention if for no better reason that it seeks to put wrongs right, rather than merely to punish those who commit them and largely ignore those against whom the wrongs are committed. It challenges contemporary practices because it asks the right questions of justice in a direct and uncompromising manner. The question: 'Who has been hurt?' matters infinitely more than: 'What law has been broken? 'The question: 'Whose responsibility is it to put it right?' also matters more than: 'Who did it and how much punishment can be justified on whatever set of pretexts?' These, surely, are important questions for true justice to enquire into which, left unanswered, will perpetuate the existence of the stagnant lake into which criminal offenders are presently cast.

Ultimately, decisions have to be made about how crime can best be reduced, rather than what measures can be justified predominantly to attempt to control it. History reminds those capable of learning its lessons of the fate of societies that have attempted to control human behaviour by *fiat* rather than by reason. Restorative justice leans far more towards reason than repression and there are increasingly evident signs that it is capable of delivering more effective criminal justice.

This much stated, there remains a necessity for caution. As Umbreit *et al.* have suggested, there is now a clear possibility that the restorative justice movement will suffer from the predictable co-opting of its philosophy (Umbreit, *et al.*, 2005a: 4).[45] This means, in effect, that as it becomes more widespread and influential, there will arise a tendency for politicians and policy-makers to 'cherry-pick' fragmented aspects of restorative justice principles and, where these sit unexceptionally alongside traditional approaches, incorporate them into legislative arrangements under the guise of restorative justice policies. Moreover, as Leslie Davey, Director of Real Justice (UK and Ireland), pointed out in a recent conference paper delivered to the International Institute for Restorative Practices in Australia:

> If we are to continue the growth of restorative justice in the United Kingdom in a sustainable, safe and accessible manner, we need to ensure that what is measured as restorative justice is, in fact, restorative justice; that systems and legislation changes are enabling rather than controlling; that standards avoid being so rigid that they stifle innovation. This means that future developments of restorative practice must be based on best evidence rather than political expediency, pressure group prejudices and vested interests. (Davey, 2005: 96)

The evaluative and collaborative work of influential writers and practitioners across the world is fast assembling an invaluable body of 'best evidence' from restorative practices and projects. If these initiatives have a common theme, it is surely that to be truly effective justice needs a human face, un-obscured by the blindfold that has hitherto been perceived as a virtue. This face must extend hope to offenders, victims and communities alike, that integrity, humanity and fairness are inseparably linked in the purpose of *doing justice better*. It must also convince those in positions of power and authority that there are better and more effective ways of doing justice than those currently in political fashion.

One central fact is undeniable: it is that restorative justice and its practices have achieved world-wide acceptance, and support for what it represents is growing in every continent as each year passes. It is encouraging to see that it has proponents in countries that have emerged from the totalitarian regimes of the former USSR,[46] in China, the Middle East and South America, all formerly noted for uncompromising approaches to criminal justice. Its principles have been endorsed by the United Nations and the Council of Europe, with a view to their incorporation into the legislative arrangements of member states. Yet in spite of these advances and because adoption of restorative justice principles and practices requires significant attitudinal, philosophical and structural change,

---

[45] A more comprehensive account of the analysis provided in this paper is to be found in Umbreit *et al.* (2005b) in an article in the *Marquette Law Review*, Vol.89, No.2 (Winter), pp.251-304.

[46] In particular countries like Hungary, Bulgaria, Poland, Slovenia and Romania all of which have, over the past four years, actively participated in the COST Action A21 project into Restorative Justice Developments in Europe under the auspices of the European Forum for Restorative Justice. The forum comprises a total of 20 member states, including all of those within Western Europe, Scandinavia and also Cyprus and Israel (http: //www.cost.esf.org). The project was due to terminate with a final conference in Warsaw in November 2006.

there remains a reluctance in countries such as Britain to embrace it substantively. This is what the 'politics' of restorative justice is all about.

There are many challenges that restorative justice faces in the future. It is a movement that has developed largely from a wide 'practitioner' base within which knowledge and understanding of 'what really works' are hard earned yet abundant. Politicians and their policy advisers have good reason to be wary of experienced practitioners because the latter are apt to 'tell it like it is'. The judgement of Derek Lewis, a politically ill-fated though much respected former Director General of the Prison Service in England and Wales,[47] provides a fitting end-note to this work:

> Crime [in this country] will not stand still. If we are content to fiddle about on the fringes of the problem, the prospects are bleak: we will drift unwittingly into a world in which increasing numbers of people are held in prison and more money is spent on the criminal justice system, but the rate of crime stubbornly refuses to drop significantly … Alternatively, we have the opportunity to adopt new and more radical approaches, learning from the experiences of other countries and developing solutions of our own. (Lewis, 1997: 234)

Prophetic words indeed!

---

[47] Derek Lewis was dismissed by the (then) Home Secretary Michael Howard from his post as Director General of the Prison Service in England and Wales in October 1995, following a report by General Sir John Learmont into the much publicised escapes from Parkhurst Prison in January 1995 (Learmont, 1995). This report followed upon that of Sir John Woodcock into the attempted escape of IRA prisoners from Whitemoor Prison in September 1994 (Woodcock, 1994). Lewis's revealing and honest account of the events leading up to his dismissal is set out in his memoir *Hidden Agendas: Politics, Law and Disorder*, London: Hamish Hamilton (1997).

POSTSCRIPT

During the brief period of three months spent on the final revision of the main chapters of this book and its submission for publication, the penal crisis in England and Wales deepened considerably. On 31 March 2007, the prison population stood at 80,300, with the maximum operational capacity of the entire prisons estate exceeded, and an overflow of prisoners held in police cells and court premises (Campbell and Travis, 2007:1). It has also to be remembered that the maximum operational capacity level of prisons takes no account of accommodation temporarily out of use for refurbishment or repair, and that it considerably exceeds the certified normal accommodation figure at which prisons can ensure that the proper standards of decent, safe, uncrowded housing of inmates are maintained and that routine regime delivery can be fully provided.

Resort to the use of police cells (or even, as occurred in 2007, those at some court centres) is no solution to these problems, and is possibly even open to challenge in the civil courts or Europe. Ironically, those sentenced to imprisonment might be said to have the 'right' to serve their sentences in facilities designed for that purpose alone, and not to be confined in police custody conditions designed for the temporary accommodation of those under arrest prior to court appearance, detained for questioning and the like.

In spite of this inexorable rise in the prison population which is expected to escalate even further in the immediate future and despite the advice of the Lord Chief Justice of England and Wales that sentencing options other than imprisonment must be used much more widely, the preferred option of the present government is evidently to create more prison places rather than send fewer people to prison.

Yet, even as recently as May 2006, the same government was issuing statements about 'maximising the use of restorative justice within the Criminal Justice System as it works well in addressing the needs of the victim and in reducing recidivism' (Home Office, 2006a: 1; and see *Chapter 2 supra*). Herein lies the paradox both of 'doing justice better and the politics of restorative justice'. At present rates it costs an average of £37,000 a year to keep an offender in prison and in 2002, when police cells were last used, the temporary accommodation of some 600 inmates cost the Prison Service £10.4 million. This seems a very high price to pay for maintaining electoral credibility under extreme media pressure to 'preserve public safety'.

Overcrowded prisons quickly become dangerous places in which the safety of inmates and correctional staff is difficult, if not almost impossible to guarantee. Those with memories extending back to the early 1990s remember the extensive riots at Manchester and elsewhere within the United Kingdom that resulted directly from overcrowded conditions and impoverished regimes. 'Dustbin' prisons merely warehouse offenders; they do nothing to reduce recidivism or improve the likelihood of law-abiding behaviour. Public protection may be an important imperative, but so also is the duty of care towards those in state custody and their immediate relatives.

All of this seems to indicate only one thing: that unless prison custody is used more sparingly and greater use of community sanctions is insisted upon, the crisis will deepen still further and make the penal system chronically pathogenic. Restorative justice offers a means of avoiding exactly this situation, of making offenders responsible and of *doing justice better*. It may represent a bitter medicine for politicians with a preference for being 'tough on crime' but it stands a far better chance of being 'tough on the causes of crime'.

David J. Cornwell
May 2007

Bibliography

Acton, H.B. (ed), (1969), *The Philosophy of Punishment: A Collection of Papers*, London: Macmillan.

Adams, R. (1972), *Prison Riots in Britain and the USA*, Basingstoke: Macmillan.

Allen, F.A. (1981), *The Decline of the Rehabilitative Ideal*, Newhaven and London: Yale University Press.

Armstrong, K.G. (1961), 'The Retributivist Hits Back', in H.B. Acton (ed), (1969), *The Philosophy of Punishment: A Collection of Papers*, London: Macmillan, pp.138-58.

Ashworth, A. (1992a), *Sentencing and Criminal Justice*, (1st Edition), London: Butterworth.

Ashworth, A. (1992b), 'What Victims of Crime Deserve', Paper to the *Fullbright Colloquium Penal Theory and Penal Practice*, University of Stirling, (September).

Ashworth, A. (1993a), 'Some Doubts About Restorative Justice', *Criminal Law Forum*, vol.4, pp.277-99.

Ashworth, A. (1993b), 'Victim Impact Statements and Sentencing', *Criminal Law Review*, pp.498-509.

Baxter, R. and Nuttall, C. (1978), 'Severer Sentences – No Deterrent to Crime', in J. Baldwin and A.K. Bottomley (eds), *Criminal Justice*, London: Martin Robertson, pp.221-6.

Bean, P. (1981), *Punishment: A Philosophical and Criminological Inquiry*, Oxford: Martin Robertson.

Beyleveld, D. (1979), 'Deterrence Research as a Basis for Deterrence Policies', *Howard Journal of Criminal Justice*, vol. XVIII, pp.135-49.

Biermans, N. (2002), 'Restorative Justice and the Prison System', *Proceedings of the 4th Annual Conference of the International Corrections and Prisons Association*, (ICPA), Ottawa: ICPA, pp.161-4.

Biggar, N. (ed), (2004), *Burying the Past: Making Peace and Doing Justice After Civil Conflict*, Washington, DC: Georgetown University Press.

Blad, J.R. (2003), 'Against "Penal Instrumentalism": Building a Global Alliance for Restorative Justice Processes and Family Empowerment', *Proceedings of the 4th International Conference on Conferencing, Circles and Other Restorative Practices*, pp.130-41

Blad, J.R. (2006a), 'The Seductiveness of Punishment and the Case for Restorative Justice', in D.J. Cornwell, *Criminal Punishment and Restorative Justice*, Winchester: Waterside Press, pp.135-48.

Blad, J.R. (2006b),'Institutionalizing Restorative Justice? Transforming Criminal Justice?' in I. Aertsen, T. Daems and L. Robert (eds), *Institutionalizing Restorative Justice*, Devon: Willan Publishing, pp.93-117.

Blair, T. (1993), 'Why Crime is a Socialist Issue', *New Statesman and Society*, (29 January), pp.27-8.

Blom-Cooper, L. and Drewry, G. (eds), (1976), *Law and Morality: A Reader*, London: Duckworth.

Bonta, J., Wallace-Capretta, S. and Rooney, J. (1998), *Restorative Justice: An Evaluation of the Restorative Resolutions Project*, Ottawa: Solicitor General Canada.

Bottoms, Sir A.E. (1977), 'Reflections on the Renaissance of Dangerousness', *Howard Journal of Criminal Justice*, vol. XVI, no.2, pp.70-96.

Bottoms, Sir A.E. (1995), 'The Philosophy and Politics of Punishment and Sentencing', in C.M.V. Clarkson and R. Morgan (eds), *The Politics of Sentencing Reform*, Oxford: Clarendon Press,

Bottoms, Sir A.E. and Brownsword, R. (1983), 'Dangerousness and Rights', in J.W. Hinton (ed), *Dangerousness: Problems of Assessment and Prediction*, London: Allen and Unwin, pp.233-7.

Box, S. (1971), *Deterrence, Reality and Society*, London: Holt, Reinhart and Winston.

Box, S. (1981), *Deterrence, Reality and Society*, (Second Edition), London: Holt, Reinhart and Winston.

Box, S. (1987), *Recession, Crime and Punishment*, London: Macmillan.

Braithwaite, J. (1989), *Crime, Shame and Reintegration*, Cambridge: Cambridge University Press.

Braithwaite, J. (1991), 'The Political Agenda of Republican Criminology', Paper to the *British Criminology Society Conference*, University of York, (July).

Braithwaite, J. (2001), *Restorative Justice and Responsive Regulation*, New York: Oxford University Press.

Braithwaite, J. and Petit, P. (1990), *Not Just Deserts: A Republican Theory of Criminal Justice*, New York: Oxford University Press.

Brody, S.R. (1976), *The Effectiveness of Sentencing*, Home Office Research Study No.35, London: HMSO.

Brunk, C. (2001), 'Restorative Justice and the Philosophical Theories of Criminal Punishment', in M.L. Hadley (ed), *The Spiritual Roots of Restorative Justice*, Albany, NY: State University of New York Press, pp.31-56.

Campbell, D. and Travis, A. (2007), 'UK Headed for Prison Meltdown', *Guardian*, 31 March, p. 1 and 14-15.

Cavadino, M. (1992), 'Theorising the Penal Crisis', in A.K. Bottomley, T. Fowles, R. Reiner and S. Walklate (eds), *Criminal Justice: Theory and Practice*, London: British Society of Criminology, pp 1-22.

Cavadino, M. (1994), 'The UK Penal Crisis: Where Next?', in A. Duff, S. Marshall, R.E. Dobash and R.P. Dobash (eds), *Penal Theory and Penal Practice: Transition and Innovation in Criminal Justice*, Manchester: Manchester University Press, pp.42-56.

Cavadino, M. and Dignan, J. (1997a), *The Penal System: An Introduction* (Second Edition), London: SAGE Publications.

Cavadino, M, and Dignan, J. (1997b), 'Reparation, Retribution and Rights', in *International Review of Victimology*, 4. pp.233-53.

Cayley, D. (1998), *The Expanding Prison: The Crisis in Crime and Punishment and the Search for Alternatives*, Canada: House of Anansi Press.

Church of England Board for Social Responsibility (1978), *Prisons and Prisoners in England Today*, London: CIO Publishing.

Civitas, (2005), *Fighting Crime: Are Public Policies Working?* (Online Briefing – November), www.civitas.org.uk/pdf/crimeBriefing Nov15/pdf.

Cooper, P. (1991), *An Enquiry Into the Role of Punishment According to Blameworthiness in English Criminal Justice*, Unpublished Ph.D. Thesis: University of Sheffield (England).

Cormier, R.B. (2006), 'Where There's a Will There's a Way: A Canadian Perspective on Restorative Justice', in D.J. Cornwell, (2006), *Criminal Punishment and Restorative Justice*, Winchester: Waterside Press, pp.149-162.

Cornwell, D.J. (1985a), 'Antilla's Dilemma: The Emergence of a "Third Alternative" in the Practice of Punishment by Imprisonment', *Prison Service Journal*, vol.57, pp.2-8.

Cornwell, D.J. (1985b), 'The Rehabilitative Ethic: Categorical Imperative or Achilles' Heel Within Custodial Punishment?', *Prison Service Journal*, vol.60, pp.4-8.

Cornwell, D.J. (1989), *Criminal Dangerousness and Its Punishment: Beyond the Phenomenological Illusion*, D.Phil. Thesis, University of York.

Cornwell, D.J. (2006), *Criminal Punishment and Restorative Justice*, Winchester: Waterside Press.

Coyle, A. (2001a), 'Relational Justice', in *Relational Justice Bulletin*, Issue 11, (August), p.3, and also quoted in F.W.M. McElrea (J), (2002a), 'Restorative Justice Issues and Trends: Where is Restorative Justice Going?' Proceedings of the 4th *Annual Conference of the International Corrections and Prisons Association* (ICPA), Ottawa: ICPA, pp.64-70.

Coyle, A. (2001b), 'Restorative Justice in the Prison Setting', Paper to the International Prison Chaplains Association Conference (Europe), www.icpa.net.

Cullen, F. and Gilbert, K. (1982), *Reaffirming Rehabilitation*, Cincinnati: Anderson.

Davey, L. (2005), 'The Development of Restorative Justice in the United Kingdom: A Personal Perspective', Paper to the *Sixth International Conference on Conferencing, Circles and Other Restorative Practices*, Penrith, Australia: International Institute for Restorative Practices (IIRP), (March).

Dignan, J. (2002), 'Restorative Justice and the Law: The Case for an Integrated Systemic Approach', in L. Walgrave (ed), *Restorative Justice and the Law*, Devon: Willan Publishing, pp.168-190.

Dilulio, J.J. Jnr. (1987), *Governing Prisons: A Comparative Study of Correctional Management*, New York: Free Press.

Doward, J. (2006a), 'Police Cells Ready as Prison Population Hits 80,000', *The Observer*, 24 September, (News), p.9.

Doward, J. (2006b), 'Violence Fears Grow as Offenders Go Unchecked', *The Observer*, 29 January (News), p.7.

Doyle, J. (1967), 'Justice and Legal Punishment', in H.B. Acton (ed), (1969), *The Philosophy of Punishment: A Collection of Papers*, London: Macmillan, pp.159-171.

Dunning, A. (2006), *World Prison Brief*, London: International Centre for Prison Studies, King's College, (June).

Dworkin, R. (1978), *Taking Rights Seriously*, London: Duckworth.

Dworkin, R. (1986), *A Matter of Principle*, Oxford: Oxford University Press.

Eaton, J. and McElrea, F.W.M. (J) (2003a), *Sentencing: The New Dimensions*, New Zealand Law Society Seminar, (March).

Eaton, J. and McElrea, F.W.M. (J) (2003b), 'Restorative Justice – An Explanation', in *Sentencing: The New Dimensions*, New Zealand Law Society Seminar, (March).

Edgar, K. and Newell, T, (2006), *Restorative Justice in Prisons: Making It Happen*, Winchester: Waterside Press.

Esmeé Fairbairn Foundation (EFF) (2004a), *Crime, Courts and Confidence: Report of an Independent Inquiry into Alternatives to Prison*, London: The Stationery Office.

Esmeé Fairbairn Foundation (EFF) (2004b), *Rethinking Crime and Punishment*, (Chairman: Baroness Linklater), London: Beacon Press.

European Forum for Victim-Offender Mediation (2000), *Victim – Offender Mediation in Europe*, Leuven: Leuven University Press.

Evans, P. (1980), *Prison Crisis*, London: George Allen and Unwin.

Ewing, A.C. (1929), *The Morality of Punishment*, London: Kegan Paul, Trench and Trubner.

Fitzgerald, M. and Sim, J. (1982), *British Prisons*, (Second Edition), Oxford: Basil Blackwell.

Fleisher, M.S. (1989), *Warehousing Violence*, London and Newbury Park, California: SAGE Publications.

Flew, A.G.N. (1954), 'The Justification of Punishment', *Philosophy*, vol.29, no.3 (October), pp.291-307. Also in H.B. Acton (ed), (1969), *The Philosophy of Punishment: A Collection of Papers*, London: Macmillan, pp.81-104. (Flew's (1967) 'Postscript' is at pp.102-4).

Foggo, D. and Grimston, J. (2006), 'Tagged Criminals Shun Curfews and Run Amok', London: *The Sunday Times*, 29 January, pp.1 and 4.

Foucault, M. (1977), *Discipline and Punish: The Birth of the Prison*, (Tr. Allen Lane), Harmondsworth: Penguin Books.

Fowles, A.J. (1989), *Prisoners' Rights in England and the United States*, Aldershot: Avebury Press.

Friendship, C., Blud, L., Erickson, M. and Travers, R. (2002), *An Evaluation of Cognitive Behavioural Treatment for Prisoners*, (Home Office Research Finding No. 161), London: Home Office Communications Development Unit.

Friendship, C., Falshaw, L. and Beech, A.R. (2003), 'Measuring the Penal Impact of Accredited Offending Behaviour Programmes', *Journal of Legal and Criminal Psychology*, 8, pp.115-127.

Galway, B., Hudson, J. and Morris, A. (1995), *Family Group Conferences: Perspectives on Policy and Pratice*, Monsey, NY: Criminal Justice Press.

Garland, D. (2002), *The Culture of Control: Crime and Social Order in Contemporary Society*, Oxford: Oxford University Press.

Gendreau, P. and Ross, R.R. (1987), 'Revivification of Rehabilitation: Evidence From the 1980s', *Justice Quarterly*, 4, pp.349-407.

Gibb, F. and Ford, R. (2006), 'Law Chief Attacks Long Sentences', *The Times*, 11 October, p.11.

Graham, J., Woodfield, K., Tibble, M. and Kitchen, S. (2004), *Testaments of Harm: A Qualitative Evaluation of the VPS Scheme*, London: Home Office.

Green, R.G. (1998), *Justice in Aboriginal Communities: Sentencing Alternatives*, Saskatoon, SA: Purich Publishing.

Griffiths, J.A.G. (1991), *The Politics of the Judiciary*, (4th Edition), London: Fontana.

Gross, H. (1979), *A Theory of Criminal Justice*, New York: Oxford University Press.

Hanks, P. (ed), (1979), *Collins Dictionary of the English Language*, London and Glasgow: Collins.

Hanson, R.K. (2001), *Age and Sexual Recidivism: A Comparison of Rapists and Child Molesters*, Ottawa: Solicitor General Canada.

Harris, A.J.R. and Hanson, R.K. (2004), *Sex Offender Recidivism: A Simple Question*, Ottawa: Public Safety and Preparedness Canada.

Hart, H.L.A. (1968), *Punishment and Responsibility*, Oxford: Oxford University Press.

Hayes, H. and Daly, K. (2004), 'Conferencing and Re-offending in Queensland', *Australian and New Zealand Journal of Criminology*, 37 (2), pp. 167-191.

Hayley, H.J. (1984), 'Retribution and the Definition of a Just Measure of Pain', in D.J. Müller, D.E. Blackman and A.J. Chapman (eds), *Psychology and Law*, London: John Wiley and Sons.

Von Hirsch, A. (1976), *Doing Justice*, (Report of the Committee for the Study of Incarceration), New York: Hill and Wang.

Von Hirsch, A. (1993), *Censure and Sanctions*, Oxford: Clarendon Press.

Home Office (1969), *People in Prison (England and Wales)*, Cmnd. 4214, London: HMSO.

Home Office (1976), *Review of Criminal Justice Policy*, London: HMSO,

Home Office (1990), *Crime, Justice and Protecting the Public: The Government's Proposals for Legislation*, Cm. 965, London: HMSO.

Home Office (1991), *Custody, Care and Justice*, Cm. 1647, London: HMSO.

Home Office (2000), *Setting the Boundaries*, London: Home Office.

Home Office (2001a), *The 2001 British Crime Survey: First Results, England and Wales*, Statistical Bulletin 18/01, (October), London: HMSO.

Home Office (2001b), *Making Punishments Work: Report of a Review of the Sentencing Framework for England and Wales*, (The Halliday Report), London: Home Office Communications Directorate.

Home Office (2002a), *Justice For All*, CM 5563, London: HMSO.

Home Office (2002b), *Protecting the Public*, CM 5568, London: Home Office.

Home Office (2002c), *Justice For All: Responses to the Auld and Halliday Reports*, London: Home Office.

Home Office (2003a), *International Comparison of Criminal Justice Statistics*, (Barclay, Tavares *et al.* (eds)), London: Home Office Research and Statistics Directorate, and www.homeoffice.gov.uk/rds/pdfs2/hosb.pdf.

Home Office (2003b), *Restorative Justice: The Government's Strategy*, (Consultation Document), London, Home Office Communications Directorate.

Home Office (2003c), *A New Deal for Victims and Witnesses: National Strategy to Deliver Improved Services*, (July), provided at www/cjsonline.gov.uk/home/html.

Home Office (2004), *The 2004 British Crime Survey*, available at www.crimestatistics.org.uk/output.

Home Office (2005a), *Crime Statistics – England and Wales*, summary data available at www.crimestatistics.org.uk/output/page63.asp.

Home Office (2005b), *Re-building Lives – Supporting Victims of Crime*, CM 6705, London: HMSO (December).

Home Office (2005c), *The Code of Practice for Victims of Crime*, London: HMSO (October).

Home Office (2005d), *Victims' Rights*, www.homeoffice.gov.uk/crime-victims/victims.

Home Office (2006a), *Crime in England and Wales 2005/6*, (A. Walker, C. Kershaw and S. Nicholas (eds)), London: Home Office Research, Development and Statistics Directorate.

Home Office (2006b), *Prison Population Projections 2006-2013 England and Wales*, Statistical Bulletin 11/06, (N. deSilva, P. Cowell and P. Worthington (eds)), London: Home Office Research, Development and Statistics Directorate, (July).

Home Office (2006c), 'Working Offenders', (Briefing Document) in *Restorative Justice: The Government's Strategy*, www.crimereduction.gov.uk/workingoffenders42.htm.

Home Office (2006d), *Prison Population*, www.statistics,gov.uk/cci (3 January).

Home Office (2006e), *Crime Statistics, England and Wales 2005/6*, London: Home Office Research, Development and Statistics Directorate.

Honderich, T. (1986), *Punishment: The Supposed Justifications*, Harmondsworth: Peregrine Books.

Hoskison, J. (1998), *Inside: One Man's Experience of Prison*, London: John Murray.

Hough, M. and Mitchell, D. (2003), 'Drug-dependent Offenders and Justice for All', in M. Tonry (ed), *Confronting Crime: Crime Control Policy Under New Labour*, Devon: Willan Publishing, pp.26-50.

Hoyle, C., Morgan, R. and Sanders, A. (1999), *The Victims' Charter: An Evaluation of Pilot Projects*, Research Findings No.107, London: Home Office Research, Development and Statistics Directorate.

Hudson, B. (1987), *Justice Through Punishment*, Basingstoke: Macmillan Education.

Hutton, N. (2003), 'Sentencing Guidelines', in M. Tonry (ed), *Confronting Crime: Crime Control Policy Under New Labour*, Devon: Willan Publishing, pp.112-39.

Ignatieff, M. (1978), *A Just Measure of Pain: The Penitentiary in the Industrial Revolution 1750-1850*, New York: Columbia University Press.

International Centre for Prison Studies (ICPS) (2006), *World Prison Populations (UK and Western Europe)*, London: King's College. Also available at: http://news.bbc.co.uk/2/shared/spl/hi/uk/06/prisons/html/nnlpage1.stm.

Irwin, J. (1985), *The Jail: Managing the Underclass in American Society*, Berkeley, CA: University of California Press.

Johnston, N. (1973), *The Human Cage: A Brief History of Prison Architecture*, New York: Walker.

Joutsen, M. (1987), *The Role of the Victim of Crime in European Criminal Justice Systems*, Helsinki, Finland: HEUNI.

Joutsen, M., Rahti, R. and Pölönen, P. (2001), *Criminal Justice Systems in Europe and North America – Finland*, Helsinki: Academic Bookstore.

Jung, H. (2003), 'The Renaissance of the Victim in Criminal Policy', in L. Zedner and A. Ashworth (eds), *The Criminological Foundations of Penal Policy*, (Essays in Honour of Roger Hood), Oxford: Oxford University Press, pp.443-62.

Kaptein, H. (2004), 'Against the Pains of Punishment: Retribution as Reparation Through Penal Servitude', in H. Kaptein and M. Malsch, *Crime, Victims and Justice: Essays on Principles and Practice*, Aldershot, UK and Burlington, VT: Ashgate Publishing, pp.80-111.

Karp, D.R. (2004), 'Birds of a Feather: A Response to the McCold Critique of Community Justice', *Criminal Justice Review*, vol.7, no.1, (March), pp.59-67.

Karp, D.R. and Todd, R.C. (eds), (2002), 'What is Community Justice? Case Studies in Community Supervision', *Pine Forge Series in Criminal Justice*, SAGE Publications.

Kessler, J. (2002), 'Research: Prisons Designs to Support Professional Corrections', Proceedings of the 4th Annual Conference of the *International Corrections and Prisons Association* (ICPA), Ottawa: ICPA, pp.212-230.

King, R.D. and McDermott, K. (1989), 'British Prisons 1970-1987: The Ever-Deepening Crisis', *British Journal of Criminology*, vol.29, pp.107-28.

Krasnow, P. (1998), *Correctional Facility Design and Detailing*, New York: McGraw-Hill.

Kyvsgaard, B. (2001), 'Penal Sanctions and the Use of Imprisonment in Denmark', in M. Tonry (ed), *Penal Reform in Overcrowded Times*, New York: Oxford University Press.

Lappi-Seppälä, T. (2001), 'Sentencing and Punishment in Finland: The Decline of the Repressive Ideal', in M. Tonry and R.S. Frase (eds), *Sentencing and Sanctions in Western Countries*, New York: Oxford University Press.

La Prairie, C. (1992), 'Aboriginal Criminal Justice: Explaining the Present, Exploring the Future', *Canadian Journal of Criminology*, vol.43, pp.281-297.

Larsson, P. (2001), 'Norway Prison Use Up Slightly: Community Penalty Lots', in M. Tonry (ed), *Penal Reform in Overcrowded Times*, New York: Oxford University Press.

Latimer, J., Dowden, C. and Muise, D. (eds), *The Effectiveness of Restrictive Practices: A Meta-Analysis*, Ottawa: Department of Justice, Research and Statistics Division Methodological Series.

Lea, J. and Young, J. (1984), *Law and Order*, Harmondsworth: Penguin Books.

Learmont, Sir J. (Gen), (1995), *Review of Prison Service Security in England and Wales and the Escape from Parkhurst Prison on Tuesday 3rd January 1995*, Cm 3020, London: HMSO.

Lewis, D. (1997), *Hidden Agendas: Politics, Law and Disorder*, London: Hamish Hamilton.

Lipton, D., Martinson, R. and Wilks, J. (1975), *Effectiveness of Treatment Evaluation Studies*, New York: Praeger Publications.

Mabbott, J.D. (1939), 'Punishment', in H.B. Acton (ed), (1969), *The Philosophy of Punishment: A Collection of Papers*, London: Macmillan, pp.39-54.

Maguire, M. and Corbett, C. (1987), *The Effects of Crime and the Work of Victim Support Schemes*, Aldershot: Gower.

Marshall, C.D. (2001), *Beyond Retribution: A New Testament Vision for Justice, Crime and Punishment*, Grand Rapids, Michigan: W.B. Eerdmans Publishing Co.

Martinson, R. (1974), 'What Works? – Questions and Answers About Prison Reform', *The Public Interest*, 35, pp.22-54. (Also in J.A. Gardiner and M.A. Mulkey (eds), *Crime and Criminal Justice*, London and Lexington: D.C. Heath and Company, pp.155-87.)

Matravers, A. and Hughes, G.V. (2003), 'Unprincipled Sentencing? The Policy Approach to Dangerous Sex Offenders', in M. Tonry (ed), *Confronting Crime: Crime Control Policy Under New Labour*, Devon: Willan Publishing, pp.51-79.

Mauer, M. (2003), *Comparative International Rates of Incarceration: An Evaluation of Causes and Trends*, available from www.sentencing project.org/pdfs/pub9036/pdf.

Maxwell, G. and Morris, A. (2001), 'Family Group Conferencing and Re-offending', in Morris, A. and Maxwell, G. *Restorative Justice for Juveniles: Conferencing, Mediation and Circles*, Oxford: Hart Publishing.

McCold, P. (2004), 'Paradign Muddle: The Threat to Restorative Justice Posed by its Merger With Community Justice', *Contemporary Justice Review*, vol.7, no.1, pp.13-35.

McElrea, F.W.M. (J) (2002a), 'Restorative Justice Issues and Trends: Where is Restorative Justice Going?' in *Proceedings of the 4th Annual Conference of the International Corrections and Prisons Association*(ICPA), Ottawa: ICPA, pp.64-74.

McElrea, F.W.M. (J) (2002b), 'Restorative Justice: A New Zealand Perspective', Paper to the Conference *Modernising Criminal Justice: New World Challenges*, London (June).

McElrea, F.W.M. (J), (2005), 'The New Zealand Experience of Restorative Justice Legislation', Paper to *The 11th Annual Restorative Justice Conference*, Fresno Pacific University, California, (September).

McElrea, F.W.M. (J) (2006), 'Restorative Justice: A New Zealand Perspective', in D.J. Cornwell, *Criminal Punishment and Restorative Justice*, Winchester: Waterside Press, pp.119-134.

McGuire, J. (ed) (1995), *What Works: Reducing Re-offending – Guidelines From Research and Practice*, London: John Wiley.

McKittrick, N. and Rex, S. (2003), 'Sentence Management: A New Role for the Judiciary?' in M. Tonry (ed), *Confronting Crime: Crime Control Policies Under New Labour*, Devon: Willan Publishing, pp.140-155.

Miers, D. (2001), *An International Review of Restorative Justice*, (Crime Reduction Research Paper 10), London: Home Office.

Mika, H. (ed) (1955), 'Special Issue: Victim Offender Mediation – International Perspectives on Research Theory and Practice, *Mediation Quarterly*, 12(3), pp.199-297.

Miles, A. (2006), 'Misery, Anger, Hurt, Confusion. Yep, a Politician Just Had Another Bright Idea', *The Times*, 19 April, p.19.

Millie, A., Jacobsen, J. and Hough, M. (2003), 'Understanding the Growth of the Prison Population in England and Wales', *Criminal Justice*, vol.3, no.4, pp. 369-387.

Monahan, J. (1975), 'The Prediction of Violence', in D. Chappell and J. Monahan (eds), *Violence and Criminal Justice*, Lexington Books.

Monahan, J. (1978), 'The Prediction of Violent Criminal Behaviour: A Methodological Critique and Prospectus', in A. Blumstein, *et al.* (eds), *Deterrence and Incapacitation: Estimating the Effects of Criminal Sanctions on Crime Rates*, Washington, DC: National Academy of Sciences, pp.244-69.

Monahan, J. (1981a), *The Clinical Prediction of Violent Behaviour*, (Crime and Delinquency Series Monograph), Washington, DC: Department of Human Sciences.

Monahan, J. (1981b), *Predicting Violent Behaviour*, (SAGE Library of Social Research), SAGE Publications.

Morris, A. and Maxwell, G. (2002), 'Restorative Justice in New Zealand', in A. von Hirsch *et al.* (eds), *Restorative Justice and Criminal Justice: Competing or Reconcilable Paradigms?* Oxford: Hart Publishing.

Morris, C. (2004), *Restorative Justice: Criminal Harms and Historical Injustice, Conflict Transformation and Peace-building: A Selected Bibliography*, re-printable and available at www.peacemakers.ca/bibliography/bib11restorative.html.

Morris, N. (1974), *The Future of Imprisonment*, London and Chicago: University of Chicago Free Press.

Morris, T. (1989), *Crime and Criminal Justice Since 1945*, Oxford: Basil Blackwell.

Mundle, C.W.K. (1954), 'Punishment and Desert', in H.B. Acton (ed), (1969), *The Philosophy of Punishment: A Collection of Papers*, London: Macmillan, pp.65-82. (Mundle's (1968) 'Postscript' is at p.81-2.)

Nagel, W.G. (1977), 'On Behalf of a Moratorium on Prison Construction', *International Journal of Crime and Delinquency*, 23, (April), pp.154-172.

New Statesman (2003), *Community Justice: Concepts and Delivery*, London, (December), available at www.newstatesman.co.uk/pdf/communityjustice 2003 supp.pdf.

Newell, T. (2002), *Restorative Justice in Prisons: The Possibility of Change*, Unpublished Cropwood Fellowship Report. (See also: Newell, T. and Edgar, K. (2006), *Restorative Justice in Prisons: Making it Happen*, Winchester: Waterside Press.)

Nugent, W.R. (2001), 'Participation in Victim-Offender Mediation and Reoffense: Successful Replications?' *Journal of Research in Social Work Practice*, vol.11, no.1, (January), pp.5-23.

Office for National Statistics (2006), *Social Trends*, (No.36), London: ONS, pp.137-8.

O'Hear, M.M. (2005), 'Is Restorative Justice Compatible With Sentencing Uniformity?', in *Marquette Law Review*, vol.89, no.2, pp.305-325.

Orr, D. (2006), 'This Government Jails People Because It Finds Helping Them Too Difficult', *The Independent*, 14 October, p.16.

Packer, H.L. (1965), 'Toward An Integrated Theory of Criminal Punishment' in *The Limits of the Penal Sanction*, London: Oxford University Press, pp.62-70.

Packer, H.L. (1973), 'The Justification of Punishment' in L. Orland (ed), *Justice, Punishment, Treatment*, London and New York: Collier Macmillan Publishers, pp.183-207.

Palmer, T. (1975), 'Martinson Revisited', *Journal of Research in Crime and Delinquency*, vol.12, pp.133-152.

Prison Reform Trust (1995), *The Prison Population Explosion*, London: PRT.

Radzinowicz, Sir L. (1972), 'Towards a Pragmatic Position', in R.J. Gerber and P.D. McAnany (eds), *Contemporary Punishment*, London and Notre Dame: University of Notre Dame Free Press, pp.238-245.

Ramsbotham, Sir D. (2003), *Prison-Gate*, London: Free Press.

Rawls, J. (1958), 'Justice as Fairness', *The Philosophical Review*, vol.LXVII, pp.164-194.

Reform International (2006), *Prison Statistics – England and Wales*, available at www.reform.co.uk/website/crime/factfile.aspx.

Restorative Justice Consortium (RJC) (2002), *Statement of Restorative Justice Principles*, London: RJC.

Rhodes, R.P. (1975), 'Political Theory, Policy Analysis and The Insoluble Problems of Crime', in J.A. Gardiner and M.A. Mulkey (eds), *Crime and Criminal Justice* (Issues in Public Policy Analysis), Lexington, DC and London: D.C. Heath and Company.

Riddell, M. (2006), 'Yes, That's Me With the Spade: How Top Judge Turned Convict', *The Observer*, 8 October, pp.24-5.

Roberts, J.V. and Roach, K. (2003), 'Restorative Justice in Canada', in A. von Hirsch, J. Roberts, A.E. Bottoms, K. Roach and M. Schiff (eds), *Restorative Justice and Criminal Justice: Competing or Reconcilable Paradigms?*, Oxford: Hart Publishing, pp. 237-256.

Roberts, J. and Smith, M.E. (2003), 'Custody Plus, Custody Minus', in M. Tonry (ed), *Confronting Crime: Crime Control Under New Labour*, Devon UK: Willan Publishing, pp.182-210.

Rodgers, B. (2005), *New Directions in Community Justice*, London: Institute for Public Policy Research.

Ross, R. (1996), *Returning to the Teaching: Exploring Aboriginal Justice*, New York: Penguin Books.

Rose, G. (2003), *The Criminal Histories of Serious Traffic Offenders*, (Home Office Research Study No. 206), London: Home Office Communications Unit, (October).

Rothman, D.J. (1973), 'Decarcerating Prisoners and Patients', *Civil Liberties Review*, 1, 8.

Rutherford, A. (1986), *Prisoners and the Process of Justice*, Oxford: Oxford University Press.

Schärf, W. (2000), 'Community Justice and Community Policy in Post-Apartheid South Africa: How Appropriate are the Justice Systems of Africa?', *International Workshop on the Rule of Law and Development: Citizen Security, Rights and Life Choices in Law and Middle Income Countries*, University of Sussex: Institute for Development Studies, (June).

Schiff, M. (2000), *Restorative Community Justice*, Cincinnati: Anderson Publishing.

Schiff, M. and Bazemore, G. (2004), 'Paradigm Muddle or Paradigm Paralysis? The Wide and Narrow Roads to Restorative Justice Reform (or, A Little Confusion May be a Good Thing)', *Criminal Justice Review*, vol.17, no.1, (March), pp.37-57.

Scottish Consortium on Crime and Criminal Justice (2005), *Reducing the Prison Population: Penal Policy and Social Choices*, Edinburgh: CCCJ.

Scottish Parliament (2006), *The Community Justice Authorities (Establishment and Proceedings) (Scotland) Order 2006*, SSI 206 (Draft), Edinburgh: HMSO.

Shapland, J., Willmore, J. and Duff, P. (1985), *Victims in the Criminal Justice Process*, Aldershot: Gower (Cambridge Studies in Criminology, 53).

Scull, A.T. (1977), *Decarceration: Community Treatment and the Deviant: A Radical Review*, (First Edition), Englewood Cliffs, NJ: Prentice-Hall.

Sharpe, S. (1998), *Restorative Justice: A Vision for Healing and Change*, Edmonton, Alberta: Edmonton Victim Offender Mediation Society.

Sharpe, S. (2003), *Beyond the Comfort Zone: A Guide to the Practice of Community Conferencing*, Calgary: Calgary Community Conferencing.

Sherman, L., Strang, H. and Woods, D. (2000), *Recidivism Patterns in the Canberra Reintegrative Shaming Experiments*, Canberra: Australian National University.

Sherman, L. and Strang, H. (2004), *Restorative Justice: What We Know and How We Know It*, available at: www.scs.upem.edu/jerrylee/research/WorkingPaper.pdf.

Shulmans Solicitors (2006), *Legal Update: Crime Victim Personal Statement*, available at: www.schulmans.org.uk/update.

Sidgewick, H. (1893), 'The Methods of Ethics', Book III, Chapter 5, (5th Edition), reprinted in F.A. Olafson (ed), *Justice and Social Policy*, Englewood Cliffs, NJ: Prentice-Hall, pp.3-8.

Sim, J. (1992), 'When You Ain't Got Nothing, You Got Nothing To Lose', in K. Bottomley, T. Fowles and R. Reiner (eds), *Criminal Justice: Theory and Practice*, London: British Society of Criminology, pp.273-300.

Smart, A. (1969), 'Mercy', in H.B. Acton (ed) (1969), *The Philosophy of Punishment: A Collection of Papers*, London: Macmillan, pp.212-227.

Steadman, H.J. and Cocozza, J.J. (1973), 'Some Evidence on the Inadequacy of the Concept and Determination of Dangerousness in Law and Psychiatry', *Journal of Psychiatry and Law*, vol.1, pp.409-426.

Steadman, H.J. and Cocozza, J.J. (1974), *Careers of the Criminally Insane: Excessive Social Control of Deviance*, Lexington: D.C. Hearth and Company.

Stenson, K. and Sullivan, R. (eds) (2000), *Crime, Risks and Justice: The Politics of Crime Control in Liberal Democracies*, Devon: Willan Publishing.

Strang, H. (2001), *Restorative Justice Programmes in Australia: A Report to the Criminology Research Council*, Australian Government: Criminology Research Council.

Strang, H. (2004a), 'The Threat to Restorative Justice Posed by the Merger with Community Justice: A Paradigm Muddle', *Criminal Justice Review*, vol.7, no.1, (March), pp.75-79.

Strang, H. (2004b), 'Is Restorative Justice Imposing its Agenda on Victims?' in H. Zehr and B. Toews (eds), *Critical Issues in Restorative Justice*, Monsey, NY and Devon, UK: Willan Publishing, pp.95-105.

Tak, P. (2001), 'Sentencing and Punishment in The Netherlands', in M. Tonry and R..S. Frase (eds), *Sentencing and Sanctions in Western Countries*, New York: Oxford University Press.

Thomas, J.E. and Pooley, R. (1980), *The Exploding Prison*, London: Junction Books.

Thornberry, T.P. and Christenson, R. (1984), 'Unemployment and Criminal Involvement', *American Sociological Review*, vol.49, pp.398-411.

Tonry, M. (ed) (2001), *Penal Reform in Overcrowded Times*, New York: Oxford University Press.

Tonry, M. (ed) (2003), *Confronting Crime: Crime Control Policy Under New Labour*, Devon: Willan Publishing.

Tonry, M. and Frase, R.S. (eds) (2001), *Sentencing and Sanctions in Western Countries*, New York: Oxford University Press.

Tonry, M. and Green, D. (2003), 'Criminology and Public Policy in the US and the UK', in L. Zedner and A. Ashworth (eds), *The Criminological Foundations of Penal Policy*, (Essays in Honour of Roger Hood), Oxford: Oxford University Press.

Treverton-Jones, G.D. (1989), *Imprisonment: The Legal Status and Rights of Prisoners*, London: Sweet and Maxwell.

Umbreit, M.S. (2001), *The Handbook of Victim Offender Mediation*, San Fransisco: Jossey Bass.

Umbreit, M.S., Coates, R.B. and Kalanj, B. (1994), *Victim Meets Offender: The Impact of Restorative Justice and Mediation*, Monsey, NY: Criminal Justice Press.

Umbreit, M.S., Coates, R.B. and Vos, B. (2004), 'Restorative Justice Versus Community Justice: Clarifying a Muddle or Generating Confusion?', *Criminal Justice Review*, vol.17, no.1, pp.81-89.

Umbreit, M.S., Vos, B. and Coates, R.B. (2005a), *Opportunities and Pitfalls Facing the Restorative Justice Movement*, University of Minnesota: Centre for Restorative Justice and Peacemaking.

Umbreit, M.S., Vos, B., Coates, R.B. and Lightfoot, E. (2005b), 'Restorative Justice in the Twenty-First Century: A Social Movement Full of Opportunities and Pitfalls', *Marquette Law Review*, vol.89, no.2, (Winter), pp.251-304.

Umbreit, M.S., Vos, B. and Coates,R.B. (2006), *Restorative Justice Dialogue: Evidence-Based Practice*, University of Minnesota: Centre for Restorative Justice and Peacemaking.

Underdown, A. (1995), *The Effectiveness of Community Supervision: Performance and Potential*, Manchester: Greater Manchester Probation Service.

Van den Haag, E. (1975), *Punishing Criminals*, New York: Basic Books Inc.

Van Ness, D.W. (2005), 'Restorative Justice in Prisons', Paper to the *Symposium on Restorative Justice and Peace*, Columbia, California, (February).

Victim Offender Mediation Association (VOMA) (2005), *VOMA Bibliography*, available at www.voma.org/bibliography.shtml.

Walgrave, L. (2003), 'Imposing Restoration Instead of Inflicting Pain', in A. von Hirsch *et. al.* (eds), *Restorative Justice and Criminal Justice: Competing or Reconcilable Paradigms?* Oxford, UK and Portland, Oregon: Hart Publishing, pp.61-78.

Walsh, D and Poole, A. (eds) (1983), *A Dictionary of Criminology*, London: Routledge and Kegan Paul.

Watson, D., Boucherat, J. and Davis, D. (1989), 'Reparation for Recidivists', in M. Wright and B. Galway (eds), *Mediation and Criminal Justice: Victims, Offenders and Community*, London: SAGE Publications.

Wiegend, T. (2001), 'Sentencing and Punishment in Germany', in M. Tonry and R.S. Frase (eds), *Sentencing and Sanctions in Western Countries*, New York: Oxford University Press.

Wiles, P. (ed), (1976), *The Sociology of Crime and Delinquency in Britain*, (Volume II: The New Criminologies), London: Martin Robertson.

Windlesham, Lord (2003), 'Ministers and Modernisation', in L. Zedner and A. Ashworth (eds), *The Criminological Foundations of Penal Policy*, Oxford: Oxford University Press.

Woodcock, A. (2006), 'Cannabis Law Back in the Spotlight', *The Independent*, 5 January.

Woodcock, Sir J. (1994), *The Escape From Whitemoor Prison on Friday 9th September 1994*, (The Woodcock Inquiry), Cm 2741, London: HMSO.

Woolf, H. (LCJ) and Tumim, S. (J) (1991), *Prison Disturbances April 1990*, Cm 1456, London: HMSO.

Wright, M. (1991), *Justice for Victims and Offenders*, Milton Keynes: Open University Press.

Wright, M. (1996), *Justice for Victims and Offenders*, (2nd Edition), Philadelphia, PA: Open University Press.

Wright, M. and Galway, B. (eds) (1989), *Mediation and Criminal Justice: Victims, Offenders and Community*, London: SAGE Publications.

Wright, R. (2002), 'Counting the Cost of Sentencing in North Carolina', in M. Tonry (ed), *Crime and Justice: A Review of Research*, vol.29, Chicago: University of Chicago Press.

Yazzie, R. (1998), 'Navajo Response to Crime', in *Justice and Healing*, 3 (2), Saskatoon, SK: University of Saskatchewan Native Law Centre.

Zedner, L. (1994), 'Reparation and Retribution: Are They Reconcilable?', *Modern Law Review*, 57, pp.228-250.

Zedner, L. and Ashworth, A. (eds) (2003), *The Criminological Foundations of Penal Policy*, (Essays in Honour of Roger Hood), Oxford: Oxford University Press.

Zehr, H. (2002a), *The Little Book of Restorative Justice*, Intercourse, PA: Good Books.

Zehr, H. (2002b), 'Restorative Justice Defined', Proceedings of the 4th *Annual Conference of the International Corrections and Prisons Association* (ICPA), Ottawa: ICPA, pp.36-51.

Zehr, H. and Mika, H. (1998), 'Fundamental Principles of Restorative Justice', *Contemporary Justice Review*, vol.1, no.1, pp.47-55.

Zimring, F.E. and Hawkins, G. (1973), *Deterrence: The Legal Threat in Crime Control*, Chicago, Illinois: University of Chicago Press.

Zion, J.W. (1985), 'The Navajo Peacemaking Court: Deference to the Old and Accommodating the New', *American Indian Law Review*, 11, p.89.

Zion, J.W. (1998), 'The Dynamics of Navajo Peacemaking', *Journal of Contemporary Criminal Justice*, 14 (1), (February), pp.58-74.

Index